THE GERM
LEGAL SYSTEM

AUSTRALIA
LBC Information Services
Sydney

CANADA and USA
Carswell
Toronto

NEW ZEALAND
Brooker's
Auckland

SINGAPORE and MALAYSIA
Sweet & Maxwell Asia
Singapore and Kuala Lumpur

THE GERMAN LEGAL SYSTEM

By

DR ANKE FRECKMANN, *Rechtsanwältin, Heidelberg* and
DR THOMAS WEGERICH, *Rechtsanwalt, executive editor (Verlag Recht und Wirtschaft), Heidelberg*

LONDON • SWEET & MAXWELL • 1999

Published in 1999 by
Sweet and Maxwell Limited of
100 Avenue Road,
London NW3 3PF

Typeset by J&L Composition Ltd, Filey, North Yorkshire
Printed and bound in Great Britain by
MPG Books Ltd, Bodmin, Cornwall

No natural forests were destroyed to make this product;
only farmed timber was used and replanted

ISBN 0421 571 004

A CIP catalogue record for this book is available
from the British Library

Foreword

"Comparative law may have been a hobby of yesterday. But it is determined to become the science of tomorrow. We must welcome rather than fear its influence."

These words could stem from one of the thousands of European continental lawyers who, since the end of the Second World War, have helped to build the European Communities which have now grown into the European Union. As of today, it is common understanding that continental lawyers can no longer afford *not* to know about foreign laws.

Yet the citation at the begining of this Foreword does not lead back to a continental, but to a prominent English lawyer. Lord Goff of Chieveley made this statement in his Wilberforce Lecture 1997 on "The Future of the Common Law" (I.C.L.Q. [1997] at 745 and 748). In the perspective of continental lawyers, their English colleagues were for centuries mainly involved in the care of their common law. They had exported their institutions and rules into many countries all over the world. Their home-law therefore was alive on many foreign continents. Hence, for English lawyers the study of foreign laws was not such a necessity as, for example, for a German lawyer.

Today, the world has changed. With the advent of the >euro<, Europe will grow together more and more. For many English lawyers the future has to do with the continent. Hundreds of thousands of business relations now tie Great Britain to the European mainland. A number of English law firms have already established branches in European cities. Hundreds of English lawyers are working in European institutions. To understand with whom they deal, where they stay and where they work, our English colleagues must try to come to some basic grips with the laws of our lands.

The present book intends to support our friends from the British Islands and from the British Commonwealth who endeavour to learn about German law. They will find in this book the description of some fundamental German legal institutions. This description is destined not only for beginners but also for those who are already advanced in their knowledge of

German law. They will certainly not be disappointed when they use this book as one of their tools in their study of how the German legal system works.

Professor Dr Otto Sandrock, LL.M., Muenster

Preface

The intention of this book is to offer the reader a broader view, or a first view, of the German legal system. It has been written primarily for students and practitioners but is also suitable for non-lawyers who want to learn about this topic. The book describes the systematic structures of the German legal system that differ from the English approach which uses the law as a tool to solve problems between conflicting parties.

"There's always the Channel" was a common saying in England and on the Continent when referring to the differences, quite fundamental differences, which existed between the case law system in England and the body of codified law in Germany. However, just as the Channel is no longer such a divisive barrier between the two land masses due to the Channel Tunnel, so the fundamental differences between English and German law are becoming part of legal history. This can be directly attributed to the influence of the European Community on the different national legal systems within the European Union. Even more marked though is that more and more parts of the German legal system have become influenced by court decisions and the English legal system is now more codified than ever before.

We hope that this book will serve as a starting point for anyone interested in the German legal system as well as for readers who would like to understand a legal system and concepts which are very different but are becoming relevant to English law.

We have tried to facilitate the reader's understanding of the German legal system by including a Glossary at the end of the book which should function as a quick pathfinder. Needless to say we take full responsibility for any errors which appear in the book. We invite you to bring to our attention any aspect of the book which you feel needs expansion, or indeed inclusion, in further editions of this book.

Please note that this edition presents the law at October 1998.

Dr Anke Freckmann
Dr Thomas Wegerich
Heidelberg, October 1998

Contents

Table of Cases

German Cases

Non-German Cases

Table of Legislation

Table of European, International and Foreign Legislation

Table of Abbreviations

AbgG	Abgeordnetengesetz
A.D.	Anno Domini
AG VwGO NW	Gesetz zur Ausführung der Verwaltungsgerichtsordnung des Landes Nordrhein-Westfalen
AktG	Aktiengesetz
Art.	Artikel
AuslG	Ausländergesetz
AsylVfG	Asylverfahrensgesetz
BayVBl.	Bayerisches Verwaltungsblatt
BauGB	Bundesbaugesetz
BauGB MaßnG	Maßnahmegesetz zum Baugesetzbuch
BB	Betriebs-Berater
B.C.	Before Christ
BGB	Bürgerliches Gesetzbuch
BGBl.	Bundesgesetzblatt
BGH	Bundesgerichtshof
BGHZ	Entscheidungen des Bundesgerichtshofs in Zivilsachen
BGHSt	Entscheidungen des Bundesgerichtshofs in Strafsachen
BImschG	Bundesimmissionsschutzgesetz
BNatSchG	Bundesnaturschutzgesetz
BRAO	Bundesrechtsanwaltsordnung
BRAGO	Bundesrechtsanwaltsgebührenordnung
BRRG	Beamtenrechtsrahmengesetz
BVerwG	Bundesverwaltungsgerichtsgesetz
BVerfGE	Entscheidungen des Bundesverfassungsgerichts
Ch.	Law Reports; Chancery Division (since 1891)
DDR	Deutsche Demoktratische Republik (German Abbreviation for the former German Democratic Republic)
EEC	European Economic Community
EEC Law	European Economic Community Law
EURATOM	European Atomic Energy Community
et seq.	et sequens

EuGVÜ	Übereinkommen der Europäischen Gemeinschaft über die gerichtliche Zuständigkeit und die Vollstreckung gerichtlicher Entscheidungen in Zivil- und Handelssachen
FGO	Finanzgerichtsordnung
FRG	Federal Republic of Germany
GDR	German Democratic Republic (for German Abbreviation see "DDR")
GG	Grundgesetz
GeschO BT	Geschäftsordnung des Bundestags
GVG	Gerichtsverfassungsgesetz
HGB	Handelsgesetzbuch
JGG	Jugendgerichtsgesetz
KPD	Kommunistische Partei Deutschlands
KO	Konkursordnung
MRK	Menschenrechtskonvention (Human Rights Convention)
M & W	Meeson and Welsby's Report, Exchequer, 16 volumes, 1836–1847
NJW	Neue Juristische Wochenschrift
NSDAP	Nationalsozialistische Deutsche Arbeiterpartei
NVwZ	Neue Zeitschrift für Verwaltungsrecht
NVwZ-RR	Neue Zeitschrift für Verwaltungsrecht – Rechtsprechungsreport
ParteienG	Parteiengesetz
RIW	Recht der Internationalen Wirtschaft
RKG	Reichskammergericht
RKGO	Reichskammergerichtsordnung
RPflG	Rechtspflegergesetz
SED	Sozialistische Einheitspartei Deutschlands
SGG	Sozialgerichtsgesetz
SRP	Sozialistische Reichspartei
StGB	Strafgesetzbuch
StPO	Strafprozeßordnung
VerfGDR	Verfassung der German Democratic Republic
VwGO	Verwaltungsgerichtsordnung (Rules of Administrative Courts)
VwVfG	Verwaltungsverfahrensgesetz (Code of Aministrative Procedure
ZPO	Zivilprozeßordnung (Civil Code of Procedure)
ZVG	Gesetz über die Zwangversteigerung und die Zwangverwaltung

Chapter One
Historical Background

This chapter covers the main developments in German legal history beginning from an unwritten and localised dispute settlement to a formal, codified and highly organised system of justice. Germany and its constituent states have created over the centuries one of the most codified legal systems in the world. Important identifying features of German law are its systematically organised state, government and judiciary along with the almost complete adoption of Roman law in the Late Middle Ages. The latter feature especially distinguishes the German legal system from common law.

1. The Germanic Period

In the Germanic Period (about 100 B.C. to A.D. 500) society was composed of independent communities (*civiates*). Their constitutions were based on a simple structure comprised of democratic, aristocratic and monarchical elements. The highest power belonged to armed freemen who assembled periodically in a *Thing* (*concilium* — council). This open-air assembly decided on relevant political questions and delivered court findings with *principes* (earls) presiding over them and preparing the relevant items. However, in cases of minor importance, the *principes* gave a ruling without convening the assembly. In some communities, *principes* administered a *Gau* (district) and delivered judicial decisions.

The structure of the judicial system during the Germanic Period was simple. The *Thing* was regarded as the highest court and heard very serious cases, such as treason and cowardice. The *Gaugericht* (district court) was responsible for cases of minor importance. However, the courts had no jurisdiction with regard to certain offences — like manslaughter — which were the result of family feuds and each family member was obliged to support the feud.

The place of trial in a *Gau* — the *Dingstädten* — was visited by the *principes* and their followers in a certain sequence. A *principe* was a visiting judge who took the chair and only his noble chairmanship gave full legal force to the judgments. However, while the *principe* conducted proceedings it was the legal community who actually decided on the judgment which the *principe* then delivered. The division between the judge conducting the trial and those who reached the judgment was a typical feature of the Germanic court system.

During the Germanic Period the law was relatively free from foreign influence. In addition, no primary legal sources (such as statutes, orders, byelaws, decrees) and only a few secondary sources (like maps and books) were in existence. As far as sources have been recorded, they derived from Roman authors, like Caesar's *De bello gallio* (51–50 B.C.) and Tacitus's *Germania* (A.D. 98).

Customary law was employed by tribes, and this simple and unwritten law governed their lives, for example, proceedings in a *Thing*. The oldest right had been the *Volksrechte* (people's rights) which had been neither recorded nor produced by a human legislator. These rights lived in the conscience of the population and were transmitted orally. The legal rules of customary law were simple and easy to remember — such as the term "*Bürgen soll man würgen*" (This is a German legal saying which means that a guarantor must honour his debt as long as the principle obligation is satisfied). Legal transactions took place before witnesses in meetings and had to be carried out symbolically, for example, the judge using his stick and the presence of the insignia of the king, thus making the legal act oral and visible.

2. SALIC-FRANK PERIOD — *FRÄNKISCHE ZEIT*

The Salic-Frank Period (about A.D. 500 to A.D. 888) was the end of the nation's migration. Germanic tribes had been gradually unified under the power of the *König der Franken* (Salic-Frank king) and constituted the *Frankenreich* (Salic-Frank empire). The Salic-Frank constitution was dominated by monarchical elements. All power belonged to one person — the king. The monarchy was the result of the growing and spacious *Frankenreich,* because people could only be held together by a strong, hierarchical, organised authority of command. A new king was elected by the aristocracy and clergy — normally the king's son was the successor to the throne. Succession to the throne was regulated by a combination of unrecorded, electoral and inheritable rules. Nevertheless, specified rules of electoral capacity and proceedings did not exist at this stage. In this period important affairs of the empire were presented before the community during the *Hoftage.* These were held by the king twice a year in order to pass resolutions on various political, social and legal affairs.

The king appointed representatives — such as earls or *Markgrafen* — who had to administer a *Gau*. These representatives were important regional dignitaries, and both the highest judges and administrators of the respective shire. The king had the right to remove them at will but he rarely made use of this power because the dismissed *Markgrafen* might have plotted against the king or started a rebellion. Over the years a common practice developed that after an earl's death his sons were installed as successors. This established custom developed into a legal tradition that one of the earl's sons claimed to be the successor to his father's position. As a result, the position of *Markgrafen* became hereditary. A feudal relationship between king and earl arose. The king, thereafter, had no right to dismiss an earl, and only a court had jurisdiction to withdraw an earl's rights provided that a serious crime had been committed by him.

During the Salic-Frank period recorded statutory law produced by a legislator appeared. It was the first time that legal rules had been recorded and intentionally produced by the people. Henceforth, there was a direct link to the *Gesetzespositivismus* (law of positivism) of modern times. Given this, the legal sources of this period may be divided into primary sources (like *Volksrechte, Kapitularen, Konzilbeschlüsse*) and secondary sources (like collections of standard proposal forms, contracts and the principle framework for various statements of claim, known collectively as *Formularsammlungen,* as well as deeds, legal books and chronicles):

(a) The *Volksrechte*[1] are of importance because they had a strong influence in the further process of codifying German law. The documentation began around A.D. 475 with the west *gotic lexes barbarorum* and reached its peak and preliminary end at the *Reichstag* in Aachen around A.D. 802.[2] The *Volksrechte,* which were recorded in Latin, contained laws of various Germanic tribes. It related their customary law and legal concepts developed by the courts and contained an outline of the systematic framework and order of procedural and private law as well as the legal consequences

---

[1] This name stems from the fact that these rights reproduced people's wills and imagination.

[2] *Volksrechte* were, for example, the *Codex Euricianus* (around 475), *Lex Salica* (around 500), *Lex Alamannorum* (around 720), *Lex Baiuwariorum* (around 740), *Lex Saxonum* (802).

of the *Missetaten* (offences). The tribe's legal "habits" were recorded by people versed in law. These people tried to clarify their customary law, took elements from Roman and canonical law and tried to interpret the law to reflect their feelings for equity. The example of written Roman law seems to have prompted a few Germanic rulers to record the law in this way.

(b) *Kapitularen* were regulations divided into chapters issued by the *König der Franken* and contained administrative rules which could be classified as orders. *Kapitularen* applied in the entire *Frankenreich* and were addressed to earls and other authorities.

(c) *Konzilbeschlüsse* (resolutions of the council) were issued by the national council under the head of the *König der Franken.*

(d) Collections of *Formularsammlung* determined how to draft actions or contracts.

(e) Royal and private deeds were executed by *Referendarius* and *Notarius*, and execution of documents is an area where the influence of Roman law can be detected.

(f) During this period, there were only a few legal books in existence. However, some chronicles were already available, like the one produced by Bishop Gregor von Tours (sixth century). There were also certain bibliographies, like Einhard's *Vita Caroli Magni* describing the exciting life of Karl the Great.

The highest court of this time was the *Königsgericht* (king's court). It was presided over by the king and in his absence by the *Pfalzgraf* (Count Palatine). The king took part as a ruler, and sometimes he passed judgment personally. The *Königsgericht* had jurisdiction upon any submitted case, if it had not already been decided by the *Gaugericht*, or if it had been decided by the *Gaugericht* but disputed by one of the a litigants. The *Königsgericht* was more or less unrestricted in how to conduct procedure because — contrary to the *Gaugericht* — it was not bound by the procedural law set down in the *Volksrechte.*

Procedure before the *Gaugericht* was strictly formal and possessed the following characteristic features: no distinction was made between criminal and civil proceedings; all actions were charges of an offence or a violation of law and, therefore, an indictable crime. Proceedings were public, oral and strictly formal at every stage. Evidence, in the form of witnesses, deeds and confessions, sometimes forced by torture, were admissible if collected by officers of the court. Parties involved in a case authorised *Fürsprecher* (mediators) versed in law to represent them, otherwise they could have run the risk of losing the lawsuit because of a wrongly filed action or motioned evidence. Proceedings were governed by the principle of party disposition, of party prosecution and of party presentation[3] and, due to this, the participating parties had to submit the respective facts of the case and to produce the necessary evidence. Courts were also strictly bound by the wording of recorded law. The reason for these procedural principles was the commonly held distrust in the ability of judges and rulers to investigate the true facts of a case and to be impartial.

Besides the *Gaugerichte*, special courts had been set up which were competent only to hear certain cases. The *grundherrliche Hofgerichte* (manor court), for instance, had jurisdiction over litigation between a *Grundherr* (lord of the manor) and his *Grundhöriger* (subject) or between subjects whose lawsuits concerned legal questions relating to the manor, for instance boundary and road litigation, or participation of inheritances. Earls or *Zentaren* presided over these courts and delivered the judgments. Proceedings in these special courts — such as the *grundherrlichen Hofgerichte* — were similar to the *Gaugerichte* but probably more simple and less formal.

3. MIDDLE AGES

The Middle Ages (888–1200) can be characterised as a period of imperialism. It started with the dissipation of the *Frankenreich* because of the king's deposition (*Karl der Dicke*, 888) and terminated with the reorganisation of the institutions in the twelfth century because of a tendency towards rationalisation.

The German emperor — as the successor to both the Salic-Frank emperor and the ancient Roman emperor — held a very powerful position and was called the *Sacrum Imperium Romanum* or *Kaiser des Heiligen Römischen Reiches* (Holy Roman Reich of the German Nations[4]). The electoral procedure to the throne was the same as the one which applied to the *König der Franken*; therefore, no rules were in force referring to electoral capacity and procedure. Moreover, Salic-Frank institutions —

---

[3] For more details concerning these judicial terms, see *ibid.*, Chap. Six, 2.

[4] The Holy Roman Reich began with Otto I's coronation in 962 and ended with Franz II's abdication in 1806.

like jurisdiction and administration — subsisted in the Middle Ages.

The emperor was the head of justice. The *Königsgericht* or *Reichshofgericht* was still the highest court with a similar jurisdiction to that of the *fränkische Königsgericht*. Despite the fact that it started as a sole tribunal, it became an appellate tribunal over the years because numerous judgments were disputed and therefore a sequence of courts was required. During this period the *Reichshofgericht* was badly organised, and the composition of the bench changed frequently. Specific procedural rules had not been in force at all, and the reformed process of the Salic-Frank period had obviously been forgotten. The *Königsgericht,* as a subordinate court, failed to develop a highly respected adjudication procedure as had happened in France and England.

The main courts were the *Grafengerichte* (earl's court). The *Gaue* or shires were still districts of the courts (and administration) and subject to the law of feudality.[5] Under this system, a shire sometimes had to be distributed under more than one successor. The consequence was a dissipation of judicial districts and a badly arranged system of justice which was therefore hard to follow at all. The law of procedure, which initially did not change, was subsequently strongly influenced by canonical procedural law. Over the years, the *Grafengerichte* were hardly ever in session and could therefore not provide effective justice. The courts constantly lost their active jurisdiction and faded to a merely aristocratic *Standesgericht* (professional tribunal). Territorial courts — like *Land-*, *Go-* and *Zentgerichte* — took their place and exercised their own jurisdiction.

In the tenth and eleventh centuries few people — except for clergymen — were able to read. The exact knowledge of the *Volksrechte* disappeared and courts referred only to their main features. The Salic-Frank law continued to be enforced and only a few primary and secondary legal sources were issued. They are as follows:

(a) A few *Kaisergesetze* (emperor's law) had been passed which specified the law of feudality. In the eleventh century, the famous *langobarischen libri feudorum* — a legal book about the law of feudality — was published in Italy. In Germany, it applied as common law as late as the thirteenth century.

---

[5] Feudality was the special relationship between the feudal lord and the vassal; the feudal lord lent a good to the vassal for a certain period of time in exchange for service and faith.

(b) Towards the end of the eleventh century, the *Investiturstreit* (investiture contest) between the pope and the emperor arose. The *Wormser Konkordat* (1122) which Henry V and Pope Calixtus II concluded finally settled this dispute, and this contained, for the first time, certain rules about bishops' elections and the emperor's position within the electoral procedure.

(c) Also of great practical importance was the *Reichsrecht* (national law) issued by the *Hohenstaufen — Kaiser Barbarossa* (1152–90) which regulated both criminal law and the *Regalien.* The latter were monopolistic rights of the emperor, such as the *Münzregal,* the exclusive right of minting, and the *Bergregal,* the exclusive right to establish and exploit mines.

(d) Numerous papal and royal deeds, mostly written in Latin, contained, among other things, privileged allowances to vassals such as immunity granted by the emperor or pope.

(e) There were also a few chronicles but these did not reach the high standard of the one written by George von Tours in the sixth century.

4. LATE MIDDLE AGES

A. CONSTITUTION

The Late Middle Ages (around 1200–1500) was a period of remarkable progress in the economy, the arts and law throughout Europe and was the beginning of the renaissance and humanism. The monarchy continued to exist as the form of government. It seemed that a central power could best guarantee the fulfilment of national business and ensure internal peace and external defence. In addition to that, a monarchical state with its simple structure was much easier to organise than a republic. Monarchical power at this time, however, was not unlimited. The emperor had to observe the law, and in the event of unlawful acts, his vassals could put up opposition to enforce the restoration of the infringed law. However, because there were still only a few recorded legal rules in force and no existing procedure at all, it was difficult to state whether the emperor breaking the law justified exercising the right of resistance.

The *Königswahlrecht* (law of succession to the throne) changed radically in the Late Middle Ages because for the first time this law had been laid down in written form. In 1200, Pope

Innocenz III formulated legal principles[6] of electoral capacity and procedure. Due to this, only special dignitaries (such as archbishops or *Pfalzgrafen*) constituted the *Kurfürstenkollegium*, and had the right to vote. Each of their votes had to be evaluated in accordance with the majority voting system. Later, in 1353, the *Reichstag* in Metz fixed electoral regulations, prepared under Karl IV, which were passed within the famous *Goldene Bulle*. This statute contained, for the first time, a very clear and precise law of succession to the throne. Thereafter, only particular *Kurfürsten* — their number raised from seven to ten through the centuries — were entitled and obliged to vote for a royal successor; in addition, the majority voting system and the principle of local and temporary unified election governed the electoral process, for instance election should be exercised in the Dome of Frankfurt and should last not more than 30 days.

During this period, the *Reichstag* was developed into a permanent institution. Similar to the *Königswahlrecht*, particular principles were introduced, for instance, the composition of the *Reichstag* or the passing of resolutions. Based on old customs, several important groups in society — like the *Markgrafen*, *Pfalzgrafen* and bishops — held a right to participate in royal resolutions. These people were regarded as the *Reichsstandschaft*, which implied a right to sit and vote in the *Reichstagshof* — which was later called the *Reichstag*. From the time of the *Interregnum* (1256–1273) 51 towns of the *Reich* (*e.g.* Regensburg, Nürnberg, Augsburg, Frankfurt, Worms and Speyer) were recognised as *Reichsstände* with the consequence that these towns had a seat in the *Reichstag*.

In the Late Middle Ages, the sovereignty of the emperor of the Reich was gradually transferred to the *Landesherren* (national sovereigns or vassals of the Reich) who were the equivalent of the *principes* of the Germanic Period and the earls and dukes of both the Salic-Frank period and the Middle Ages. For centuries, the *Landesherren* developed and enhanced their role and position to a *Landesherrschaft* or *Landeshoheit* (national sovereignty) of supreme power over their governed territories within the *Heiliges Römisches Reich Deutscher Nationen*. They were considered to be the equivalent of the emperor in their *Land* (territory) and their legal position, especially towards the *Kaiser* of the Holy Roman Empire, was fixed in two important statutes (*Reichsgesetze*): the *Confoederatio cum*

---

[6] After the death of Heinrich VI in 1197, two kings — Phillip von Schwaben and Otto von Braunschweig — were elected and the Pope attempted to act as an arbitrator to settle this dispute while determining these rules.

principibus ecclesiastius (1220) and the *Statutum in favorem principum* (1232). Most of the *Landesherren* developed a strict and well organised national sovereignty by degrees: they established new, non-feudal offices (mostly filled with lawyers), levied taxes, built up an army and sometimes recorded the law applying in their territory which was called *Landesrecht* (law of the *Land*).

Towns growing in size and stature through the craft and export trade with well organised administrations and *Stadtrechte* (law of towns) were an important feature of the Late Middle Ages. Over time, nearly every town passed a constitution and developed its own *Stadtrecht*. The *Stadtrecht* addressed constitutional and administrative questions as well as problems concerning private, criminal and procedural law. It was recorded and, unlike the *Landesrecht,* was quite advanced and consumer friendly. A particular *Stadtrecht* was issued in those towns in which citizens were allowed to issue *Satzungen* (charters) to regulate their own affairs, such as the law of succession. Each town administered its affairs by administrative bodies with some towns also installing a *städtischer Rat* (town council), like Lübeck for instance, or a *Stadtgericht* (municipal court), in Magdeburg and Leipzig. Also of some importance were regulations issued by the *Handwerkerzunft* (guild). They laid down strict rules about how to learn a trade, how to become a guild member and that only members of the respective guild were allowed to practice their craft in the town.

B. JURISDICTION

Jurisdiction became increasingly complicated in the Late Middle Ages. Differences now had to be made between higher, upper and lower jurisdictions and specific courts were responsible for definite groups of people or particular legal affairs. A court's jurisdiction was also restricted with regard to territorial applications, personal scope and *Landesrecht*, law of feudality, *Stadtrecht* or canonical law. Moreover, criminal and civil proceedings were separated for the first time in legal history.

Criminal procedure was changed fundamentally by the *Landesfriedensgesetze* (twelfth and thirteenth centuries). Not only could the injured person or his relatives institute criminal proceedings, now public prosecutions were carried out *ex officio* just as establishing the facts of the case and passing judgments. Instead of principles of party disposition, prosecution and presentation, the *Offizialmaxime* and *Amtsbetrieb* (principle of *ex officio* proceedings) and the *Untersuchungsgrundsatz* (principle of investigation) were in effect and governed criminal trials.[7] The admissible means of evidence were the *Zweizeugenbeweis* (evidence by two witnesses) and confession. The accused's testimony — mostly given under the pressure of torture — was recorded for the first time. But in proceedings the accused had no opportunity to defend himself because the inquiry was secret and after the judgment was pronounced it had to be enforced at once and the convicted person could not file an appeal against his conviction. Therefore, criminal proceedings had become more and more an *Inquisitionsprozeß* (inquisitorial proceedings).

Contrary to criminal proceedings, civil procedure kept its former principles, like party disposition, party presentation and party prosecution. Modern means of evidence, such as testimonial evidence, appeared in civil proceedings along with written trial conduct. Roman and canonical procedural law strongly influenced civil procedure and, due to this, it bears the name *römisch-kanonischer Zivilprozeß*, which was still in effect, in some parts of Germany, until the enforcement of the *Reichszivilprozeßordnung* in 1877 (Code of the Reich Civil Procedure). During this time, numerous arbitration proceedings were conducted in the *Austraegalgerichte,* a permanent court of arbitration. In addition to this, the *Reichshofgericht* was reorganised. This was governed and specified under the *Mainzer Landfrieden* (1235) and the jurisdiction of it to hear cases was enhanced. This royal court could now attract a civil case which was pending at a lower court level (for instance of the *Länder* or *Reichsstädte*) by evocation in order to give a finding — in other words: in this case we see a right to withdraw a matter from the cognisance of another court. A case could also be heard in the *Reichshofgericht* because of an appeal to be lodged against a ruling of the lower court (of the *Länder* or *Reichsstädte*). However, the *Reichshofgericht* had no or only limited jurisdiction if the respective *Landesherr* held a privilege which was the *privilegium de non evocando, privilegium de non appellando* or the *privilegium de non evocando et non appellando* — the latter did not possess any *Kurfürsten* because of the *Goldene Bulle* (1356). These rights may be regarded as a restriction of the jurisdiction of the *Reichshofgericht*.

C. LEGAL SOURCES

In the Late Middle Ages, the law was rationalised and recorded in statutes and legal books. In towns and *Länder*,

---

[7] For more details concerning these judicial terms, see *ibid.*, Chap. Seven, 3.

numerous legal rules and institutions of private, procedural, constitutional and administrative law were formulated. Roman and canonical law began to modestly influence German law. It was the beginning of the era of the influence of Roman and canonical law: students who had studied law in Bologna returned to Germany, where they became highly respected and were able to make use of Roman law in cases in which national legal rules were not at hand. In addition courts made use of canonical and legal rules under Roman law. Roman law also penetrated the work of notaries, for instance, Italian scholars versed in law had written precedent books which described special rules for certification.

(a) One group of legal sources of this time could be classified as universal law which was in force throughout the Christian world. This canonical law passed by the church had been developed and rationalised in a precise way. Its legal sources were the *Corpus iuris canonici* (a comprehensive clerical digest of law) literature of canonical professors and single deeds and statutes of clerical orders. The precise and highly developed canonical law was a yardstick for procedural law for the next centuries.

(b) Common law as a further set of legal sources applied in the entire German Reich: numerous *Reichsgesetze* (laws of the Reich) had been passed during this time which concerned different fields of law. The *Mainzer Reichslandfriede* (1235) issued by Friedrich II, for instance, was important for the rationalisation of criminal law whereas the *Reichskammergerichtsordnung* (1495) contained precise rules of jurisdiction and judicial procedure.

Next, the *Goldene Bulle* (1356), written in Latin, laid down the provisions for a king's election to the throne, and was the most important constitutional law until the end of the old Reich.

Furthermore, the *Corpus iuris civilis*, as another common law source was in force as it was interpreted by *Glossatoren* (Glossators), Italian professors who studied the Justinian *Corpus iuris civilis* at Bologna and developed the Roman law with their *Glossen* (comments); younger Glossators continued their work. *Accursius* finished the work of the Glossators in the *Accursische Glosse* (1230). From the fifteenth century, this was printed in several volumes. Courts made use of this annotated law until the codification of modern civil law (like the *Preußische Allgemeine Landrecht*, 1794) and even until the enforcement of the *Bürgerliche Gesetzbuch* (German Civil Code, 1900).

Next, the *Libri feudorum* (eleventh century) as a further common law source was a ruling upon the law of feudality and continued to apply together with Roman law.[8] But contrary to France and England, it applied in Germany as a subsidiary source of law, namely, only in cases in which no special regional feudal rules had been in effect. In addition to this statute, numerous feudality orders prevailed and some of them were recorded, such as the *Sachsenspiegel* (around 1220) and the *Schwabenspiegel* (around 1270).

(c) In addition, the so-called particular law was in force. As another group of legal sources it can be regarded as the law of regulations and orders which — in contrast to the *Reichsrecht* — applied only in certain German areas (*e.g.* city law in certain towns like Münster, Leipzig, Magdeburg and *Land* law in certain *Länder* like Sachsen),[9] and was the law of regulations and orders. These recorded legal rules — different to modern rules — were not issued as one-sided orders by the highest body of community; the idea of binding law towards everyone created by orders, however, was unknown in these days. Nevertheless, the following particular sources could be regarded as the precursor of legislative orders and authority:

Sometimes legal sources were formulated by means of granting a one-sided privilege, for instance a master imposed rights on an addressee who — in return — undertook certain duties.

In addition, *Satzungen* (charters) were issued; legal sentences were agreed and this put a constantly binding effect upon the participating parties and their successors but not upon third parties.

Next, *Weistümer* (wisdom) as legal rules were set up. Wisdoms were judgments in which a court or body (like *Reichstag* or *Kurfürstenkollegium*) stated in an abstract way, without referring to a particular case, that a legal rule with a definite content, was applicable. In those days, it was necessary to set up numerous wisdoms because the creation of new law was impossible according to the former school of thought.

---

[8] In Germany, the *Weimarer Reichsverfassung* (1919) abolished the law of feudality whereas in England it still exists but with minor importance.

[9] The legal structure of particular law existed on two levels, it was like *Land* law on the first level and like city law on a second level.

During this time, numerous public registers recording peoples' births, deaths and marriages were created, and *Schöffensprüche* (findings of lay magistrates) were recorded in some upper courts and, therefore, strongly influenced the jurisdiction of other courts.

Last but not least, numerous legal books presenting the approved law of the time were published. The most outstanding law book was the *Sachsenspiegel* (around 1220) written by Eike von Repgow. It dealt with constitutional, criminal, private and procedural law and was laid down in a very precise, judicially sensible, figurative and affectionate way. Further legal books were drafted in a similar way, such as the *Schwabenspiegel* (around 1270).

5. EARLY MODERN TIMES

A. CONSTITUTION OF THE REICH

Early Modern Times (about 1500–1800) was the era between the discovery of America (1492) and the French Revolution (1789) and its aftermath was the period of counter-reformation and renaissance. Around 1500, a period of reformation began because of growing discontent with the national situation. The *Reichsstände* demanded constitutional reforms to strengthen the executive power. Emperor Maximilian I (1493–1519), however, opposed these proposals with his plans to strengthen royal power. A compromise was reached at the *Reichstag* in Worms (1495) with the following content: *Ewiger Landfriede* (permanent freedom) prohibited feuds in the whole *Reich;* a permanent *Reichskammergericht* as the highest court of appeal was set up; a moderate but permanent tax, the so-called *Gemeiner Pfennig*, was introduced; a permanent *Reichsregiment* (army of the *Reich*) was founded, and 10 *Reichskreise* (districts of the *Reich*) were set up in order to secure the *Ewigen Landfriede* and to enforce the judgments of the *Reichskammergericht.*

During this time, the *Reichstag* turned into a permanent institution as well. It was now summoned by the emperor and consisted of three committees: first, the *Kurfürstenkollegium* — composed of *Kurfürsten* whose number rose over the centuries form seven to ten; secondly, the *Fürstenkollegium* composed of 204 *Reichsstände*, such as bishops, earls and dukes, and thirdly, the *Städtekollegium* consisted of 51 powerful *Reichsstädte.* The *Reichstag* of these days had definite powers, but the proceedings for passing resolutions had become complicated and required a unanimous consent between emperor and all committees. The *Reichstag*, however, held in principle an unlimited legislative authority, but in practice, it never really exercised legislative power. This was because on one hand it was difficult and time-consuming to pass resolutions, and on the other the common idea prevailed that new law could not be produced by a human legislator and only existing law could be stated and reformulated.

Now we would like to draw your attention to the emperors position within the Reich: the imperial powers, formerly far-reaching, had shrivelled up to the following remnants. The emperor still held various rights in the *Reichstag*, such as to summon the *Reichstag*, to submit proposals, to prevent adoption of resolutions by means of refusing to consent to the respective proposal. The emperor was still the highest feudal lord, commander-in-chief of the army and leader of diplomatic negotiations. He appointed the presiding judge of the *Reichskammergericht*, chose — together with the *Reichsstände* — the assessors' offices in the *Reichskammergericht* just as the offices in the *Reichshofrat* — its powers rivalled with those of the *Reichskammergericht*. He held the *Reservatrechte* in non-contentious proceedings, such as the right to appoint notaries, to legitimate children born out of wedlock, to confer academic degrees (which had often been delegated to universities) and to raise people to the peerage.

During this period, there was a strong demand to change the place of canonical and religious affairs within the constitution and to reorganise the legal relationships between emperor and *Reichsstände*.

(a) The *Augsburger Religionsfrieden* (1555) may be seen as an important improvement with regard to this. It acknowledged the Lutheran and the Catholic religions as being equal, and introduced the principle of *cuius regio eius religio* (whoever reigns shall determine the religion) which meant that a *Landesherr* could determine his subject's religion in his territory, on the provision that other followers of a different religion had the right to leave the territory unharmed.

(b) Another important improvement was introduced with the *Westfälische Friede* in 1648 — a peace treaty which marked the end of the terrible *Dreißigjähriger Krieg* (thirty-year war) which had disturbed Europe since 1618. This peace treaty came into existence after two congresses — in Münster with the emperor, Catholic *Reichsstände* and foreign ambassadors and in Osnabrück with Protestant *Reichsstände* and foreign ambassadors. The *Westfälische Friede* was guaranteed by the contracting foreign empires. Besides a few territorial changes, it contained constitutional amendments, such as the acceptance of the reformed, Lutheran religion with equal rights and status and, moreover, the acceptance of the right of non-alignment granted to the *Reichsstände.* The treaty also recognised the institute of *itio in partes* in religious affairs, with the consequence that the *Reichstag* had to be subdivided into a Catholic and a Protestant assembly and that the consent of both assemblies was now required for passing a resolution in the *Reichstag.*

B. CONSTITUTION OF THE *LÄNDER*

The sovereignty of the *Länder* (especially in protestant territories) grew gradually to an absolute state authority. The reformation and the newly introduced principles of *cuius regio eius religio* by the *Augsburger Religionsfrieden* (1555) were the main reasons for the growing power of the *Länder.* The *Landesherren* levied higher taxes, re-recorded their so-called reformation of *Landrecht*, and each *Land* had a different state machinery.[10] Moreover, they improved their civil service; for instance in Prussia, the *Berufsbeamtentum* (permanent civil service) was created during the reign of Friederich Willhelm I. Due to this, civil servants had to regard their payments not as remunerations but as fulfilments of the unalterable duties of faith of loyalty towards the Prussian king. Because of low payments a strict and economical fiscal administration was set up.

C. CIVIL LAW AND PROCEDURE

During this time civil law and its procedure developed constantly. Due to this, numerous statutes of civil law and procedure were passed and the *Reichskammergerichtsordnung* (1495) now contained specific rules of jurisdiction, organisation and proceedings in the *Reichskammergericht.* In addition, numerous statutes of the *Landrecht* and *Stadtrecht* were passed

---

[10] In Prussia, for instance, the highest public authorities were the *Generaldirektorium* as the finance and economy office, the *Kabinettsministerium* which was responsible for foreign affairs and the *Geheimer Rat* which was responsible for justice and intellectual affairs. These authorities had jurisdiction all over Prussia and constituted the *Staatsrat*. Subordinated authorities were the *Kriegs-* and *Domänenkammern*, responsible for particular territories in Prussia, and below them stood the *Landräte*.

in order to clarify uncertainties arising from the question of which law — common or particular law — applied in the respective case. The *Nürnberger* (1479), *Wormser* (1498) and *Frankfurter* reformation (1578), the *Freiburger Stadtrecht* (1520) and the *Württembergisches Landrecht* (1555) laid down how to deal with this problem. Finally, *Polizeiverordnungen* (police regulations) were issued which regulated public order.

The *Usus modernus Pandectarum* written by Professor Samuel Stryk was a further and important source of civil law and procedure during this period. As a legal book it was based on the system of how *Glossatoren* and *Konsilatoren* had interpreted Roman law. This legal work represented the legal practice and jurisprudence in Germany until it was displaced by the *Preußisches Allgemeines Landrecht* (Prussian Common Land Law, 1794) in Prussia and in other German territories by the findings of the *Historische Rechtsschule* (historical law school).

The first codification[11] of civil law occurred in the eighteenth century. Codification of laws were possible because a detailed plan and conception was in existence pursuant to which a legal code could be drafted in a systematic order. The plan and concept upon which the codification of the law is based had been developed and created by the *Naturrechtslehre* (natural law theory or doctrine[12]). Codification of the law was also enhanced by the fact that for the first time the sovereign had the power and the will to issue codifications. The creation of new law produced by a human legislator was now widely accepted. The first codification of civil law was the *Codex Maximilianeus bavaricus civilis* (1756) — the Bavarian Civil Code — which was written in German, contained Latin phrases, and its contents were like the *Usus modernus Pandectarum.* Furthermore, the *Preußisches Allgemeines Landrecht* of 1794 has to be underlined as being one of the most important sources in German legal history. This eminent code contained rules of private, commercial, criminal and parts of administrative law. This statute was very precise, clear and systematic and applied in all Prussian territories.

In addition to the developing civil law, civil proceedings were fundamentally changed by the *Reichskammergerichtsordnung* (RKGO, 1495). For the first time a permanent *Reichskammer-*

---

[11] Codifications are statutes of a comprehensive extent which set out in order at least a part of the legal system in a strictly systematic and complete way.

[12] The doctrines of Hugo Grotius (1583–1645) in *De iure belli ac pacis libri tres* (1625) and *De iure naturae et gentium libri octo* (1672) were important as were those of Christian Thomasius (1655–1728).

gericht (RKG) was set up in Speyer (1526–1689) and later in Weimar (1693–1806). This court had to compete with the *Reichshofgericht* in Vienna which was presided over — contrary to the RKG — by the king. The emperor appointed the presiding judge of the RKG and — together with the *Reichsstände* - the *Assessoren* (associate judges) who were partly nobles and legal scholars. The RKG was the highest court of appeal in civil cases but had no jurisdiction in criminal cases. An appeal to the RKG supposed that, first, the case had been adjudicated in a lower court (of *Länder* or *Reichsstädte*) beforehand; secondly, it had to reach a specific value of the matter in dispute; and thirdly, the court's *Landesherr* should not hold a *privilegium de non appellando* against which a party intended to appeal. If a case did not meet these requirements, the RKG was allowed to hear the case only where a miscarriage of justice would otherwise take place. The proceedings to be conducted in the RKG were still in the form of the *römisch-kanonische Zivilprozeß*.

Judges of the RKG had to make use of the common law *ex officio* and by virtue of the principle *curia novit iura* (the judge knows the law).[13] For the first time they were obliged by law to make use of a specific source of law. In addition, particular law[14] applied in accordance with the principle *Stadtrecht bricht Landrecht, Landrecht bricht gemeines Recht* (town law breaks regional law, regional law breaks common law). In other words, the hierarchy of various legal sources was established at this stage. Due to this development, findings of subordinate courts now complied with the adjudication of the RKG. In addition, this trend was enhanced by the fact that for the first time only learned judges composed the bench and participated in trials, required under the *Hof- und Landgerichtsordnungen* (1571). These regulations led to a comprehensive reception of Roman and canonical law. This development, however, did not change the content of the legal judgments but — rather — the method of adjudication. Before this time, the legal basis of adjudication had been a few recorded legal judgments which judges knew — laws, privileges, wisdoms, legal books and customs. This kind of adjudication had now been replaced by comprehensive Latin texts regulating the civil law. A further typical feature of this time was that proceedings now became more complicated, lay people could no longer understand civil procedure and advocates quite often took responsibility for conducting people's lawsuits.

---

[13] For more details concerning this term, see *ibid.*, Chap. One, 4, B.

[14] For more details concerning this term, see *ibid.*, Chap. One, 4, C.

D. Criminal law and procedure

Many learned Italians (like the *Konsilatoren Bartolus* and *Baldus*) who had studied the criminal part of the *Corpus iuris civilis* developed doctrines to eliminate the arbitrariness — but not the harshness — of criminal law. The *Halsgerichtsordnung* of the *Fürstenbistum Bamberg* (1507, *Constitutio criminalis Bambergensis*) was a comprehensive and excellent Criminal Code which was strongly influenced by these doctrines. This statute partly served as the literal transmitted pattern for the *Peinliche Gerichtsordnung* of Karl V (*Constitutio criminalis Carolina*, 1532). The so-called *Carolina* was the most important *Reichsgesetz* which had ever been passed in the old Reich because of its extent and content. The *Carolina* contained rules of criminal proceedings and substantive criminal law, was written in clear and understandable German language and was more precise than former statutes. Criminal proceedings were now instituted *ex officio* and implemented mainly as an inquisitorial system; inquiries — which were secretly conducted — and not the actual trial presented the main part of procedure.

In the eighteenth century, codification of criminal law was deeply influenced by the *Aufkläurngszeit* (Age of Enlightenment[15]). Under this influence the *Länder* started to codify their criminal law, passing, for example, the *Codex iuris criminalis bavarici* (1751) or *Constitutio criminalis Theresiana* (1768) as comprehensive Codes which aspired to completeness and, moreover, specified acts which constituted a criminal offence. This specification was an important progression from the *Carolina.* Afterwards, the *Josephinische Kriminalgesetze* (1787–1788) and the quite modern *Preußisches Allgemeinen Landrecht* (1794) were passed — both of them containing penalties for crimes.

6. Liberal Constitutional State

The period of the Liberal Constitutional State can be fixed between 1806 and 1900. In Germany the upheaval was less radical than in France where the years of the Great Revolution (1789–1794) removed almost any institutions which were typical of the Middle Ages. Nevertheless, in Germany, the constitution of the Reich and several institutions which referred to the

---

[15] *Montesquieu* (1689–1755) laid down in his *Esprit des loi* (1748) the principle *keine Strafe ohne Gesetz* (no punishment without law) which Feuerbach (1801) later formulated as the principle of *nulla poena sine lege.*

Heilige Römische Reich Deutscher Nationen as a political and judicial creation were removed too.

A. UNIFICATION OF GERMANY

The unification of German States was — apart from the struggle for liberty, equality and participation in the law-making process — the most important aim of the population. This political wishful thinking had been satisfied in a small way by the *Bundesakte* (1815) which was supplemented later by the *Wiener Schlußakte* (1820). Both documents established an international — not constitutional — federation of sovereign *Bundesstaaten* (single states), the *Deutscher Bund*, whose highest parliamentary body was the *Bundestag* in Frankfurt. In 1833, the German *Zollverein* (customs union) was set up. This development was a further step on the long way to unification and the idea was to extend the Prussian principle of free trade all over Germany. The *Zollverein* had been entered into by numerous contracts agreed between the single *Bundesstaaten* (except for Austria) and was the basis of a homogeneous economic area covering these states.

The next stage of German unification was the *Frankfurter Reichsverfassung* or *Paulskirchenverfassung* (March 28, 1848). It had been drafted by an assembly of several hundred deputies from all federal territories in the *Frankfurter Paulskirche* which is why the city of Frankfurt even today is commonly known as the "*Wiege deutscher Demokratie*" (cradle of German democracy). The deputies, intellectually high-ranking men, were mainly members of the well-educated and financially well-off bourgeoisie. Due to a resolution of the *Bundestag*, they had to work out a *Reichsverfassung* resting on the idea of liberty and equality just as liberal-conservative aims. Constitutional civil rights were prominent in parts of the *Paulskirchenverfassung* because they formed part of the modern conception of an exemplary constitution. Nevertheless, the *Deutsche Verfassungsgebende Nationalversammlung* did not have the power to enforce the *Paulskirchenverfassung* upon the *Bundesstaaten*. As a result, it never entered into force.

The last stage of unification is represented by the *Reichsverfassung* — also called *Bismarck'sche Reichsverfassung* (1871). This constitution was very complicated, invented by Chancellor Bismarck — the dominant political power of this historical period — and designed for him. A typical feature was that the constitutional powers of the *Bundesstaaten* were more comprehensive than those of the *Bund*. Contrary to the *Paulskirchenverfassung*, it did not contain constitutional liberal rights but granted and transferred certain *Reservatrechte* (prerogative rights) to a few *Bundesstaaten* — for instance Bayern, Baden, Hamburg, Bremen. Because of these *Reservatrechte* — concerning such practically important areas like post, train, telegraphy and tax on consumption, beer and spirits — the *Bundesstaaten* were able to influence and regulate the named areas at will. These rights could only be removed by an amendment of the constitution and, in addition, required the consent of the respective *Bundesstaat*.

During this period, the new empire was both a state and a *Bundesstaat* which was constituted of 25 *Bundestaaten*.[16] Sovereignty was held by the assembly of all German earls and free towns (Lübeck, Hamburg and Bremen) which were represented in the highest and most important *Reichsorgan*, the *Bundesrat*. Besides the *Bundesrat*, the *Reichstag* was active as a parliamentary representation of 397 deputies. These deputies had been elected in a common, equal, confidential and direct election which stood in contrast to the *Dreiklassenwahlrecht* (electoral proceedings of three classes) according to which the deputies of the Prussian *Landtag* were elected. In addition, any deputy of the *Reichstag* could claim equal rights in the law-making process. The executive power in the Reich, however, was allotted to the emperor — it was up to him to appoint or dismiss the *Reichkanzler* (as the prime minister) and other civil servants of the Reich. In the law-making process the emperor held minor rights; for instance he had to ratify statutes which had passed the *Bundesrat* and *Reichstag* — but: the emperor had no right to refuse his consent. Nevertheless, he represented the Reich in international affairs and was — together with the *Reichskanzler* — responsible for foreign policy. This system worked well with such outstanding personalities and political characters like Wilhelm I and Bismarck — but it failed with their successors who did not have comparable political strength.

B. CONSTITUTIONS OF THE *LÄNDER*

The *Wiener Bundesakte* (1815) put the obligation on all *Bundesstaaten* to pass their own constitution. These constitutions contained only a few democratic elements and can be divided into three groups:

---

[16] Prussia as one of those *Bundesstaaten* held an institutional predominance: its king was the hereditary emperor and his appointed prime minister was acting as the *Reichskanzler*.

(a) *South-German constitutions*[17] with a monarchical, aristocratic character and — like the French "*Charte constitutionnelle*" (1814) and the famous English constitution drafted by Montesquieu — provided two chambers: one chamber was reserved for the aristocracy and the other chamber was occupied by deputies who were socially and financially well-off, belonged to the educated class, must have reached a certain age and — in most cases — had been elected indirectly.

(b) *North-German constitutions*[18] followed the modern constitution of Belgium (1831) — with one important exception: the provision that all power comes from the people themselves was not adopted. This provision would have stood in contrast to the understanding of German kings, the *Bundesakte* and the monarchical principle in the *Wiener Schlußakte*. Therefore, from a modern point of view we cannot think of the nineteenth century German constitution as a democratic one.

(c) In Prussia it took a long time until a formal constitution was passed.[19] Wilhelm IV had been in distress because of the revolution in 1848 (the *Verfassungsoktroi*) and, due to this, imposed a formal constitution on his people. It provided that deputies of the chamber had to be elected in electoral proceedings in accordance with the three classes (*Dreiklassenwahlrecht*) which represented the existing three tax classes. In Prussia electoral law differentiated between rich and poor people in order to preserve the status quo. Obviously, this has nothing in common with democratic ideas at all.

The principle that the government was legally bound by the laws had been in existence before — but was now formally accepted and laid down in the constitution. In addition, together with the participation of the authority of the State in executive, legislative and judicial power (by Montesquieu), the *Grundsatz der gesetzmäßigen Verwaltung* (principle of lawful administration) was enacted into the constitutions of the *Bundesstaaten* as well. This principle is a characteristic feature of a *Rechtsstaat* (Constitutional State) and entails separation of

---

[17] Such as Baden and Bayern (1818), Württemberg (1819), Hessen-Darmstadt (1820).

[18] Such as Sachsen and Kurhessen (1831), Braunschweig (1832), Hannover (1833).

[19] In Austria, a formal constitution was issued as late as 1867.

powers, the court's independence, the guarantee of human and political rights and the foreseeability of statute-making governmental actions. It was no longer sufficient that authorities tried to uphold the law — their actions also had to be based on legal grounds. In addition, the principle of *nulla poena sine lege* which had been realised in some statutes before was in force everywhere in the nineteenth century. Finally, civil judgments now had to be justified in written form — or at least orally — under specified legal provisions. Judges had to account to the parties that they had adjudicated by the virtue of law and not merely according to their sense of justice.

The *Bundesstaaten* laid down a few civil rights. The rights of liberty (*Freiheitsrechte*[20]) as expressed in the American constitution (1776–1787) and the French Declaration of Human and Political Liberty (1789) had been applied in Germany by the *Bundesstaaten* – either in their constitutions or other statutes. Nevertheless, the constitutions did not provide the principle of equality (*Gleichheitsgrundsatz*). This principle indeed prevailed in adjudication over centuries because judges were obliged to rule without reference to someone's class. In a substantive legal system, however, people did not only have different rights according to their class but also a different legal capacity. As a result, the endeavour to enforce equality was weakly enforced in the nineteenth century. Moreover, for the first time the duty to attend school (*Schulpflicht*) was in existence in Germany just as the obligation to serve in the armed forces — introduced in the Prussian *Hardenberg'schen* reform (1814).

C. CODIFICATION IN ALL AREAS OF THE LAW

In the second half of the nineteenth century, there was a strong tendency to codify any area of the law. Numerous statutes had been issued since 1871. Important examples are the *Reichsjustizgesetze* of 1877 such as the *Zivilprozeßordnung* (Code of Civil Procedure), *Strafprozeßordnung* (Code of Criminal Procedure), and the *Gerichtsverfassungsgesetz* (Judicature Act) which apply, with certain amendments, even today. Furthermore, the *Reichsstrafgesetzbuch* of 1871 (Criminal

---

[20] The acknowledged rights of liberty were as follows: personal freedom (abolition of slavery); freedom of property (abolition of lord manor's power — *Grundherrschaft)*; freedom of settlement (dissolution of corporate bindings); freedom of commerce and economy (abolition of the obligation to be in guilds (*Zunftzwang*); abolition of the right to banish tradesmen (*Gewerbebannrechte*); freedom of marriage (abolition of marriage restrictions); freedom of faith and of conscience just as freedom of press and associations.

Code of the Reich) and the *Kulturkampfgesetze* (1871–1875) which tried to overcome clerical resistance had been issued as well as the statutes of industrial property law, for instance on Copyright and Trademark Protection. In addition, Codes of Social, Insurance and Labour Law had been passed in *Bismarck's* era of political power (1881–1889) which made Germany at the time the most advanced social-political state in the world.

During the 1850s, there was a strong endeavour to codify civil law. In 1871 a commission of lawyers and professors started working on the *Bürgerliche Gesetzbuch* (BGB, Civil Code) which was passed in the *Reichstag* on July 1, 1896 and came into effect on January 1, 1900. This excellent legislative work is outstanding because of its systematic framework and precise wording which has allowed it to remain in force until today — although amended. Further details with regard to this masterpiece of legal handicraft — especially the amazing fact that the Civil Code was able to serve as the "bible" of the German system of private law in democratic times as well as during the Monarchy and the Fascists period — are set out in more detail in Chapter Two.

The French *Code d'instruction criminelle* (1808) had brought about important reforms in the field of criminal procedure. These reforms applied — after strong and long lasting disputes — in all of the German *Bundesstaaten* (around 1850) bringing the following innovations: preliminary proceedings and trial procedure were separated into two independent procedural parts whereas the main trial developed to become the most important part. The *Inquisitionsprozeß* was abolished, though the principles of investigation and of *ex officio* proceedings continued to exist. The Department of Public Prosecution now had two functions: to conduct the preliminary trial and to be the public prosecutor in the main trial. The principles of orality, public trial and directness prevailed. The principle of free evaluation of the evidence was valid just as the principle *in dubio pro reo* (innocent until proven guilty). Like the Germanic *concilium* and the English jury, *Schwurgerichte* (criminal chamber of courts) had been set up consisting of judges and *Geschworene* (jurors). These, however, were later replaced by the *Schöffengerichte* (criminal courts with professional judges and lay assessors) in order to save expenses ("*Emmingersche Justizreform*") in 1924.

7. SOCIAL LIBERAL STATE

A. THE WEIMAR REPUBLIC (*WEIMARER REICHSVERFASSUNG*) (1919)

Towards the end of the First World War (1914–1918), on October 28, 1918, a new government was formed with the *Reichskanzler* Prinz Max von Baden and state secretaries of all the political parties. The *Reichskanzler* now only had the political power to exercise his official functions with the consent of the *Reichstag*. The Constitutional Monarchy became a Parliamentary Monarchy. In addition, as allied governments refused to enter into peace negotiations with the German sovereigns, Wilhelm II declared his abdiction (November 9, 1918). On the same day the republic was proclaimed. This was the end of the *Bismarck'sche Reichverfassung*.

The *Nationalversammlung* — gathering on February 6, 1919 — drew up a "*Notverfassung*" — a provisional constitution to prevent further political deadlock. Friederich Ebert was elected as *Reichskanzler* and Philipp Scheidemann took the office of the Prime Minister (*Ministerpräsident*). Their main task consisted of setting up a new Republican Constitution of the Reich. On July 31, 1919 — after the *Versailler Friedensvertrag* (June 6, 1919) had empowered Germany to reform their internal relations — the *Weimarer Reichverfassung* was passed by peoples' representatives within the *Reichstag*. The *Weimarer Reichsverfassung* was the first constitution to contain *Grundrechte* (Constitutional Civil Rights). It also transferred public power from the *Länder* to the Reich by abolishing the *Reservatrechte* of the *Bismarck'sche Reichsverfassung* — the competence to decide upon, for instance, tram, post and to levy taxes, were now allotted to the Reich.

The *Reichstag* as the highest political body in the Reich was a committee of peoples' representatives — a revolutionary feature was that now (for the first time in German legal history) women were allowed to run for a seat in Parliament; generally deputies could be elected from the age of 25 onwards. Moreover, the electoral system changed from a majority vote system into a *Verhältniswahlsystem* (proportional representation) which diminished the power of single candidates and strengthened the power of the listed parties. Another political body was the *Reichsrat* consisting of representatives of the *Länder* — the former *Bundesstaaten*. It was the successor of the former *Bundesrat* but was less powerful than before — nevertheless, the *Reichsrat* was able both to initiate and hinder the enactment of new statutes. The position of the *Reichspräsident* corresponded with the former position of the emperor with the major exception being that he was elected. He had the usual duties of the head of state, such as to be the Reich's representative, to appoint civil servants, to be the commander-in-chief of the army, to have the prerogative of mercy, to appoint the *Reichskanzler* and the ministers and to break up the *Reichstag* under specific requirements and announce new elections.

During the *Weimarer* time, the *Reichstag* had to deal with very difficult problems, and political disorder along with social and financial problems of the State added to these difficulties.[21] The *Weimarer Reichsverfassung* itself tended to obstruct the work of the *Reichstag*. Numerous tiny political parties were allowed to be present in the *Reichstag* because of the unlimited admission of political parties. Therefore, conducting negotiations and passing resolutions was difficult. Furthermore, deputies became politicians by career because the enormous demands of the *Reichstag* required that they had to gather almost every day; their re-election was now a question of existence and their interest was more to gain the voter's favour than to pass effective resolutions. The consequence was that since 1930 deputies in Parliament have refused to pass unpopular resolutions in order to hold their place in Parliament. It was now left to the *Reichspräsident* to overcome economic, social and political problems by issuing emergency decrees. The legal basis of these decrees (Article 48 II of the constitution) was questionable indeed, because it was a so-called *Notverordnungsrecht* (right of emergency decrees[22]), and the *Reichspräsident* was able to issue these decrees only because the term *öffentliche Sicherheit und Ordnung* (public peace and order and public security) was interpreted in a very broad way.

During this time, the Government tried to overcome the economic crisis, among other things, by ordering deep salary cuts and by limiting national expenditure — a political agenda which at the end of the day, did not work at all. The contrary happened: the unemployment rate rose to an extreme level. Left and right wing political parties became more and more successful at polls, because people were not satisfied with the situation. It has to be pointed out that the, at least to some extent, the

---

[21] The revolution caused disorder and subversion, with political assassinations of ministers Erzberger (1921) and Rathenau (1922), the occupation of the *Ruhrgebiet* (industrial area), passive resistance (1923), massive inflation of the German currency (1923) and the international economic crisis (1929) made the development from a liberal to a social constitutional state difficult.

[22] Pursuant to Art. 48 II, the *Reichspräsident* could take measures to restore the former condition while he abrogates for a limited time the *Grundrechte* in case of a present, serious disturbance of public peace and order or public security or in case of their endangering.

liberal *Weimarer* Constitution led to the political system being misused by non-democratic parties and politicians. This was the historical soil which prepared the ground for the fascistic catastrophe and opened the door for the Nazi regime. The result: on January 30, 1933, Adolf Hitler was formally appointed as *Reichskanzler.*

B. NATIONAL SOCIALISM (*NATIONALS SOZIALISTISCHE ZEIT*) (1933–1945)

Between 1933 and 1945 Germany ceased to be a constitutional and democratic state. Hitler became a dictator after he had induced the *Reichstag* to grant him unlimited power (*Ermächtigungsgesetz* (Enabling Act) 1933). He then took combined power as *Führer, Reichskanzler* and *Reichspräsident*. During his dictatorship he removed all representations of the *Länder,* abolished trade unions and replaced them by the *Deutsche Arbeiterfront,* he also forbade any activities of political parties — except for the *Nationalsozialistische Deutsche Arbeiterpartei* (NSDAP). Obviously, the most terrible attempt was to "eliminate the Jews" as he had expressed and to some extent predicted in his book *Mein Kampf* ("My Fight" — which was written during a period Hitler had to serve in prison). In the *Gesetz zur Wiederherstellung des Berufsbeamtentums* (April 1933) all "non-Aryan" people and those without National Socialist views were excluded from public service. From 1933 boycotts of Jewish shops were organised and officially directed mass riots were used to plunder. Finally, the *Nürnberger Gesetze* (1935) forbade marriages of "germanic" people and Jews, and in 1938 the Jews were forbidden to conduct any trade or business. In a way, this development was merely the beginning of what happened later. Hitler tried to achieve the "*Endlösung der Judenfrage*" — a cynical expression that describes the final solution of the Jewish question. Even if the dictator did not manage to fulfil this aim more than six million people lost their lives in this dark period of German history.

During the Second World War the Nazi regime attempted to become the leading power in the world. Given that this section of the book deals with legal history, it must be noted that during the Fascist era (1933–1945) there was a dictatorship which abolished the democratic legal system which had been developed. The Third Reich radically amended the existing German legal system to suit the aims of the Nazi state, however, following the end of the Second World War the allies repealed all of these Nazi laws. See Chapter Three for a more detailed analysis of this period of German legal history.

C. OCCUPYING POWERS (*BESATZUNGSMÄCHTE*) (1945–1949)

In the time between 1945–1949, the French, American, English and Soviet *Besatzungsmächte* (occupying powers) governed Germany. Germany and Berlin had been divided into four occupation zones pursuant to both the agreement in Yalta between Stalin, Roosevelt and Churchill in February 1945 and the convention between the occupation troops' commanders-in-chief of America, the Soviet Union, England and France on July 5, 1945. The occupation zones were defined by the *Kontrollrat* in Berlin which was composed of four commanders-in-chief of the occupying powers. Their main aim was to abolish National Socialism, to disarm Germany and to re-erect a constitution and a resumption of responsibility of the countries own affairs — in other words: to build up what had been destroyed during the past 12 years of the Nazi regime. One can imagine that it took several years until the German State managed to recover.

D. CONSTITUTION (*GRUNDGESETZ*) (1949) AND UNIFICATION (1989)

The *Grundgesetz der Bundesrepulik Deutschland*[23] (Constitution of the Federal Republic of Germany, FRG) came into force on the March 23, 1949. It contained similarities to the *Paulskirchenverfassung* (1848) and the *Weimarer Reichsverfassung* (1918) and introduced a canon of effective basic rights, as part of constitutional civil rights, constitutional principles and system.

Since 1949, the *Bundesrepublik Deutschland* and the *Deutsche Demokratische Republik* (German abbreviation: DDR; English abbreviation: GDR, German Democratic Republic) existed as two separate states. The constitution (November 7, 1949) of the GDR was based on different principles to the *Grundgesetz* of the *Bundesrepublik Deutschland* (FRG — Federal Republic of Germany), for instance the *Sozialistische Einheitspartei Deutschlands* (SED) governed the country, not the people of the DDR, and property was nationalised. For four decades the GDR existed as a socialist state which was strongly influenced by the former Soviet Union.

In 1989, there was pressure to reform the GDR; the opening and abolition of the *Berliner Mauer* (Berlin Wall) (November 9/10, 1989) and a few amendments of the constitution of the former GDR were carried out. On May 18, 1990 the two German States agreed to a *Staatsvertrag* (international treaty) and, finally, on July 1, 1990 *Währungsunion* (monetary union)

---

[23] For more details see Chap. Three.

was set in force. On November 3, 1990, both states signed the so-called *Einigungsvertrag* (Treaty of Re-Unification) in which the GDR joined the FRG on the basis of Article 23 of the *Grundgesetz*. Berlin became the capital of the unified German State.

E. LEGAL SOURCES

In the twentieth century the law of administration and its procedure has been codified and specified — such as the *Verwaltungsgerichtsordnung* (Law of Administrative Court Procedure, 1960) and the *Verwaltungsverfahrensgesetz* (Law of Administrative Process, 1974). The growing field of administrative law in the twentieth century was influenced by the change from an executive administration during the nineteenth century into an administration of community services in the twentieth century. Moreover, during this century numerous acts have been passed to specify further distinct fields of law — such as taxation, company, competition, labour, criminal, and civil law and procedure.

SELECTED BIBLIOGRAPHY

Textbooks

Dulckeit, Schwarz, Waldstein, *Römische Rechtsgeschichte* (9th ed., 1995).
Eisenhardt, *Deutsche Rechtsgeschichte* (2nd ed., 1992).
Koschaker, *Europa und das römische Recht* (4th ed., 1966).
Mitteis, Lieberich, *Deutsche Rechtsgeschichte* (19th ed., 1992).
Söllner, *Einführung in die römische Rechtsgeschichte* (4th ed., 1989).
Willoweit, *Deutsche Verfassungsgeschichte, Von Frankreich bis zur deutschen Wiedervereinigung* (3rd ed., 1997).

Chapter Two
Sources of German Law

1. Codification

One of the most striking differences between the English common law system and the German system is that Germany has had a codified law since the Age of Enlightenment during the seventeenth and eighteenth centuries. The widely divided structure of the German territory in the nineteenth century and the efforts made to reach national unification led to the introduction of statutes and the prevailing importance of statute law in the most important areas of the legal system. It is fair to say that some common law countries — like the U.S., India and Canada — have compiled and drafted quite a number of codes, but even so: the idea of structuring the existing law and presenting it as a whole in different sets of statutes is the basic principle of civil law countries and reflects the philosophical idea of the law of reason.

From a practical point of view the most relevant modern Codes are the *Bürgerliches Gesetzbuch* (Civil Code), the *Strafgesetzbuch* (Criminal Code), the different Commercial Codes (such as the *Handelsgesetzbuch* (Commercial Code), the *Aktiengesetz* (Company Law), the *GmbH-Gesetz* (Code of Limited Liability Company) and — above all — the *Grundgesetz* (Constitution). So Germany is in line with most of the other European legal systems which also arrange the existing law in a structured way (*e.g.* Spain, Italy, France) — except for the English, Scottish and Irish systems.

Nevertheless, the impact of national (and international) jurisdiction on the shape and content of German law is steadily gaining importance — in fact we could say that this brings all the most notable changes to the German legal system, because a code that is getting older and older is overlapped by several layers of case law. From a comparative point of view this is quite a remarkable development, because the modern German legal system is developing in the opposite direction to the English common law system. On the English side of the channel there is now a tendency to codify certain practically important areas of the law, whereas in Germany one has to accept the formation of a system in which case law is, if not yet prevailing, on its way to becoming a dominant factor within the legal system.

This is so because changes in society take place at a faster pace today than compared to, for instance, in the nineteenth century. The reaction of legislative bodies towards new demands and needs of society are inevitably slow — whereas the importance of judicial decisions to set up rules is increasing in every branch of law.

Given this, we can now witness a process that brings the two legal systems in Germany and England closer together which cannot be a surprise if one takes into account that — to use the practically most important example — the Civil Code is now in its "late nineties". This eminent statute, which is ruling relevant legal parts of the German citizen's everyday life, has survived four political revolutions (1918, 1933, 1945 and 1989), has served during a monarchy (1900–1918), a dictatorial Fascist regime (1933–1945) and two democratic systems (1919–1933, 1945 until today). Furthermore, the Civil Code represents the legal basis by which millions of citizens of the former *Deutsche Demokratische Republik* (German Democratic Republic) have become familiar with the needs and the legal environment of a competitive and market-orientated society. These historical facts do prove the impressive standard of the legislative skills behind the Civil Code. On the other hand new social, political, economic and legal circumstances and problems have prepared the ground for changes of the law that are inevitable to meet the requirements and obviously necessary adoptions.

There are, for instance, new areas like *Arbeitsrecht* (labour law), *Verbraucherkreditgesetz* (Consumer Credit Act) and *Gesetz zur Regelung des Rechts der Allgemeine Geschäftsbedingungen* (Code regulating the Law of General Terms and Conditions of Trade or Business). These are some of the most relevant parts of German consumer law — just to give you a few examples to show the different ways the legislative bodies have chosen to keep the Civil Code fit for the needs and requirements of modern society. Labour law, for instance, was originally contained in just a few paragraphs — §§ 611 *et seq.* — of the Civil Code, but is today a legal discipline of its own and is ruled in special sets of statutes outside the Civil Code whereas the other areas we just mentioned above supplemented the original Civil Code.

2. HIERARCHY OF LEGAL SOURCES — THE LEGAL PYRAMID

The German legal system has different legal sources and moreover a certain structure of legal norms which can be compared to a pyramid. As we mentioned before, the most important sources of the law are laid down in statutes, which is written law that is generally applicable to all members of society. Case law is also a source in its own right, and we have to take into account the huge body of *Gewohnheitsrecht* (customary law) and also legal writings as a persuasive source of law.

A. GERMAN NATIONAL LAW

The different types of legal norms do have to be seen in a strictly hierarchical order; any norm that is of lower rank has to comply with a norm of higher rank — if there is a conflict of rules in a certain case, the higher rule prevails. The most eminent written law is contained in the *Grundgesetz* (Constitution) which forms the top-end of the legal pyramid. Two examples may point out this extraordinary position.

In the words of Article 1 III GG: "The following basic rights shall bind the legislature, the executive and the judiciary as directly enforceable law".

Moreover Article 20 III GG states that: "The legislature shall be subject to the constitutional order, the executive and the judiciary shall be bound by law and justice".

If one studies the content of the above norms one can notice, that Article 1 III GG in connection with Article 20 III GG seals the priority of the constitution in comparison to any other law. From a theoretical point of view this is a true democratic concept which points out that the existence of the constitution itself is justified, because it is accepted by the majority of people as *the* basic order of the community.

Gesetze (law, act or statute) come next to the constitutional norms in terms of practical importance. In the German concept of law the statutes are the basis and anchor of the legal system. The term statute is formally defined as a legal rule that is abstract and generally binding on anyone, enacted by the responsible legislative bodies in formal legislative proceedings and published in the *Bundesgesetzesblatt* (Federal Law Gazette). *Staatsverträge* (State Treaties) do have the same effect and impact as statutes.

Next to statutes are several forms of *Rechtsverordnungen* (statutory instruments) and *Satzungen* (byelaws or charters of public organs). Those types of legal norms are set into effect by certain public authorities and have the function of explaining the ambit of statutes in more detail. Therefore, the legislative power for delegated legislation has to be given within the statute itself.

The role of *Verwaltungsvorschriften* (administrative provisions or regulations) is increasingly important. In practice those rules affect the ordinary citizen as well, because the executive is bound by the principle of equality which in the German system is one of the basic rights and laid down in Article 3 I GG.[1] Therefore, public authorities (and any civil servant) have a duty to handle and decide a comparable case of citizen Mr A in the same way as the one of Mrs B. In other words the interpretation of regulatory orders in a certain way leads to a self-restriction and a duty of the executive body to take into account the demands of Art. 3 I GG in any single decision.

Beside the sources of law we have mentioned so far there is another specific point which has to be stressed. Due to the fact that the German political and legal system is federal, one has to differentiate between federal law and *Land* law. Germany is a federal state but it is divided into 16 *Länder.* There are legislative bodies at both levels,[2] with different powers. The most important principle with regard to this fact is that federal law overrides *Land* law (the German formula is: *Bundesrecht bricht Landesrecht*) — a pure matter of fact which is laid down in the German constitution as well: Article 31 GG is the relevant norm in this context, and solves the basic and potential conflict between federal law and law of the *Länder* in favour of the former. With regard to the principle of federation, therefore, Article 31 GG is a fundamental rule for the understanding of the German legal system.

Interestingly enough, the collision rule does not differ between the rank of federal and *Länder* law — in other words: federal delegated legislation prevails over statute law in one of the *Länder*. This fact underlines that the spiritual fathers of the German constitution were — due to historical reasons and especially experiences during the period of the "Third Reich" — dedicated followers of the federal concept. A concept which has the fundamental advantage of securing the certainty of law with respect to society as a whole.

B. LAW OF NATIONS (*VÖLKERRECHT*)

This body of legal rules stands independently at the same level as national law. Again one can see that the Constitution is a

---

[1] For more details, see *ibid.*, Chap. Three, 7, B, (3).
[2] For more details, see *ibid.*, Chap. Three, 5, A.

rich source for the most important regulations: Article 59 II GG states that treaties concerning political relations of the Federation or the federal legislation need either the approval or the contribution of the authorised national legislative bodies. That means treaties under the reign of the law of nations become part of German law by being officially announced as (and transformed into) a national statute — the *Europäische Konvention zum Schutz der Menchenrechte und Grundfreiheiten* (European Convention for Human Rights) can be used as a very prominent example.

Anyway, the basic rule of Article 59 II GG has to be seen in connection with Article 25 GG which deals with those parts of the law of nations that becomes part of the national legal system without any act of transformation: the general rules of the law of nations does form an integral part of German law. In theory, these rules even prevail in comparison with national statutes and they are binding on any German citizen.[3] The only problem is that up until now there have not been many rules accepted as being "general" in the sense of Article 25 GG. A precondition is that a majority of states acknowledges a certain rule as being fundamental[4] — as has happened for the principle of a fair trial[5] or of proper legal protection for foreigners.[6]

It has to be underlined that those generally accepted rules of the law of nations are in a legal class of their own. In other words (and to use the pyramidal picture once again): general rules in the sense of Article 25 GG do rank lower than the German national constitution, but they are still superior with regard to "ordinary" national statutes.

C. EUROPEAN COMMUNITY LAW (*EUROPARECHT*)

Another important source of private German law is E.C. law which fulfils a double function as a body of law in its own right and as an integral part of the national legal system. In terms of ranking of legal rules and sources it should be highlighted that E.C. law supercedes national German law — including the constitution.

(1) Primary and secondary E.C. law

One must differentiate between primary and secondary E.C. law. The first refers only to the three founding treaties of

---

[3] See the wording of Art. 25 GG.
[4] BVerfGE 15, 25, 34.
[5] BVerfGE 63, 332, 338.
[6] BVerfGE 60, 253, 303.

the European Community (and its later amendments), the *Einheitliche Europäische Akte* (Single European Act) signed on July 1, 1987 and the treaty on the foundation of the European Union signed on February 2, 1992.

More important with regard to our topic is the body of secondary E.C. law — which in terms of practical importance is by no means law of a second rank. Secondary E.C. law includes statutory orders, directives, decisions of the European Court and also recommendations, official statements of EEC organs and treaties with other (non-E.U.) states.

(2) National basic rights versus (secondary) European law

The most relevant practical question lies with the problem of how to handle conflicts of law arising between secondary E.C. law — implemented in a legally correct way by competent legislative organs — and German national law, especially constitutional law. Are German courts — namely the *Bundesverfassungsgericht* (Federal Constitutional Court) in Karlsruhe — allowed to judge on and to examine norms of European law using the national basic rights (Articles 1 to 19 GG) as relevant criteria?

The majority of German scholars and the jurisdiction of the European and national courts nowadays stand on a common ground in that E.C. law (secondary and of course primary) prevails in comparison with the body of national legal rules and even the catalogue of basic rights. The main legal argument for this opinion is that the functioning of E.C. institutions must not be undermined — the so-called *principe del' effet utile.* Another reason in favour of this point of view is that Germany as a member of the European Union has accepted E.C. law as an integral part of the national legal system.

Even if this might sound logical enough, it took the German Constitutional Court at least seven key decisions and almost 20 years to decide this question. The starting point was the famous *Solange I* decision given on May 29, 1974.[7] In this case the court held that *as long as* there is no catalogue of basic rights on the European level which is adequate (and comparable) to the standards of the German constitution, the Constitutional Court shall have the competence to use the national constitution (and the national basic rights) to judge on the question on whether a certain EEC statutory order complies with national law.

This in fact meant nothing less than the following principle:

[7] BVerfGE 37, 271.

national law prevails if in conflict with European law. A legal opinion which obviously runs counter to the common and widely accepted aim of creating a European Union. And, therefore, it is no surprise that the Federal Constitutional Court had to adapt its judgments to the requirements of the process of European Unification.[8] The most remarkable move in this direction came in the case of *Solange II*.[9] On October 22, 1986 the court held that "*as long as*" the EEC organs — and especially the *Europäische Gerichtshof* (European Court of Justice) — will make sure that basic rights are obeyed in a proper way, the German Federal Constitutional Court will no longer use the national Constitution as criteria for the binding effect of (secondary) EEC law on German courts or authorities. This was an impressive change of opinion that can be seen as a sign of the growing success of European integration.

D. CUSTOMARY LAW (*GEWOHNHEITSRECHT*)

Customary law is recognised to be a source of law in its own right, closely related to judge-made law. It consists of long-practised customs that are followed and appreciated by a majority of people who are convinced about the legality of the custom. It must be stressed that there is customary law on a federal basis and on the basis of the different *Länder*. But given the enormously high degree of codified law and judge-made law in Germany today, there is little room (and little practical importance) for customary law at all.

E. JURISDICTION (*RECHTSPRECHUNG*)

As another important source of law we have to take into account the exceptionally important role of the judiciary in practice. Despite the fact that Germany has a codified system, it is — of course — not just regulated by statutes. Therefore, especially in the second half of our century, it is simply not correct to put a common law system as we have it in the United Kingdom for instance in strict contrast to the German codified system. Judge-made law in a statute-dominated legal system is gaining more and more influence as the system gets older. No legislative body, however thoughtful and wise, is able to incorporate the uncertainties of social changes at the time of

---

[8] To recapitulate the long and (as some say) "painful" route the court had to take see the following judgments in BVerfGE 52, 187, 202; BVerfGE 58, 1, 27 — Eurocontrol; BVerfGE, NJW 1983, 1258.

[9] BVerfGE 73, 339, 387.

drafting a new code. No one is able to foresee all the possible cases that might arise in the future.

This is the point where the role of the judiciary becomes relevant: judges have to interpret the law[10] and to keep it in check with changing situations. The fact that the methods and tools of interpretation in Germany are basically different from the British approach helps to make this task more accessible — but nevertheless the development of existing law by means of judicial decisions is one of the main methodological guarantees to help a codified system survive in practice. Methods and tools of interpretation in Germany differ from the British approach primarily because of the different legal systems. A codified legal system has to take a different approach in order to solve a particular case which involves using specific tools of legal interpretation in comparison with a legal system based on case law like the English one.

It is fair to say that courts nowadays have a dominant position in legal practice — which is extraordinary if one considers that the German system of the nineteenth century used to be influenced and dominated by academics.[11]

From a comparative point of view it is interesting to stress that the German legal system is generally unfamiliar with the theory of binding effects of precedent. This might sound strange to common law jurists at first hand, but is a consequence arising from the different systematic approaches. In Germany, a judgment only has and develops a certain effect *between* the parties of a legal procedure — usually plaintiff and defendant. Furthermore, due to Article 20 III in connection with Article 97 of the German constitution a judge is bound only by statutes and the law — not by precedent. From this theoretical background it is therefore possible that a court of first instance (usually the *Amtsgericht* — County Court) could take a different legal opinion than — for instance — the *Bundesgerichtshof* (Federal Court of Justice).[12]

Of course in reality it is general practice that decisions of higher courts do influence the minor courts. Why should a court of first instance hold a certain opinion if there is no doubt that the court of second instance will dismiss it anyway? Moreover, whenever a higher court doesn't hold a certain decision in an

---

[10] For more details, see *ibid.*, Chap. Two, 3.

[11] As a result of this fact one can notice the professional approach of statutes particularly in the late nineteenth century. For more details, see *ibid.*, Chap. One, 7, C.

[12] For more details regarding the court structure in Germany, see *ibid.*, Chap. Five, 2.

appeal case and sends the case back to the first instance again — then the minor court is bound by the decision of the higher one.

There are even more procedural situations which create a binding effect. Again we have to realise and to accept the special and dominating role of the Federal Constitutional Court: due to § 31 I BVerfGG (*Bundesverfassungsgerichtsgesetz* — Code of the Federal Constitutional Court) any other German court, constitutional organ (on federal and *Länder* level) and authority has to obey the effect of decisions and judgments coming from the highest German court. In certain cases these judgments have the same effect as statutes. Furthermore, whenever a court of second instance, in other words a Court of Appeal, *e.g.* the *Oberlandesgericht* (Regional Appeal Court) in civil cases, the *Oberverwaltungsgericht* (Higher Administrative Court) in public law matters[13] — intends to take a different legal opinion than a higher court, the court cannot decide straight away but has to ask for the (then binding and final) decision of the next higher court.

3. STATUTORY INTERPRETATION (*GESETZESAUSLEGUNG*)

A. GENERAL

Any lawyer has to deal with language, because legal norms are written down in statutes. Therefore, any lawyer is also — in the true sense of the word — an interpreter, because his task is to understand and "translate" the legal wording for other people — be they clients or students or colleagues. Statutory interpretation is basically different from the interpretation methods in England which shall be discussed in greater detail in this chapter. First of all there is no approach similar to the British strict and narrow interpretation system asking for the objective sense of a rule, and there is also no restriction on the bare wording of a certain paragraph as commanded by the doctrine of literal interpretation.

And why is that so? Primarily because of the theoretical background: in Germany the so-called jurisprudence of valuation (*Wertungsjurisprudenz*) prevails. It is a classical doctrine which was taken forward during the second half of the nineteenth century by the then famous Professor of Law Phillipp Heck (1858–1943).[14] Due to this theory, dealing with the law means

---

[13] For more details, see *ibid.*, Chap. Five, 2.

[14] Although thoughts in the same direction are found in Rudolf von Jhering's (an even more prominent lawyer) publications at the same time. For details see Heck, *Das Problem der Rechtsgewinnung* (2nd ed., 1932) and von Jhering, *Der Kampf ums Recht*, (4th ed., 1832).

to find out the legislative valuation originally intended with a certain statutory decision.

The German Civil Code, for instance,[15] was enacted on January 1, 1900 and has to be seen as the legislative result of a typical mixture and collection of conservative and liberal thoughts which were prominent during that historic period. The legislative intention was to unify private law in the then young State (which was founded as "*Deutsches Reich*" only 29 years earlier) — but obviously the law — and social and political circumstances — has changed during the last 98 years.

Consequently, a lawyer who has to work, who has to interpret an old code like the Civil Code, has to try to adjust any legal rule to modern requirements. The concept of the doctrine of *Wertungsjurisprudenz* allows exactly this: in order to understand basic ideas of the statute (and the relevant norm itself) any interpreter has to take into account the respective historical situation which lead to the enactment.

Having this knowledge is the starting point to understand the sense and the spirit of a certain legal rule. In other words the interpreter has to determine the objective content expressed by the legislator — the remarkable point of fact is that he has to find out the objective intention *transformed* to the time of applying the rule. Given this pliant technique of dealing with old codes and statutes it becomes clear that even the oldest legal rule can be adapted to today's requirements.[16]

B. TOOLS OF INTERPRETATION

(1) Introduction — the "*Savigny'sche Quart*"

Basically there are four methods of interpretation: literal, systematical, historical interpretation and the search for the so-called "*ratio legis*", the objective sense of a certain norm. This classical canon was introduced to the scientific legal world by the famous Professor Friedrich — Carl von Savigny. From his point of view interpretation is a "scientific deal, starting point and basis of any application of the law, but also . . .

[15] Which we would like to take as an example because of its importance as the eminent statute regulating the day-to-day lives of German citizens.

[16] A fact which might give you an idea of why it was possible for the Civil Code to survive two World Wars, the Fascist era and two democratic systems without being abolished or radically changed at any stage. Today the Civil Code — though frequently amended and being expanded across the former GDR — is well on course to celebrating its centenary.

art".[17] This famous quotation very clearly shows the double-edged position of legal interpretation: on the one hand practising the four main interpretation methods — the so-called "*Savigny'sche Quart*" — is nothing else but pure legal handicraft; on the other hand it is also an intellectual challenge to juggle terms and to therefore persuade by means of distinguishing. At this point it has to be stressed that the different methods are not mutually exclusive but complement each other. Together they serve a common aim: the ascertainment of an objective meaning of a legal rule which has caused problems in a particular case.

Given this it becomes quite clear that statutory interpretation in Germany is in methodological terms totally different from the British approach: asking for the objective sense of a norm, the *ratio legis*, goes far beyond a self-restriction only to the wording of a certain paragraph as commanded by the English doctrine of literal interpretation. Furthermore — and this, too, is a fact that has to be taken into account in order to understand methodological differences between the two countries — the extensive use of extrinsic materials as well as the application to historical interpretation is quite common in continental Europe. The consequences of this fundamental divergence will be discussed below. Please note that since *Pepper (Inspector of Taxes) v. Hart* [1993] A.C. 591 in which the House of Lords significantly relaxed the general prohibition as it relates to Acts of Parliament, the English approach to statutory interpretation has become more similar to that taken in Germany.

(2) Literal interpretation

We have now introduced you to the main methods of statutory interpretation. Nevertheless, literal interpretation is naturally the first choice to begin within statutory interpretation. The interpretation of the sense of any expression has boundaries. Which is the explanation that does not necessarily lead to misinterpretation? This is exactly the balance which has to be found.

The basic point is that any interpretation which is strictly against the wording is inadmissible whereas an extensive interpretation is allowed as a basis for further investigation. This of course is not difficult at all if there are official legal definitions to refer to. The German legislator quite often uses such definitions to prevent any doubt as far as the intention and spirit of a

---

[17] Savigny, *System des heutigen Römischen Rechts* (1st–8th eds, 1840–1849), Vol. 1, pp. 206 *et seq.*

certain norm is concerned. To give an example: § 90 BGB, for instance, explains the legal term "*Thing*" — a word which in the sense of this code only refers to physical objects such as a pencil, a book or a personal computer. Consequently, § 90 BGB does not apply to any non-physical object such as — for instance — gas. If there is in a particular case no such legislative assistance, the common literal meaning in the context of the whole statute has to be examined. The result is a mixture of literal and systematical interpretation.

The use of specialised literature or even an ordinary dictionary is permissible, for colloquial speech terms personal understanding is decisive. Another important question is to establish whether the wording used by the historical legislator or modern language is relevant. The time of enacting a certain statute matters because otherwise the legislative intention could be missed. But no rule is without exception, because generally modern comprehension turns the scale. In this way the law tries to adapt even the oldest enactments to today's legal requirements — an advantage which keeps the statutory law applicable and almost independent from the time factor.

(3) Systematical interpretation

Systematical reasons — in other words the context of a certain rule is placed within a statute — functions as an evidentiary fact, because any rule is part of a wider legislative surrounding which has to be interpreted without any logical contradiction. The result of a methodical operation like this is the so-called "horizontal" and "vertical" harmonisation of regulations — or to put it more simply, a uniform understanding of a certain term within a statute (= horizontal) and a congruity with law of a higher rank (*e.g.* constitutional law = vertical).

With regard to systematical interpretation the following four methodical thoughts are essential:

(a) Certain sections under a common headline usually deal with a special legal problem. §§ 823–847 BGB for instance contains the German law of torts. § 847 BGB entitles one to damages for pain and suffering — a systematical interpretation leads to the result that this paragraph only refers to torts mentioned in this particular chapter of the Civil Code.

(b) The further rule concerns the meaning of a certain expression in different parts of a statute. Due to this, no legal rule should be interpreted in a way which makes another rule redundant. Therefore, statutory interpretation has to find out whether the interpretation question has the same or a different meaning with regard to the entire statute.

(c) Another rule deals with systematical conclusions from basic principles of the legal system or a certain field of the law. The German *Sachenrecht* (law of property) for example restricts contractual freedom, because one has to consider the limiting effects of enumerative legal institutes — the *numerus clausus* effect. This means the restricted admission to those legal institutes which the law of property provides.

(d) Finally, there is a comparative interpretation of foreign law in important cases. A principle which is not unknown in the United Kingdom, because British courts are used to taking into account the decisions of judges throughout the Commonwealth and the U.S. as well.

(4) Historical interpretation

The Federal Constitutional Court has decided that legislative intentions (laid down in parliamentary drafts), recorded discussions in Parliament, special political committees and the genetic development of a certain statute are fundamental parts of any statutory interpretation.[18]

In this respect we are introduced to another striking difference between Germany and the United Kingdom: the *mischief rule*[19] and its restricted canon of appropriate questions which demands a method of interpretation which is subjective and historical as well as teleological. In Germany, meanwhile, a more objective view is decisive. Of course, the original and "real" legislative intention — necessarily a subjective one — should be obeyed by the interpreter, but much more important is the objective content expressed in a legal rule as we understand it today.[20] Particularly in older rules the former legislative intention can be neglected whereas the objective sense is gaining priority steadily.

This way of dealing with legal rules goes hand in hand with other means of interpretation such as the search for the "*ratio legis*". Moreover, the historical interpretation gives a good example of the practical influence of the doctrine of *Wertungsjurisprudenz*.

---

[18] BVerfGE 79, 121 *et seq.*; see also BGHZ 46, 80.
[19] See Lord Coke in *Heydon's Case* (1854) 3 Co. Rep. 7 a.
[20] BVerwGE 74, 125.

(5) *Ratio legis*

Now we should turn our interest to the main interpretation method which — due to its practical importance — has already been mentioned. The search for the *ratio legis*[21] of a certain norm is the most significant means of statutory interpretation — in other words: the heart of the *Savigny'sche Quart*. Compared to the British way of statutory interpretation we notice a fundamental difference once again: because of the traditional priority of case law, statute law is — at any event from a theoretical point of view — merely a secondary source of law. Enacted law is often seen as a disturbing foreign body within the fine-spun net of precedents — with the help of judicial interpretation it becomes wrapped up in a curtain of precedents. K. C. Allen has described this kind of prejudice against statutes by using a striking metaphorical picture:

"It is a long judicial experience, that a sound and vigorous principle, once imprisoned within a formula of words, is like Gulliver bound by the Lilliputians".[22]

So, how does this methodical technique fit into German statutory interpretation and the method of *ratio legis*? The simple answer is: it does not fit at all. It has already been pointed out that due to German legal theory any rule follows a certain aim which can be recognised and valued by the underlying conflict of social interest. In many cases a legal rule is designed to solve more than one problem or expressively names its original legislative intention.[23] If that is not the case, the interpreter has to find out the relevant social conflict, compare it to the norm and then decide whether the rule is applicable or not. For this purpose a comparative analysis between abstract regulation and the concrete case has to be made, the so-called "*Subsumtion*". As a result of this: the rule fits if both elements — abstract and concrete — are congruent.

The decisive part of this process — which is not the handicraft but the more artful part of legal interpretation — is a valuation: any interpreter should ideally come to a conclusion

[21] From the Greek word *telos* — meaning "the sense".
[22] Allen, *Law in the Making* (6th ed., 1958), page 496.
[23] *e.g.* § 433, BGB as basic rule of the German law of contract. See also § 1 BImschG (*Bundesimmissionsschutzgesetz* — Law Concerning the Protection against Harmful Effects on the Environment through Air Pullution, Noise, Vibrations and Similar Factors) and § 1 BNatSchG (*Bundesnaturschutzgesetz* — Federal Nature Conservation Law).

which is practically useful and — this point should of course not be neglected — does not infringe ideals of justice.

Furthermore, there are other principles to be considered when applying the technique of *ratio legis*: general rules in a certain field of law have to be interpreted extensively, exceptional rules more strictly. Moreover, any legal interpretation has to take into account the possible (practical) consequences, because unlawful results would be contrary to the sense and aim of the respective norm. Finally, economic and ecological aspects have to be obeyed if (and whenever) relevant for the solution in a given case.

C. SPECIAL INTERPRETATION METHODS

Above this — and hopefully at this stage not surprisingly for you as reader — a good deal of attention has to be paid to the German constitution, the *Grundgesetz*, which was set into effect on May 24, 1949.[24] Even the official designation is interesting, because the legislator opted for "*Grundgesetz*" instead of "constitution" in order to underline its provisional character in a then divided German State which had hardly managed to recover from the political, economical as well as legal effects of a lost Second World War.

The provisional character of the constitution, while no longer strictly relevant, since the reunification of East and West Germany in 1990, is nevertheless of interest to a foreign lawyer who aims to understand the German techniques of handling the law and legal norms properly. In understanding the German method, one should always bear in mind the extraordinary position of the *Grundgesetz* within the legal system in this country.

First of all, the *Grundgesetz* contains rules of the highest rank[25] and has a tremendous impact on the interpretation and application of any other norm. This is exceptionally so with regard to constitutional rights — laid down primarily in Articles 1 to 19 GG — as these are fundamental regulations which influence private law as well. General clauses of the Civil Code such as § 242 BGB allow at least a vicarious effect for constitutional rights. Another outstanding constitutional norm

---

[24] As a somewhat strange (but in a way "typical" German) historical footnote it should be mentioned that Bavaria — which is always proud about its independence and special role among the German *Länder* — did not vote for the *Grundgesetz*. The political intention behind this move was to achieve more independence from federal restrictions and duties.

[25] For more details, see *ibid.*, Chap. Two, 2, A.

which is important for the interpretation process is Article 3 GG.[26] It is the fundamental regulation which guarantees equal rights for men and women and also for members of any race and religion. Therefore, the German legal interpreter — unlike the British counterpart who is not bound (and sometimes restricted) by a *written* constitution — always has to think about the *Grundgesetz* as the most important barrier and guideline for any interpretation work which has to be done.

Does all this theoretical knowledge help in practice? The answer to this question is this, the outstanding importance of the *Grundgesetz* generally demands the canon of interpretation methods that we have already introduced you to — in particular, the *Savigny'sche Quart* is applicable. But in addition — and due to the special position of the constitution within the German legal system — there are supplementary principles to be considered as well. The simple theoretical reason for this fact is that the *Grundgesetz* presents the most relevant and also far-reaching regulations with regard to German society as a whole. It combines legal and political questions — from a legal point of view a demanding fact that asks for the following principles of legal interpretation: a) Unity of constitution; b) Effectiveness of constitution; and c) Priority of constitution.

Again, what does this mean? The principle of unity of constitution reminds the interpreter to balance conflicting constitutional rules to ensure that each norm shows to advantage. Effectiveness of constitution means that legal rules have to be interpreted as exactly as possible to avoid any difficulties which might arise from the fact of constitutional abstractness.[27] Priority of constitution is simply the principle which demands that any other norm of a minor rank — regulations enacted in the German Civil Code for instance — have to comply with the *Grundgesetz*.[28]

This special method of dealing with the constitution in the legal day-to-day life is called "interpretation conforming to the constitution" (*verfassungskonforme Auslegung*). If one wants to judge dogmatically and in a strict sense about this method, it has to be seen as interpretation of minor legal rules[29] in the light of the *Grundgesetz* rather than a methodical category of its own.

---

[26] For more details, see *ibid.* Chap. Three, 7, B, (3).

[27] As you can imagine, the historical legislator has laid down the *Grundgesetz* — which, as basic law, contains relatively few regulations — in abstract language to enable the law to keep pace with changing social conditions.

[28] This fundamental principle was also part of the decision of the Federal Constitutional Court in BVerfGE 7, 207. As you can see a very early decision of the court that has never given up its legal opinion.

[29] Seen from the constitutional angle, any other rule is (by definition) of minor legal rank.

Nevertheless, obeying the principles we just mentioned opens up the paths to interpret the law in a more effective way.

D. EXCURSUS: "THE PREVAILING VIEW"

The term "prevailing view"[30] means an understanding of a certain sense of a legal rule which is shared by a majority of interpreters in literature and judicature. It is quite obvious (and has been pointed out before) that leading authors, practitioners, professors and also the decisions of higher courts influence the outcome of any interpretation process by publishing legal opinions and annotations to a legal problem in legal magazines[31] or textbooks.

One point is undisputed: opinions are in no way able to displace the legislative sense of a norm or statute — however leading and well reputed the author may be. On the other hand, an important and generally accepted view will be followed by other legal interpreters who are convinced about the reasoning. Moreover, newly arising legal questions have to be mastered by using the already tested methodical equipment — and, finally, no interpreter can afford to ignore legal positions or published comments that are presented by well-known authorities of the law such as judges or professors. By the way: this is a phenomenon which is basically comparable to the effect of persuasive authorities in the United Kingdom's legal system. Therefore, from a comparative point of view, it is worthwhile to note that the development and application of prevailing opinions is quite similar to the doctrine of *stare decisis* which establishes the binding effect of precedents. Both methodical tools can be described as conservative elements to keep the existing legal system in check.

E. AMENDMENTS OF INTERPRETATION METHODS

There are further principles and models of reasoning which are practically important and helpful to find out what a

---

[30] The German equivalent is "*herrschende Meinung*", usually abbreviated in judgments or textbooks as "h.M."

[31] The leading legal magazine in Germany is the *Neue Juristische Wochenschrift* (NJW) which has a weekly circulation of close to 60.000 copies. The NJW, published by C.H. Beck law publishers of München and Frankfurt a.M., has a long standing tradition in the national legal literature and celebrated its 50th anniversary in 1997. Another eminent weekly legal magazine is the "*Betriebs-Berater*" (BB) which focuses on economic, labour and tax law. BB is published by the Verlag Recht und Wirtschaft, also an established publishing house situated in Heidelberg.

certain legal norm meant at the time of its enactment by the historical legislator, and — even more important — to find out what its actual meaning and relevance is. In any event the interpreter has to be aware of the fact that his decision for or against a certain model already influences his result of statutory and legal interpretation. Furthermore, as we have set out above, the interpretation process has to take into account the *ratio legis* of the respective norm.[32]

(1) Analogy

This term describes using a legal rule in an appropriate manner although its suppositions are not fulfilled literally.[33] In other words: analogy means reasoning from parallel cases. To refer to the quotation of von Savigny (mentioned above) once again it is fair to say that using analogy as a tool of interpretation definitely is legal art rather than handicraft, because the interpreter always has to find and to point out a comparable legal essence. Reasoning by means of analogy was developed by the courts. The judges were more or less forced to do so, because this is the way to use a certain regulation in equivalent cases which had originally not been noticed and foreseen by the historical legislator. In this respect, analogy is the method used to update the law to requirements of the modern society.

Generally, the application of analogy as an acceptable tool of interpretation is admissible if unregulated legal positions are similar, or if enacted law is lacking at all, but a similar rule can be drawn upon. The interpreter has to ask and answer the following questions:

— Is there a gap in the law?

— If so, is the gap according to legislative intention?

— If not, is the legal situation between the gap and the analogously applied rule comparable with regard to the legal content?

[32] As this is the most important factor to obey we would like to draw your attention to the pertinent decisions of the Federal High Court of Justice in BGHZ 2, 184; BGHZ 18, 49; BGHZ 78, 265.

[33] For details see Palandt — Heinrichs, *Introduction to the Civil Code*, p. 7. See also Tröndle, *Commentary to the German Criminal Code*, § 1 StGB, p. 9: with regard to criminal law, analogy is forbidden if the result would lead to a legal disadvantage for the accused. This important restriction — which finds its roots in Art. 103 II GG — gives evidence of a truly democratic principle within the German legal system.

Only if all the named assumptions fit in a certain case, an analogy between different norms will be allowed as methodically correct.

(2) Teleological reduction

As a means of interpretation teleological reduction is the opposite of analogy — the aim of the interpreter in this case is to restrict the application of a certain norm even against its wording. This makes all the difference to a simple restrictive interpretation which in cases of several possible ways of understanding a legal term uses the most narrow one. Teleological reduction goes far beyond that by disregarding the words that are set up by the legislator. Can that lawfully be done? The answer is yes, at least if the intention is to filtrate the *ratio legis* of a term or regulation, the "real", actual and objective sense.

Nevertheless, reviewing teleological reduction from a strict methodical angle, it cannot be seen as an interpretation method like the ones we have introduced you to earlier on. Instead of that, teleological reduction can be described as an admissible correction to the wording with a view to results that are welcome (and wanted) in practice. Therefore, any interpreter making use of this method has to be careful, because teleological reduction is only justifiable if it is necessary in a given case to ascertain the objective spirit of the relevant norm.[34]

(3) Further amendments

The demonstrated canon of models of reasoning could not claim to be complete without the methodical means of the restrictive and extensive interpretation, the "*argumentum a majore ad minus*", the "*argumentum a fortiori*" and the "*argumentum ad absurdum*".

Each of these methods of Latin origin basically explain themselves. Extensive and restrictive interpretation methods are relevant whenever the wording of a certain legal term allows more than one interpretation — in this case the former votes for a "wide" understanding, the latter for a narrow and "strict" one. Both ways are admissible provided the interpreter does not disregard or underestimate the *ratio legis* of a legal rule, term or statute.

The "*argumentum a majore ad minus*" says that if the histor-

---

34 BGHZ 59, 236: this is a very interesting decision which refers to the "classical" example in § 181 BGB.

ical legislator has set up a certain legal consequence in a special case, this consequence is necessarily all the more applicable in a similar case. We would like to give an example to point out the practical relevance of this fact: according to Article 14 GG, the basic norm which deals with the law of property, the State has to pay compensation for any *lawful* act of expropriation. Given this fact, the interpreter can easily conclude by applying the "*argumetum a majore ad minus*" that the State has to pay as well — and for even better reasons — in the case of an *illegal* expropriation.[35]

Of course, the "*argumentum a fortiori*" means the opposite, so we can now turn our interest to the "*argumentum ad absurdum*" — a principle which takes British lawyers and students back to familiar ground, because it is the equivalent to the "Golden Rule".[36] Having said that, the message of the "*argumentum ad absurdum*" is obvious: statutory (or any other) legal interpretation shall never produce legal results which are absurd or contrary to the legislative intention.[37]

4. APPENDIX: LEGAL WORKING TOOLS

It is different to do research in a case law system than in a common law system. Due to the differences in the theory of statutory interpretation there are consequently differences in the way we handle legal information. Therefore, this section is supposed to provide you as a non-German reader with a basic understanding and knowledge of how to get around and how to deal with the legal tools in Germany.

First of all, there is one formal source of law: the legislation. Any statute which is passed by the legislative bodies of *Bund* or *Länder* is published in official law gazettes, either the *Bundesgesetzblatt* (Federal Law Gazette) or the law gazette of the *Länder* which has issued the new regulation. It has to be mentioned that there is the *Bundesgesetzblatt I* — which only contains statutes and prescriptions — and *Bundesgesetzblatt II*, which is the place to publish, for instance, international treaties agreed by the *Bund*. Anyway, being official publications, the *Bundesgesetzblätter* are not very easy to handle in practice. This is the reason why German publishing houses offer

---

[35] In Germany this method of reasoning is called "*Erst Recht-Schluß*" — as to this stimulating way to put forward ones own arguments see the *Bundesgerichtshof* in: BGHZ 6, 290.

[36] See *Re Sigsworth* (1935) Ch. 89 and *Becke v. Smith* (1836) 2 M. & W. 191.

[37] See BGHZ 56, 171.

comprehensive compilations of statutes; probably the best known of them are the so-called *Schönfelder* and the *Sartorius* which represent the actual legislation in private and public law.

Furthermore, quasi-official law reports have to be taken into account. In these volumes the federal courts publish the most relevant and important cases in a series which is usually edited by the judges themelves. Therefore, we have to look at the *Entscheidungen des Bundesverfassungsgerichts* (decisions of the Federal Constitutional Court), the *Entscheidungen des Bundesgerichtshofs in Zivilsachen und in Strafsachen* (decisions of the Federal Court of Justice in civil matters and in criminal matters), the *Entscheidungen des Bundesarbeitsgerichts* (decisions of the Federal Labour Court), *Entscheidungen des Bundesfinanzhofs* (decisions of the Federal Tax Court) *und Entscheidungen des Bundessozialgerichts* (decisions of the Federal Social Court). In addition to the named documentations most of the highest courts at *Länder* level publish a similar series which is a starting point for any legal research as well.

From a practitioner's point of view an even better starting point is delivered by the many legal magazines competing on the German market. It is very difficult to provide an objective overview, because due to the general tendency of specialisation and particularisation within the legal system there are simply too many legal magazines today to introduce you to each and every one of them. However, probably the most important and widely read law journal is the *Neue Juristische Wochenschrift* (NJW) — a weekly magazine that provides a general overview of the German legal world. In addition to the NJW there are several specialised magazines which should be mentioned. For economic, tax and labour law there is the *Betriebs Berater* (BB) and, focusing on international economic law, the *Recht der Internationalen Wirtschaft* (RIW), both of which are particularly well regarded and widely subscribed-to law journals. Another distinguished magazine, dealing with comparative law, is the well-established *Zeitschrift für Vergleichende Rechtswissenschaft* (ZVglRWiss), a journal on comparative law, whose scientific roots date back to the nineteenth century. From an editorial perspective the RIW and the ZVglRWiss are most interesting to an English reader, because both magazines take a fairly regular look across the channel.

In addition to this, textbooks and commentaries are a very important source to learn about German law. In particular the commentaries are interesting to look at, because this special way of interpreting and introducing a certain field of the law features differences with regard to the Anglo-American system. If one takes the *Bürgerliches Gesetzbuch*, for example, as probably the most important codified source of civil law. The Code consists of more than 2300 paragraphs, dealing with the Law of Succession (see §§ 1922 *et seq.* BGB) as well as with the legal problems of buying and selling of goods (see §§ 433 *et seq.* BGB) and questions of compensation for damages (see §§ 823 *et seq.* BGB) — to name just a few legal topics. The way to make a reader familiar with the legal question is very simple and logical: each norm is described and commented on by following the sequence of sections of the Code; the relevant legal literature and jurisdiction is delivered in addition to this.

Therefore, commentaries — usually written by eminent legal academics, experienced judges and/or lawyers — are a first class basis to do legal research — provided one knows where to begin with the research, because it is evident that each code has a certain structure.

To give you a — and probably *the* — typical example of a commentary, we would like to mention the *Palandt,* a massive book which has managed to become a household name in legal circles, and which is now in its 57th edition since the first appearance in 1939. *Palandt* provides a commentary of the relevant codes with regard to German civil law, concentrating on the norms of the BGB. If one takes into account that a team of not more than seven commentators manages to produce one edition per year and to include any relevant new material, one can only admire the efficiency and achievement of the editorial team, and can understand why this commentary has an outstanding reputation as an institution of the civil law. Of course, there are several competitors to the *Palandt* — commentaries which tackle the subject of civil law (or almost any other field of the law, because commentaries are obviously not restricted to a certain area) with different editorial concepts. A few of the most important of them are listed in the selected bibliography section below.

To finish this tour d'horizon through German legal literature and legal working tools we would like to mention textbooks. As in England — and most of the other European countries — there is a huge market in legal textbooks. It would be misleading to name too many or just a few of them, but you will find a selection below. Unfortunately there is a lack of general literature on German law written in English. In this respect, the process of European integration is likely to bring a change for the better.

SELECTED BIBLIOGRAPHY

I. Commentaries

Jarass, Pieroth, *Grundgesetz für die Bundesrepublik Deutschland* (4th ed., 1997).
Jauernig *Bürgerliches Gesetzbuch* (8th ed., 1997).
Rebmann, Rixecker, Säcker, *Münchener Kommentar zum Bürgerlichen Gesetzbuch* (Vol. 1. Allgemeiner Teil (§§ 1.240)), *AGB-Gesetz* (3rd ed., 1993).
Palandt, *Bürgerliches Gesetzbuch* (57th ed., 1998).
Staudinger, *Kommentar zum Bürgerlichen Gesetzbuch* (12th ed., 1993).
Tröndle, *Strafgesetzbuch und Nebengesetze* (48th ed., 1997).

II. Textbooks

Allen, *Law in the Making* (6th ed., 1958).
Baumann, *Einführung in die Rechtswissenschaft* (8th ed., 1989).
Baur, Walter, *Einführung in das Recht der Bundesrepublik Deutschland* (6th ed., 1992).
Bischof, *Europarecht für Anfänger* (2nd ed., 1996).
Ebke, Finkin, *Introduction to German Law* (1996).
The European Law Students' Association (ELSA), *Guide to Legal Studies in Europe 1996–1997* (1996).
Gramm, *Jura erfolgreich studieren* (2nd ed., 1997).
Heck, *Das Problem der Rechtsgewinnung* (2nd ed., 1932).
Larenz, Wolf, *Allgemeiner Teil des Bürgerlichen Rechts* (8th ed., 1997).
Rinken, *Einführung in das juristische Studium* (3rd ed., München 1996).
Savigny, *System des heutigen Römischen Rechts* (1st–8th editions, 1840–1849, Vol. 1).
von Jhering, *Der Kampf ums Recht* (4th ed., 1832).

Chapter Three
The German Constitution

1. Historical background

After its defeat in May 1945, the German state authority was taken over; with power subsequently exercised by the four *Besatzungsmächte* (occupying powers). In addition, the German territory was divided into four occupation zones; later on, the occupying powers were supported by smaller entities (the *Länder*) which were created in every occupying zone. Their task was to support the occupying powers while trying to restore public order in every zone.

The original idea was to re-establish Germany, but it soon became clear that this aim could not be realised — it failed mainly because the USSR and the Western Allies pursued different objectives and rapidly became estranged from one another. During the London Conference in December 1947 the Western Allies attempted to prevent the separation of Germany into two different states but this attempt was not crowned with success.

Thereafter, the three western occupying powers (USA, United Kingdom and France) authorised the *Ministerpräsidenten* (minister-presidents) of the 11 newly established *Länder* to set up a constituent *Parlamentarischer Rat* (parliamentary council) for the western part of Germany which should work out a constitution. The minister-presidents consented to this in order to shape only a provisional "*Grundgesetz*" ("Basic Law") rather than a *Verfassung* (constitution); they wanted to emphasise the provisional character of the Western German State. The provisional character was later set out in the preamble of the *Grundgesetz*. Originally it was stated that the German people should "achieve in free determination the unity and freedom of Germany". This political goal has altered because the reunification of East and West Germany has now been realised. Today it is said that the 16 *Länder* have completed German unification.

But let us get back to the historical agenda of the Constitution. In August 1948, experts presented a first draft of the *Grundgesetz* as a basis for a discussion to the Constitutional Convention which took place in *Heerenchiemsee.* During 1948 and 1949, the *Parlamentarische Rat* — composed of members of the Parliament of the *Länder* — sat in Bonn and revised and worked out a final version of the *Grundgesetz* on which the Allies had an important influence as well. The final version of the *Grundgesetz* was agreed by the *Parlamentarischer Rat* on May 8, 1949 (see Article 145 I GG), and the Allies accepted the *Grundgesetz* with a few reservations on May 12, 1949. After the consent of the Parliaments of the *Länder* — except for Bayern which nonetheless expressly confirmed its affiliation to Germany — the *Grundgesetz* came into force on May 24, 1949.

Only a few months later and with the support of the USSR, the German Democratic Republic (GDR), as the eastern part of Germany, was founded by the *Volkskongress,* who wrote its own constitution. The new state came into force on November 7, 1949. The post-war development in the eastern part was mainly influenced by basic changes in industry and agriculture. The most important measure was the *Bodenreform* (land reform) under which comprehensive expropriation was carried out. This led to legal battles after reunification, because the people concerned tried to get back their former property.

At the beginning the *Grundgesetz,* the constitution of the GDR, started from the continuation of a uniform German State; because it was also said in Article 1 I VerfGDR (Constitution of the German Democratic Republic, 1949) that Germany is an indivisible democratic republic. But over the years the federal republic and the GDR developed as independent states, and the *Grundlagenvertrag* of 1972 spoke for the first time ever of "the two German States". Contrary to the opinion of the GDR — the Western point of view was that there still existed only one uniform German territory with uniform German citizenship.

The fulfilment of one of the substantial aims of the *Grundgesetz* which was pointed out in its preamble — namely the unification of the two separate "States" — took 50 years to be realised. The Berlin Wall came down on November 9, 1989, and — after long discussions for and against the unification — the Governments of the two German States came to the decision to unify the states while the GDR accessed the territory governed by the *Grundgesetz*. From a constitutional point of view, unification was completed on November 3, 1990. Now, the *Grundgesetz* covers Germany as a whole. This does in fact mean that the provisional character of the *Grundgesetz* has come to an end; the term *constitution* does now makes sense.

2. LEGAL POSITION AND STRUCTURE OF THE CONSTITUTIONAL LAW

The *Verfassungsrecht* (constitutional law) is part of public law and contains the legal principles of the common fundamental and constitutional order in Germany. Constitutional law deals with legal rules governing the basic order of the State (especially the form of government), its organisation and the highest bodies of the State which are the constitutional organs (such as the Federal President). In addition, it contains the material principles of economic and social life, the political system and the legal position of the citizen within the State. These fundamental principles are codified in the German *Grundgesetz*.

The framework of the *Grundgesetz* has a special order and is subdivided according to the matters concerned. It starts with the basic rights (Articles 1 to 19 GG) followed by the federation and the *Länder* (Articles 20 to 37 GG), the main constitutional organs (Art 38 to 69 GG), the federal legislation (Articles 70 to 82 GG), the implementation of federal legislation with federal administration (Articles 83 to 91a GG), adjudication (Articles 92 to 104 GG), finance (Articles 104a to 115 GG) and last but not least defence (Articles 116 to 146 GG).

The legal rules set forth in the *Grundgesetz* form the highest and most important source of law within the hierarchy of legal rules in Germany.[1] This means that all legal sources possessing a lower rank in the hierarchy of legal sources — such as national law, customary law, statutory instruments and byelaws — are null and void if they infringe the *Grundgesetz*. It also follows from this that any law with a lower rank than the *Grundgesetz* has to be interpreted in a way that the orders and prohibitions laid down in the *Grundgesetz* shall become effective in the best way possible.[2]

Because of its legal position within the hierarchy of legal sources, the *Grundgesetz* can, as a rule, be amended but only by formal statutes and in accordance with the proceedings specified in Article 79 GG. Amendments must be carried out by two thirds of the members of the *Bundestag* (Federal Parliament) and two thirds of the votes of the *Bundesrat* (Federal Council).[3] But there are also certain constitutional rules which cannot be changed: the law dividing the federation into *Länder*, the principle of

---

[1] For more details, see *ibid.*, Chap. Two, 2.
[2] For more details, see *ibid.*, Chap. Two, 3.
[3] For more details, see *ibid.*, Chap. Three, 5.

the participation of the *Länder* in the law-making process and the principles governed under Articles 1 and 20 GG.

There is also a hierarchy of legal norms within the *Grundgesetz*. The highest rank goes to those legal norms which have been declared as unchangeable (Article 79 III GG). The remaining constitutional legal rules have the position of ordinary constitutional law. A lesser legal effect goes to those constitutional rules which may be restricted or specified in detail and more precisely (such as the basic rights governing the freedom of the person (*e.g.* Articles 2 I and 12 GG), or the basic right guaranteeing property pursuant to Article 14 I GG).

Constitutional law, therefore, deals primarily with the standard of living and legal relations in Germany. As a result, this field of law has to be demarcated from those laws concerning relations to other states:

(a) For instance, the *Völkerrecht* (public international law) governs the sovereign — which means non-private — legal relations between the subjects of international law. To it belongs, for instance the law of diplomatic relations, the law of international organisations, and contracts under public international law.

(b) Another separate branch of law is the *Recht der europäischen Gemeinschaften* (European Communities Law). "European Communities" is the collective term for the European Coal and Steel Community, the European Economic Community (EEC) and the European Atomic Energy Community (Euratom). The law of these Communities regulates relations between the members of the European Communities and their relations to non-Member States. The law consists of contracts, statutory instruments and directives.

3. FUNDAMENTAL STRUCTURAL PRINCIPLES

The fundamental structural principles of the Federal Republic of Germany are laid out in Article 20 GG which states:

(1) The Federal Republic of Germany shall be a democratic and social federal state.

(2) All public authority emanates from the people. It shall be exercised by the people through elections and referendums and by specific legislative, executive and judicial bodies.

(3) The legislature shall be bound by the constitutional order, the executive and the judiciary by law and justice.

Due to this legal norm, the German State is a democratic republic, social and federal state based on the rule of law. In total, there are five fundamental structural principles which have to be obeyed, because of the importance of the constitutional concept in general: *Demokratie* (Democracy), *Republik* (Republic), *Rechtsstaat* (Constitutional State), *Sozialstaat* (Social State) and *Bundesstaat* (Federal State). In addition to this, the protection of the environment laid down in Article 20 a GG has to be added to these principles; this Article came into force in 1994 as a result of a revision of the basic law. Article 20 GG enjoys special protection because any amendment effecting the principles outlined above is prohibited. These most fundamental principles are unchangeable.

The named principles have to be recognised and followed by everyone. Article 20 GG has been referred to as the *Verfassung in Kurzform* (constitution in short form), a saying which underlines the outstanding status of the norm within the German legal system. But anyway, as a structural principle Article 20 GG also fulfils the task of making clear the theoretical concepts which were originally intended by the historical legislator. Furthermore, it has to be stressed that the five principles are not only in effect at state level, the same structure has to be in effect in each of the 16 *Bundesländer* due to Article 28 GG. This principle is called *Homogenitätsgebot*, which can be translated as "homogeneous system" and means that the constitutional basis within the *Länder* is in line with the Federal State. The contents of each of the fundamental principles of the constitution are described separately below.

A. DEMOCRACY (*DEMOKRATIE*)

By definition the word *Demokratie* (Democracy) means that the *Staatsgewalt* (state authority) is in the hands of the people. If you read the text of the German constitution you will discover that Article 20 II 1 GG states that "*Die Staatsgewalt geht vom Volke aus*" — in other words the prerequisites for Germany to be a democratic state are fulfilled.

This has not been the case during long stretches in German history. For centuries, Germany — like England — had a monarch or a feudalistic state organisation due to its lack of unity. Nevertheless, the installation of the democratic organisation of the State is an achievement of eminent importance, because during the Hitler era the most remarkable threat to any free country came from Germany itself.

The design of the German constitution is taking up theoretical ideas which have already been implemented in the so-called *Weimarer Reichsverfassung* — the constitution of the first German democracy which was in force between 1919 and 1933. We have already introduced you to Article 20 II 1 GG — the rule which places state power in the hands of the people, but also important for the practical functioning of a democracy is Article 20 II 2 GG which completes this basic rule of law. There it is stated that:

"*Das Volk übt die Staatsgewalt in Wahlen und Abstimmungen und durch besondere Organe der Gesetzgebung, der vollziehenden Gewalt und der Rechtsprechung aus.*"

This is the concept of a *repräsentative Demokratie* (representative democracy) which means that the people exercise their state power by means of political elections and opinion polls and through certain organs of legislation, administration and jurisdiction. The participation at elections and polls, therefore, is the main task of the citizen with regard to his or her active role within a democracy. The fact that the citizen takes part in the political process through representatives he or she has chosen can be double checked and compared with democratic practice: legislation is (mainly) the task of the Parliament; administration only works correctly when there is a legal competence to act and — finally — the judiciary decides cases in court "*Im Namen des Volkes*" (In the Name of the People).

B. REPUBLIC (*REPUBLIK*)

This structural principle is easy to explain, because it is defined as the contrary of a *Monarchie* (Monarchy): the latter state has a king or queen as head of the State whereas it is typical for a republic to have a head of state who comes into office after success in an election. Due to Article 54 GG the *Bundespräsident* (Federal President), as formal number one in the hierarchy of the State, is voted into office for a period of five years with the option of becoming re-elected once (see Article 54 II 2 GG for details).

C. CONSTITUTIONAL STATE (*RECHTSSTAAT*)

The fundamental principle of Germany as being a *Rechtsstaat* (Constitutional State) is not mentioned expressly in Article 20 GG. Nevertheless, it is general opinion and common legal knowledge that the essential points and structures of this *Staatsform* (form of government) are contained within this basic norm. In fact, the principle of constitutional state is to be seen as one of the most important and distinctive features of Article 20 GG. In addition to this several aspects of the principle of a constitutional state are laid down in other sections of the constitution, for instance in the catalogue of basic rights and other important parts of the constitution.

In this section we would like to draw your attention to the most relevant points with regard to the principle of a constitutional state. First of all, as we have just stressed, there is a requirement that every citizen be protected by the catalogue of *Grundrechte* (basic rights). A state that cannot guarantee this will never qualify as a *Rechtsstaat*. Furthermore, Article 19 IV GG states that every citizen is entitled to receive legal protection against acts or omissions of the State. The essential basis of this claim is called *Rechtsschutzgarantie* (guarantee of legal protection), and has to be regarded as a stylistic factor of a constitutional state.

The principle of a constitutional state basically means that the State and all its organs are bound by the law. In other words they are restricted by the legal system as a whole. Furthermore, the State has to grant freedom and justice to all citizens in order to fulfil the requirements of Article 20 GG.

Another very important factor is the system of *Gewaltenteilung* (separation of powers) between the *Regierung* (government), *Verwaltung* (administration) and *Rechtsprechung* (judiciary). These kinds of checks and balances also ensure that none of the single powers will be able to suppress one of the others to the disadvantage of the citizens. Within this system of separated powers the state organs are bound by the law; any act or omission of state organs has to be lawful and qualified by a certain legal norm. This principle is called *Vorrang des Gesetzes* (priority of the law) and expresses that statutes are the most important basis within a lawful constitutional system. This aspect is completed by another principle which is called *Vorbehalt des Gesetzes* (reservation of the law) — which means that interference into the private sphere of a citizen also needs to be justified by a legal norm.

Again, closely connected to the named essentials of a *Rechtsstaat* are two further principles which have to be mentioned as very important aspects: the *Vertrauensschutzprinzip* (fidelity clause) and the *Bestimmtheitsgrundsatz* (principle of certainty). The first principle means that the citizen generally can trust in acts or omissions of the state organs. With respect to this it is — at least in general terms — unlawful to create *rückwirkende Gesetze* (retroactive legislation). Because of the possible (and obviously negative) consequences to a citizen, there is a total restriction on retroactive legislation in criminal law; Article 103 II GG states this expressively and without any uncertainties. This legal position was implemented by the legislator for powerful reasons, as no one should be found guilty for an offence which was not punishable at the time when he or she committed the deed. If you think about the concept of the fidelity clause, the principle of certainty is not difficult to explain, because it also means that with regard to acts or omissions of state organs, the citizen has to have a fair chance to estimate developments in advance.

Finally, it is worth mentioning the *Verhältnismäßigkeitsgrundsatz* (principle of proportionality). Again, this is a very important aspect of the constitutional state which can be concluded from the catalogue of basic rights, but does form a single aspect of Article 20 GG as well. The principle of proportionality is formed from three parts which are: *Geeignetheit* (suitability), *Erforderlichkeit* (necessity) and *Angemessenheit* (adequacy). These three aspects have to ensure that the lawfulness of acts of state organs is given. In general any action has to be suitable in general in order to reach a certain aim; in other words it has to be necessary and there should be no alternative in a certain case. Finally, the adequacy of the single act must be established. The act of the state organ in question must be in justifiable proportion with regard to the aims that should be reached.

To conclude, the introduction to the elements of the constitutional state: one should always bear in mind that a lot of aspects we have just mentioned are contained in several basic rights as well. But the *Rechtsstaatsprinzip* as a constitutional concept of its own underlines the intention of the historical legislator who obviously wanted to stress the points that form the basis of a truly lawful state organisation.

D. SOCIAL STATE (*SOZIALSTAAT*)

It would be unfair to refer to the principle of social state as being a *Stiefkind* (stepchild) of the constitution. Nevertheless, in comparison to the other basic structural principles we described before, it is of less practical importance. Germany is a social state. This fact is pointed out in the constitution in Articles 20 I GG and 28 I GG. It is interesting that the historical legislator pronounced Germany as being a *sozialer Bundesstaat* (Social Federal State). We will come back to this in the next section, when we introduce you to the concept "federal state". Basically the principle of social state demands that the German legal system — or more precisely: government, judiciary and administration — has to respect the *Menschenwürde* (human dignity) of any citizen and has to take care that social circumstances for people living in Germany meet a certain standard. Therefore, this part of Article 20 GG can be understood as a kind of *Gesetzgebungsauftrag* (legal order) as well as law in action. Moreover, the principle of social state as an integral part of the German constitution is important to understand and to interpret the basic rights laid down in Articles 1 to 19 of the constitution.

E. FEDERAL STATE (*BUNDESSTAAT*)

As we mentioned above due to Article 20 I GG, Germany is a *Bundesstaat* (Federal State). This norm has to be seen in connection with Article 28 GG which states that the:

"*verfassungsmäßige Ordnung in den Ländern muß den Grundsätzen des republikanischen, demokratischen und sozialen Rechtsstaats im Sinne dieses Grundgesetzes entsprechen.*"

This sentence of the constitution can be translated as "the constitutional order in the *Länder* has to comply with the basic principles of a republic, democratic and social Constitutional State" as laid down in the *Grundgesetz*. Given this fact it is easy to understand that Articles 20 and 28 GG are basic rules of central importance within the constitution. The principle of *Föderalismus* (federalism) is a key factor within the German legal system, because along this line the relationship between the *Bund* (Federal State) and the sixteen different *Länder* is organised.

In this context it has to be stressed that the Federal State and the *Länder* have a legal capacity of their own, self-government and self-administration. Due to Article 70 GG the *Gesetzgebung* (legislation) falls within the remit of the *Länder*. But obviously, Articles 71 to 75 of the constitution do contain a catalogue which transfers the most eminent questions of legislation into the hands of the Federal State, especially the *konkurrierende Gesetzgebung* (concurrent federal legislation). This principle is laid down in Article 72 GG and refers to important legal areas like civil law, criminal law, competition and commercial law. With respect to this the *Länder* basically have the privilege of legislation — as long as the *Bund* does not claim its own right to act. One can imagine that this concept of different competences leads to the fact that important legal questions (which should be ruled in the same way throughout the country) are solved on the higher level of the Federal State.

Nevertheless, in practice the legal position of the *Länder* is quite strong. The *Bundesrat* (Federal Council) is — together with the *Bundestag* (Federal Parliament) — the main organ to exercise political power.

4. CONSTITUTIONAL ORGANS

State organs are institutions of the German State which are regarded as acting on behalf of the German State. The most important are the *Bundestag* (Federal Parliament), the *Bundesrat* (Federal Council), the *Bundesregierung* (Federal Government), the *Bundespräsident* (Federal President) and the *Bundesverfassungsgericht* (Federal Constitutional Court). But the highest courts and public authorities, the *Bundesrechnungshof* (Federal Audit Office) and, last but not least, the *Bundesbank* (Central Bank of Germany) are also regarded as state organs of the Federal Republic of Germany.

The term "state organ" has to be distinguished from the term "constitutional organ" because the latter are only those organs whose status and material powers are directly regulated by the constitution. The highest constitutional organ is the *Bundestag* because it is directly elected by the people. The remaining constitutional organs are the *Bundesrat*, *-regierung*, *-präsident* and the *Bundesverfassungsgericht* whose main principles are outlined below.[4]

A. FEDERAL PARLIAMENT (*BUNDESTAG*)

(1) Election

The legal status of the *Bundestag*, its organisation and powers are laid down in Articles 38 to 48 GG. The *Bundestag* is directly elected by the German people, represents the German people and is, as a result, the only constitutional organ which obtains direct legitimation from the people. It can therefore, be regarded as the highest constitutional organ in Germany.

The deputies of the *Bundestag* are elected in a general, direct, free, equal and secret election for a four-year term. They are — due to Article 38 I GG — the representatives of the German

[4] For more details concerning the *Bundesverfassungsgericht*, see Chap. Three, 8.

people, not bound to any instruction or directive and only subject to their conscience. Every German citizen has the right to vote after attaining the age of 18 years. Every German citizen is eligible for election upon reaching the age of 21 years. The question of who is regarded as a "*Deutscher*" in the sense of the *Grundgesetz* and, therefore, has these rights as outlined above, is laid down in Article 116 GG — as a rule it is anyone possessing German citizenship.

The *Bundestag* is re-elected after a four-year period which is called the *Legislaturperiode* (legislative period). The legislative period of the former *Bundestag* terminates with the meeting of the newly elected *Bundestag* (Articles 39 I GG). The composition of the *Bundestag* may change every four years. As far as basic political decisions have to be rendered, its individual content depends on the personnel which is connected to the party-political composition of the *Bundestag* — the personnel might change when another government takes the chair after the legislative period. Thus, the concrete composition of persons sitting in the *Bundestag* is decisive and with respect to this, the principle of discontinuity applies.

But on the other hand the *Bundestag* is also an organ or institution which continues to exist irrespective of its composition for the time being, and it is independent from elections. In this respect the organ exists continuously.

(2) Autonomy and powers

The *Bundestag* is autonomous and this power is outlined in Article 40 I 2 GG. Thereafter, the *Bundestag* has the right of self-regulation in all of its affairs. The *Bundestag* exercises this power in its concrete, personnel composition. It can issue its own *Geschäftsordnung* (Standing Orders) — the GeschO BT. The *Bundestag* is completely independent from other constitutional organs. Due to this, no other body or authority is allowed to exercise any kind of authority in the building of the *Bundestag.*

The power of the *Bundesrat* is not explicitly governed in the *Grundgesetz*. It is, however, generally described as the highest constitutional organ representing the will of the electorate and has comprehensive powers. The *Bundestag* is, for instance, the only body empowered to elect other state organs, to control the executive, to represent the people and to exercise legislative, budgetary and consenting functions. But only a few provisions of the *Grundgesetz* expressly transfer powers to the *Bundestag*, for example, the election of the Chancellor in Articles 63, 67 and 68 GG, the right to initiate legislation, deliberation and taking decisions by federal law (§§ 76 *et seq.* GG). If no special provision is on hand, as a rule, the respective affair will be subject to the comprehensive power of the *Bundestag*. But the power of the *Bundestag* is restricted by two principles: at first the *Bundestag* is only responsible if the respective matter falls within the sphere of the Federation (principle of the federal state); and secondly, no other (federal) organ should be responsible for the matter concerned (principle of the separation of powers).

(3) Organisation

Only a part of parliamentary work is performed in full session. The resolutions to be passed in plenary session are often prepared in the sub-classifications of the *Bundestag*, namely parliamentary groups and parliamentary committees.

(a) Parliamentary group (*Fraktion*)

The parliamentary groups are associations of at least 5 per cent of the members of the *Bundestag* which belong to the same political party or to those political parties which on the strength of parallel political affiliations do not compete in any *Land* (§ 10 I 1 GeschO BT). The *Bundestag* can be subdivided into the different parliamentary groups.

The *Grundgesetz* does mention the parliamentary groups (though only casually) in Article 53 a GG. A fundamental regulation concerning the status and task of the parliamentary groups has been laid down for the first time in §§ 45 *et seq.* *Abgeordnetengesetz* (AbgG — rules concerning the Members of the *Bundestag*) which came into force on January 1, 1995. Due to § 46 I and II AbgG, parliamentary groups are associations with legal capacity and, therefore, are able to sue and be sued. The law makes clear in § 46 III AbgG that they are not part of the public administration and cannot carry out public authority.

Parliamentary groups are part of the constitutional organ "*Bundestag*" and, due to this, are at least indirectly, a constitutional organ. They take part in performing the tasks of the *Bundestag* (§ 47 AbgG) and have two main functions:

(a) Parliamentary groups are also known as "Parties" in Parliament because they bring to Parliament the political intent of the political party they represent. Hence, they are important for political work in Parliament. Today the existing parliamentary groups reflect the majority and opposition in Parliament and drive the main political debates.

(b) Parliamentary groups are also mediators between Parliament and the deputy: while the political positions are united in parliamentary groups, the single deputy obtains a permanent and effective influence on parliamentary events and, due to this, can effectively exercise his rights which follow from Article 38 I 2 GG.

Any parliamentary group (having 5 per cent of the Members of Parliament) has certain rights. An association which does not reach such a figure can be acknowledged only as a mere group. Only parliamentary groups — and not groups in general — have certain rights in Parliament. This cannot be furnished under Article 21 GG (concerning political parties) but follow from the status of the deputy and, therefore, from Article 38 I 2 GG. There it states that any deputy is subject only to his conscience and is not bound by any instruction or directives. The rights of a parliamentary group — such as the right to propose speeches or to file applications in the Parliament, committees and forums — depends mainly on the respective personal strength of the group. As a matter of principle, the strongest parliamentary group provides the President of the *Bundestag*.

With regard to the power of parliamentary groups within Parliament, a group may influence the composition of offices (*e.g.* President of the *Bundestag*) and, especially the composition of the parliamentary committees (§§ 11, 12 GeschO BT). In addition, if you consider that the committee's composition depends mainly on the number of deputies belonging to a parliamentary group, and when smaller committees have to be set up, groups representing a political minority might not be taken into consideration. But due to the principle of equal representation for all and the order to protect minorities, these small parliamentary groups do enjoy certain protection: there must be the same access to the committees and forums for all parliamentary groups.

(b) Parliamentary committee (*Ausschuß*)

Parliamentary committees are set up as sub-organs of the Parliament in accordance with the *Grundgesetz* and the Standing Orders of the *Bundestag*. As a rule they are established in order to prepare parliamentary negotiations in full session (§§ 54 *et seq.* GeschO BT). Their power is in accordance with the scope of the responsibilities of the *Bundestag* with explicitly assigned tasks. Generally they prepare the plenary sessions, especially while they deliberate draft bills between the first and second reading. Therefore, they have a high practical importance, because usually they are composed of people who are specialists and experts in the field concerned. The committees consist of deputies of the parliamentary groups whose individual number — as outlined above — is in accordance with their strength in Parliament (§§ 54 *et seq.* GeschO BT). Committees do not render independent, final decisions but rather perform preparatory work for the parliamentary process. Their meetings take place in chamber.

Due to Articles 45 a and c GG certain committees have a compulsion to be formed such as the Committee for Foreign Affairs, the Defence Committee and the Petition Committee. Further committees are usually set up during a legislative period just as the Committee for Internal Affairs, the Committee on Legal Affairs and the Budgetary Committee were. In addition to this, particular tasks can be carried out by the so-called *Untersuchungsausschuß* (investigation committee) which will be set up if one quarter of the Members of the *Bundestag* demands to furnish such a committee in order to investigate a certain affair (Article 44 GG). The investigation committee's competences and the proceedings to be conducted have to act in accordance with the provisions of the Code of Criminal Procedure and the Judicature Act to which Article 44 II GG refers.

(4) Deputy or Members of the *Bundestag* (*Bundestagsabgeordneter*)

Due to Article 38 I 2 GG members of the *Bundestag* are the representatives of the German people as a whole and are not bound by any instructions or directives and are only subject to their conscience. This free mandate, which stands in contrast to an imperative mandate, prohibits a voter giving legally binding instructions to a deputy, or the party or its organs instructing him in a legally binding way.

The rights of Article 38 I 2 GG cannot be regarded in isolation but are rather connected with Article 21 GG: the deputy is simultaneously a representative of the political party for which he has been elected and is also involved in the policy making decisions; the same applies to the parliamentary group. Due to this, any influence exercised by the parliamentary group or party on the deputy is inadmissable. The *Fraktionsdisziplin,* the discipline of the parliamentary group or party, in reaching a uniform approach and appearance in parliamentary work, is acceptable. This also comprises the influence on single deputies as far as the loyalty and common political work it requires. But the *Fraktionszwang,* the obligation to vote according to parliamentary policy, is forbidden because, in this case, the deputy would be bound by instructions and would not be able to decide according to his conscience — this infringes his rights guaranteed in Article 38 I 2 GG.

A deputy of the *Bundestag* is elected in general, direct, free, equal and secret elections. He is the holder of a public office whose content follows from the *Grundgesetz*, special provisions (*e.g.* AbgG and GeschO) and also from the character of the Parliament as a representation of the people. The most important rights and duties are laid down in Articles 47 and 48 GG. Thereafter, nobody may be hindered from undertaking the office as a deputy; because of this a notice of termination or dismissal is inadmissible as well (Article 48 II GG). Deputies have the right to speak and the right to file applications in the *Bundestag*. Deputies also benefit from the *Indemnität* (indemnity) prescribed under Article 46 I GG which is a statutory bar to the right to bring an action. It is the exemption from punishment of Members of Parliament for statements made or votes cast in Parliament — with the exception of a defamatory statement. In addition, Members of Parliament have a further privilege which is the parliamentary *Immunität* (immunity) which is laid down in Article 46 II GG. This means that a deputy can be held responsible or arrested for an act subject to penalty only with the consent of the *Bundestag*. These principles intend to guarantee the possibility of an open and free discussion in Parliament. The operation and function of Parliament is protected by these means.

(5) Party (*Partei*)

Article 21 GG provides the main principle of the political parties, their proper position and functions are as follows:

(1) The parties shall participate in the forming of political will of the people. Their foundation is free. Their internal organisation must comply with democratic principles. They must publicly account for the sources and intended use of their funds just as their property.

(2) Parties which, by reason of their aims or the behaviour of their adherents, seek to impair or abolish the free democratic basic order or to endanger the existence of the Federal Republic of Germany shall be unconstitutional. On the question of unconstitutionality the Federal Constitutional Court shall decide.

(3) Details shall be regulated by Federal law.

The political parties have to promote their political opinions, and to set up their party programme with the main political current and trend which they represent and on whose basis they nominate their candidates for election. They, therefore, exercise a double function: on the one hand they are non-public institutions within society; on the other hand they participate in the forming of political will in the political and public field and, due to this, approach the position of a state organ.

Pursuant to Article 21 III GG, details concerning political parties are provided in the *Parteiengesetz* (ParteienG — Law concerning the Political Parties). This Code governs in detail the organisation and structure, the formation of will and the rights of their members. It is defined in § 2 ParteienG that parties are:

"associations of citizens who set out to influence either permanently or for a long period of time the formation of political opinion at federal or *Land* level and to participate in the representation of the people in the *Bundestag* or the State Parliament provided that they offer sufficient guarantee of the seriousness of their aims in the general character of their circumstances and attendant conditions, particularly with regard to the scale and strength of their organisation, the number of inscribed members and their image in public opinion."

In the first place the Civil Code (§§ 21 *et seq.* BGB) applies for the foundation and organisation of a party supplemented by Article 21 GG and the ParteienG. A political party is generally an association with or without legal capacity. In any case the party is able to sue and be sued (§ 3 ParteienG). Members of political parties can only be natural persons. Due to § 1 ParteienG political parties are necessary and important for the liberal and democratic fundamental order. Their participation in the process of forming a political will is the main task under public law which is specified under the *Grundgesetz*. They especially have to influence the political development in the Parliament and Government and have to take care of a permanent, lively connection between the people and the State. The parties must have written programs which shall reproduce their political aims and intents. The minimum content of the byelaws is laid down in § 6 II ParteienG.

Political parties which, by reason of aims or behaviour of their adherents, seek to impair or abolish the free democratic basic order, are unconstitutional — this is said in Article 21 II GG. The *Bundestag*, *Bundesrat* or the Federal Government may file an application with the Federal Constitutional Court to review the constitutionality of a political party. As far as such an application is legally justified, the Federal Constitutional Court will state the unconstitutionality of the party concerned. Connected with such a statement is the dissolution of the political party and the prohibition to constitute a political party of a substitute. Further legal consequences are laid down in §§ 32 and 33 ParteienG. Up until this time two left-wing political parties — the "*Sozialistische Reichspartei*" (SRP)[5] and the "*Kommunistische Partei Deutschland*" (KPD)[6] — have been declared as being unconstitutional.

B. FEDERAL COUNCIL (*BUNDESRAT*)

Through the *Bundesrat*, the *Länder* participate in the legislation and administration of the Federal Government just as in the affairs of the European Union (Article 50 I GG). The *Bundesrat* takes part in the federal legislation and administration. It is not an institution of the *Länder* although it is composed of representatives from the *Länder*. It is rather like the *Bundestag* — a federal organ. Participation in the sense of Article 50 GG, however, establishes only a right of participation. The *Bundesrat*, therefore, is not a second, independent chamber of legislation.

Unlike the *Bundestag*, the *Bundesrat* is a permanent organ. It has neither a personnel discontinuity nor discontinuity with regard to the subject matter. The *Bundesrat* consists of members of the 16 *Land* Governments which appoint and recall them (Article 51 I GG). Due to this, the *Bundesrat* is not directly democratically legitimated (unlike the Senate in the USA for instance which is elected directly from the people). The legitimation of the *Bundesrat* derives from the fact that the people elect the *Land* Parliaments who then, at least through the election of the minister-president, determine the composition of the *Land* Governments, and the *Land* Governments send their deputies to the *Bundesrat*.

In proportion to the region's size, they have three,[7] four[8] or six[9] votes (Article 52 II GG). Each region can delegate to the *Bundesrat* as many members as it has votes. A region is sufficiently represented in the *Bundesrat* as long as at least one member is present who represents the others who failed to appear. In

---

[5] See BVerfGE 2, 1 *et seq.*
[6] See BVerfGE 5, 85 *et seq.*
[7] Such as Bremen, Hamburg, Saarland, Mecklenburg-Vorpommern.
[8] Such as Berlin, Brandenburg, Hessen, Rheinland-Pfalz, Sachsen, Sachsen-Anhalt, Schleswig-Holtstein, Thüringen.
[9] Such as Bayern, Baden-Württemberg, Nordrhein-Westfalen, Niedersachen.

addition, each region must vote unanimously, and an infringement of this order to vote in uniformity leads to the invalidity of a region's votes. Moreover, the members of a *Land's* Government are bound by instructions from their respective Government and have to act in conformity with these instructions. The powers of the *Bundesrat* are not governed under Article 50 GG but rather are laid down in special provisions of the *Grundgesetz*:

(a) The *Bundesrat* takes part in the formal law-making process governed under Articles 76 *et seq.* GG, for instance, while it has the right to introduce bills and has to consent to a bill which has been adopted by the *Bundestag* before it may become law.[10]

(b) The *Bundesrat* also participates in affairs concerning the European Union (Articles 23 and 52 III a GG).

(c) In addition, certain *Rechtsverordnungen* (statutory instruments or ordinances) also require the consent of the *Bundesrat* before they can be passed (Article 80 II GG).

(d) The *Bundesrat* must also consent to federal supervising and controlling measures (Article 84 III and IV GG), new organisations of federal authorities of a middle and a lower rank (Article 87 II 2 GG) and measures which are subject to the *Bundeszwang* (federal enforcement) — the latter are measures to be taken by the Federal Government in order to enforce the federal obligations owed by every *Land* (Article 37 GG).

C. FEDERAL GOVERNMENT (*BUNDESREGIERUNG*)

The Federal Government is a collegiate federal organ which consists of a Federal Chancellor and Federal Ministers (Article 62 GG). Its constitutional position results from the principle of the separation of powers as part of the second, executive power (Article 20 II and III GG). It is incumbent on the Government to exercise all tasks which are not subject to the sphere of competences of either the legislative organs or the jurisdiction. In addition, the Federal Government has to be demarcated from the (remaining) administration because it is the head of the executive power: usually the tasks of the Federal Government can be described as with guidance, control and leadership of the entire German State whereas the rest of the administration deals with the mere task of executing the law.

---

[10] For more details, see *ibid.*, Chap. Three, 5, B.

(1) Federal Chancellor (*Bundeskanzler*)

The Chancellor is elected in a secret ballot by the majority of the members of the *Bundestag* (Article 63 GG). He deals with the current business and has effective and comprehensive political power. A significant feature of his office is that he establishes the *Richtlinien der Politik* ("national policy guidelines") for which he is also responsible. Only within these "national policy guidelines" can each of his Federal Ministers run his respective sphere of responsibilities independently and under his own responsibility (Article 65 GG). The Chancellor's power to give guidelines as a kind of frame for the political agenda is not restricted by law but is a general power and forms the main basis of foreign and domestic policy. Moreover, the Chancellor may propose the Federal Ministers to the Federal President for appointment or for removal (Article 64 GG).

The Chancellor's term of office can terminate because of a voluntary resignation, through death, when a newly-elected *Bundestag* meets for the first time or when a vote of no confidence is taken and simultaneously a new Federal Chancellor is elected. In these cases, the Federal President has to dismiss the Chancellor from office (Article 67 GG).

(2) Federal Ministers (*Bundesminister*)

As we have already mentioned, the Federal Ministers form — together with the Chancellor — the Federal Government. The Ministers run the business independently in their respective sphere of responsibility and within the scope of the "national policy guidelines". The number and the sphere of responsibility of any ministry is not laid down and specified under the *Grundgesetz* but has been established in accordance with tradition and necessity. Any Minister exercises his tasks independently and under his own responsibility. No direct responsibility of the Minister exists towards the *Bundestag*.

The Federal Ministers are appointed and dismissed by the Federal President on the Chancellor's proposal. Their term of office terminates with any disposal of Chancellor's office, especially when a new *Bundestag* is coming together.

(3) Authority of the Federal Government

The authority of the Federal Government as a collegiate organ is restricted to the extent that the Chancellor gives the "national policy guidelines", and within the scope of these guidelines the ministers run the business of their Ministries.[11] Conflicts because of different opinions between Federal Ministers are decided by the Federal Government.

The powers of the Federal Government are not enumerated in detail in the *Grundgesetz* but follow from the character of government. The following tasks are explicitly transferred: the Government participates in the law-making process (Articles 76 I and 82 I GG) and can be empowered to pass statutory instruments (Article 80 I GG) and administrative provisions (Articles 84 II, 85 II and 86 GG).

In addition, it is very difficult to describe the Government's tasks and responsibility in a comprehensive way. The following responsibilities, however, are the Government's by tradition and are of particular importance: foreign or defence policy, organisation in the federal territory (provided no special provisions are in effect) and control of the executive administration by the *Länder* (see Articles 84 III to IV and 85 III to IV GG).

D. FEDERAL PRESIDENT (*BUNDESPRÄSIDENT*)

The Federal President is the head of the state but is only provided with very limited power. He is elected by the *Bundesversammlung* (Federal Electoral Assembly) which consists of members of the *Bundestag* and *Bundesrat* (Article 54 III GG). Any German citizen is eligible for this office after attaining the age of 40, provided he or she has the right to vote for the *Bundestag* (Article 54 I GG). The term of office of a Federal President is five years; thereafter, re-election is permissible only once. The Federal President is represented by the *Bundesrat*.

The Federal President is not allowed to belong to the Federal Government or a legislative body of either the Federation or *Länder*. He undertakes a neutral position within the State. The legal powers of the Federal President are exclusively regulated in the *Grundgesetz*. For instance, the President participates in the law-making process because his signature ratifies the law (Article 82 GG), represents the State on national and international levels (Article 59 GG), appoints and dismisses the members of the Federal Government (Articles 63 and 64 GG) or may declare a state emergency (Article 81 GG).

In comparison to the legal position of the President of the *Weimarer Reichsverfassung* the constitutional position of the

---

[11] The Federal Government usually sets up its own *Geschäftsordnung der Bundesregierung* (Standing Orders of the Federal Government).

Federal President, as laid down in the *Grundgesetz,* is less powerful, because for the exercise of certain official enactments he has to have the counter-signature of the Chancellor or the respective Minister.

5. LEGISLATION (*GESETZGEBUNG*) OF THE FEDERATION

A. POWER TO LEGISLATE BETWEEN THE FEDERATION AND THE *LÄNDER*

It is said in Article 30 I GG that it is the task of the *Länder* to exercise state authority and to fulfil state functions provided that the *Grundgesetz* does make another arrangement. According to this basic rule set forth in Article 30 GG, the provision of Article 70 I GG sets up the principle that "The *Länder* shall have the right of legislative power as far as this *Grundgesetz* shall not delegate legislative power to the Federation." Thus, Articles 71 to 75 GG mainly deal with the allocation of legislative power to the Federation. As a result, the power to legislate is delegated to such a comprehensive extent that not much has been left over for the legislation of the *Länder.* Therefore, the exclusive legislative power of the *Länder* takes action only with regard to special fields not being enumerated in the *Grundgesetz*, for instance, constitutional law and administration of the *Länder,* the local law, police and regulatory law as well as art, television, new media, schools and education.

The ordered and transferred legislative power to the Federation pursuant to Articles 71 *et seq.* GG is compulsory and can not be changed by law or by agreements entered between the Federation and the *Länder.* In addition, no holder of legislative power is allowed to waive them or — without a constitutional authority — to delegate them.

With regard to the allocation of responsibilities to the Federation, the *Grundgesetz* makes a difference between the three types of legislative power which are outlined below. In addition there are also unwritten powers.

(1) Exclusive legislative power (*Ausschließliche Gesetzgebungszuständigkeit*) of the Federation

The exclusive legislative power of the Federation is governed under Article 71 GG and means that the *Länder* shall have the power to legislate in the sphere of exclusive legislation of the Federation only if and as far as a federal law expressively grants authority to do so. Then, such a granted authority is only possible with regard to single questions and not concerning an entire special field. It also applies to legislation but does not bind the *Länder.* In practice the *Länder* are, as a matter of principle, excluded from legislating in this area.

The special fields of exclusive legislation of the Federation are listed especially in Articles 73, 105 I, 143 a and 143 b GG (*e.g.* foreign affairs, defence and civil defence, citizenship, transport system, postal system and telecommunications, protection of industrial property and copyright). Beyond this, exclusive legislation can be assumed as well in those cases in which the *Grundgesetz* states that a further regulation is performed by federal law (see Articles 14 III 2 and 21 III GG).

(2) Concurrent (*Konkurrierende*) legislative power

The concurrent legislative power between the Federation and the *Länder* is set forth in Article 72 GG and can be regarded as the biggest and most important field of legislation. It is said in Article 72 I GG that the *Länder* shall have legislative power in the field of concurrent legislation as long as and as far as the Federation has not made use of its legislative competence. The Federation has the power to legislate within this field under two prerequisites which must be met: first, the special field must be enumerated in the catalogue of Articles 74, 74a and 105 II GG and secondly, there must be a necessity for a uniform regulation throughout the federal territory (Article 74 II GG).

(a) As a result of this, the Federation has legislative power if the object to be regulated is subject of the concurrent legislative power. Its subjects are mainly enumerated in the catalogue of Articles 74 and 74 a GG. The following regulative fields are important: civil law, criminal law, execution of a sentence, organisation of the court system, judicial proceedings, law of trade and industry, labour law (including the works constitution), remuneration and supply of the members of the public services of the *Länder.*

(b) As outlined above, the Federation only has the power to legislate if there is a requirement for a uniform regulation throughout the Federal Territory (Article 72 II GG). This is the case if and as far as a uniform regulation by Federal Territory is required in order to establish equivalent living conditions within the entire Federal Territory or to safeguard the legal and economic unity for the benefit of the national interest.

Given these suppositions, there is a necessity for federal legislative activity. The legal consequence of this is that only when the Federation is not exercising its legislative power does it revert to the *Länder.* Therefore, this legislative power is regarded, not only by the courts, as a power of the Federation.

(3) Skeleton legislation (*Rahmengesetzgebung*)

The skeleton legislation of the Federation is set forth in Article 75 GG and means that the Federation is allowed to pass *Rahmenvorschriften* (general or outline provisions). Their completion is incumbent on the *Länder.*

With respect to the skeleton legislation, a similar principle applies as to the concurrent legislative power. The Federation is competent as far as, first, the subject to be regulated lies within a special field belonging to the skeleton legislation pursuant to Article 75 GG (*e.g.* public service, nature conservation, landscape conservation and water resources management) and secondly, the prerequisites of Article 72 II GG — as indicated above and to which we may refer — are fulfilled as well. The Federation has limited legislative power in the sphere of skeleton legislation, it is not allowed to pass a complete regulation but is restricted to passing general provisions. The Federation provides the important framework legislation for the *Länder*; in addition, the federal law demands and ensures that the skeleton legislation is completed by the *Länder.* Only in exceptional circumstances is the federal legislator allowed to pass provisions which enter into particulars.

The *Länder* are competent to pass a complete law on this special field if the Federation could not pass a law because of the lacking prerequisites of Article 72 II GG or the Federation does not make use of the given skeleton legislative power.

(4) "Unwritten" power to legislate

Although an explicit allocation in the *Grundgesetz* does not exist, the Federation has exceptional legislative powers provided that the subject to be regulated has close and inseparable reference to the specific subjects governed under Articles 73 *et seq.* GG.

Also acknowledged is the *Annexkompetenz* of the Federation which is the legislative power to regulate all questions arising during the preparation and implementation of a special field explicitly delegated to the federation.

Last but not least, there are particular subjects which have to be regulated by the Federation because of their individual nature. This is the case, for instance, if the regulation of a question by the *Länder* is compulsorily excluded because the regulation can be exercised only by a federal regulation which is uniform for each of the states.

B. LEGISLATIVE PROCEDURE (*GESETZGEBUNGSVERFAHREN*)

The legislative procedure is governed under Articles 76 to 82 GG and can as a rule be subdivided into three different parts — the proceedings to introduce a bill, the main proceedings and the termination proceedings — which are outlined below (see Schedule 1).

(1) Introduction of a bill in the *Bundestag*

The first part of the legislative procedure is the part in which a bill is introduced in the *Bundestag*. The legislative procedure is initiated with the introduction of a bill (Article 76 GG): the introduction of a bill can be started from the Federal Government, the *Bundestag* and the *Bundesrat*.

In practice the Federal Government normally initiates legislation and the course of proceedings is generally as follows: the competent ministry submits a *Referentenentwurf* (draft of the head of section) to the *Bundeskanzleramt* (Office of the Federal Chancellor); other ministries and the *Länder* may take part as well in the decision-making process. Next, the *Kabinettsvorlage* (cabinet bill) is passed by decision of the cabinet and becomes the *Regierungsentwurf* (government draft). This government draft is then passed on to the *Bundesrat* (Article 76 II GG). The sense of submitting the bill to the *Bundesrat* is that the *Bundestag* will already know — during the parliamentary debate — the opinion of the *Bundesrat* on the government draft. The opinion of the *Bundesrat* can be considered in the draft bill and conflicts can be avoided in advance.

Draft bills of the *Bundestag* must be introduced by a parliamentary group or 5 per cent of the members of the *Bundestag* whereas the deputies may belong to different parliamentary groups (§ 76 GeschO).

Bills of the *Bundesrat* as an organ (not of single *Länder*) however are not directly passed to the *Bundestag* but go through the Federal Government. The Government then has to specify its opinion therewith (Article 76 III GG).

(2) Main proceedings

Federal law has to be passed by a formal vote in the *Bundestag* (Article 77 I 1 GG). The taking of a decision is the material act regarding legislation. But prior to adoption of a resolution in the *Bundestag*, a debate on the respective draft bill takes place. These debates are structured in quite a complicated way. As a matter of principle, the draft bills are debated on in three readings (§§ 78 to 86 GeschO BT).

(a) First reading: when the bill is read for the first time, no applications for amendments or votes take place but perhaps a general debate. Normally the draft bill will be transferred to a certain committee for an in-depth discussion.

(b) Second reading: a general debate in the *Bundestag* takes place and certain provisions of the bill might be discussed on the basis of the committee's report. Applications for amendments can then be filed. The discussion ends with the vote on the draft bill in which each member of the *Bundestag* has to participate.

(c) Third reading: applications for amendments can be only filed by deputies who have the strength of a parliamentary group. In this reading the final vote on the bill is performed. As long as there have not been any amendments adopted in the second reading, the third reading can continue to proceed directly after the second .

The *Grundgesetz* makes a difference with regard to the required majority in order to take an effective decision. As a matter of principle a simple majority of the members of the *Bundestag* is demanded (see Article 42 II GG), and only a law amending the constitution requires a qualified majority of the members of the *Bundesrat* and the *Bundestag* (two thirds, see Article 79 II GG).

As already mentioned, apart from the *Bundestag* the *Bundesrat* also takes part in the law-making process: the law will be passed onto the *Bundesrat* after it has obtained the required majority in the *Bundestag* (Article 77 I 2 GG). On principle, the power and authority of the *Bundesrat* to participate in the legislative proceedings depends on the type of law to be adopted:

(a) As a matter of principle, the laws are *Einspruchsgesetze* which means that the *Bundesrat* can convene the committee of conciliation within a period of three weeks (Article 77 II GG) or can file an objection within two weeks after the conclusion of the proceedings with the mediation committee (Article 77 III GG).

(b) A *Zustimmungsgesetz* must be distinguished from the type of law as just indicated. First of all, a law is a *Zustimmungsgesetz* if it is prescribed as such by the *Grundgesetz* (see Articles 84 I, 85 I, 104 a III 3, 105 III and 79 II GG). A law requiring consent is only adopted if the *Bundesrat* gives its consent to it. The *Bundestag* is not obliged to declare its consent and the consent cannot be replaced or outvoted by the *Bundestag*.

The legislative proceedings of the participation of the *Bundesrat* might become complicated and Schedule 1 gives you a broad overview of the course of the legislative proceedings. Because of the very complicated legal norm of Article 77 GG, Article 78 GG shows the five cases in which a law which had been adopted by the *Bundestag* can come into existence. Due to this Article, a bill passed by the *Bundestag* shall become law if the *Bundesrat*:

— consents to it (in case of an *Einspruchsgesetz* or *Zustimmungsgesetz*);
— has not (or delayed) applied to convene the committee of conciliation (Article 77 II GG);
— has not lodged an objection within the period of Article 77 III GG;
— withdraws the objection; or
— is overridden by the *Bundestag*.

(3) Termination proceedings

A bill which has been adopted pursuant to Article 78 GG is signed by the Federal President (Articles 58 GG) and thereafter is promulgated in the *Bundesgesetzesblatt* (Federal Law Gazette). Each law must specify the exact date to which the law enters into force (Article 82 II GG).

(4) Law amending the constitution

A law amending the constitution has to be adopted in a proceeding where a high standard has to be met before such a law is passed (Article 79 GG). To begin with, the legislative proceedings regarding a law amending the *Grundgesetz* contain a few particularities in comparison with the proceedings outlined above (Article 79 I and II GG): first, the wording of the *Grundgesetz* must be amended explicitly. Then, the law amending the constitution requires in all cases the consent of the *Bundesrat*. Finally, for passing such a law a qualified majority of two-thirds of the members of the *Bundestag* and the *Bundesrat* is required.

On the substantive side the legislator has to observe Article 79 III GG which says that certain basic principles cannot be changed or amended at all. These principles include: the division of the Federal Republic into the *Länder*, their participation in the legislative process, the basic principles set forth in Articles 1 and 20 GG and the provision of Article 79 III GG itself.

C. PASSING STATUTORY INSTRUMENTS

Article 80 GG governs the passing of statutory instruments and regulates the following in section 1:

"By virtue of law the Federal Government, a Federal Minister or a *Land* Government can be authorised to pass statutory instruments. Thereby the content, purpose and the extent of the granted authority shall be determined in the law. The legal basis has to be indicated in the regulation. It is provided by virtue of law that an authority can be transferred additional powers, so it requires for its transfer an authority of a statutory instrument."

This Article intends to discharge the *Bundestag* from its legislative task because in certain cases the authority to establish rules of law is transferred to the executive power by operation of law. But you should keep in mind that generally the legislation is reserved for the Parliament as the ordinary legislator; this is required by democratic principle and the principle of a constitutional state (especially the separation of powers).[12]

As a result, the passing of statutory instruments by the executive power requires a definite and concrete legal authorisation in order to be effective. The reason behind this requirement is to prevent the Parliament losing its legislative power. In addition, such an authorisation must be laid down in federal law. For an authorisation by the virtue of regional law the provisions of the regional constitution apply which quite often has the same wording as Article 80 GG. As far as such a provision under regional law does not exist, it is impossible to go back to Article 80 GG because this legal norm applies neither directly nor indirectly by an analogous interpretation; then, the conditions to be met follow from the democratic principle and the principle of a constitutional state.[13]

---

[12] For more details, see *ibid.*, Chap. Three, 3, C.
[13] BVerfGE 55, 207 (226).

At this stage we must emphasise that in order to understand the term "statutory instrument" correctly one has to bear in mind that this secondary legislation must be distinguished from formally enacted law. A statutory instrument is not legislated by the legislative power (the Parliament) but by the executive power (the administration) and rests on a legal authorisation that must be effective and has to fulfil the requirements which are governed under Article 80 I GG. Finally, the statutory instrument is regarded as material law and ranks in the hierarchy of legal sources under the formally enacted law by Parliament.

6. IMPLEMENTATION OF FEDERAL LAWS

A. ADMINISTRATIVE RESPONSIBILITY AND TYPES OF ADMINISTRATION

The division of powers between federation and *Länder* is not distributed into special fields but in accordance with functions to be performed. The allocated legislative power to the Federation for a certain field, therefore, does not mean that the Federation also has the power to carry out the law. The reason for this is laid down in Article 83 GG which states that "The *Länder* implement Federal laws as their own affairs as far as this *Grundgesetz* determines or permits nothing else". Therefore, in the first instance the assumption of a region's administrative responsibility applies — as it has also been specified in Articles 30 and 70 GG. Exceptionally, the Federation has the legislative power and also the additional administrative powers provided that this has explicitly been prescribed in Articles 84 *et seq.* GG.

Furthermore, the enforcement of the law is not a mere appendix to passing a law, and it is not possible to conclude from legislative to administrative competence — this conclusion can also not been drawn vice versa. The reason is that the *Länder* might have the administrative competence by operation of Article 83 GG, although they might have had no legislative competence. These points have to be checked in every single case.

The *Grundgesetz* regulates only the implementation of federal laws and the region's administration on behalf of the Federation. Comparable to the legislative competences, the *Grundgesetz* makes a difference between different administrative types while carrying out federal laws. With regard to this, the attachment to one of the administrative types — which are outlined below — is decisive because along this line acts the substructure of federal authorities and federal powers towards the *Länder*. But the implementation of regional law is — because of Article

30 GG — not subject to the *Grundgesetz*. It belongs to the sole competence of the *Länder* and, with regard to this, a supervision exercised by the Federation is generally inadmissible.

B. IMPLEMENTATION OF FEDERAL LAW THROUGH THE *LÄNDER* AS THEIR OWN AFFAIRS

As a rule, federal law is implemented by the *Länder* independently (Article 83 GG). Generally, the *Länder* then regulate the setting up of public authorities and the applicable administrative proceedings. However, federal law might prescribe something else provided that the *Bundesrat* has previously consented to it (Article 84 II GG).

The implementation is supervised by the Federal Government in respect that the law must be implemented legally (Article 84 III 99). This supervision is called *Rechtsaufsicht* (supervision limited to the question of legality of administrative activities) and covers measures like the notice of defects (Article 84 IV GG) or the single instruction by operation of law — but again only with the consent of the *Bundesrat* (Article 84 V GG).

C. THE *LÄNDER'S* ADMINISTRATION ON BEHALF OF THE FEDERATION (*BUNDESAUFTRAGSVERWALTUNG*)

Administration of the *Länder* on behalf of the Federation is governed under Article 85 GG. It means that federal law is implemented by a region's administration and not by the Federal administration. Therefore, the acting authorities are those of the respective *Land*, and the authorities do not act in the capacity of a federal organ. The *Grundgesetz* provides the administration by commission in particular areas and the most important areas are: administration of federal highways (Article 90 II GG), nuclear energy administration (Article 87 c GG), federal defence administration (Article 87 b II 1 GG) and finance (Articles 104 a III 2 GG).

Again, with regard to this, the Federation supervises the region's implementation of the law. Federal supervision extends to the lawfulness and expedience of the implementation (Article 85 IV GG). This is the *Fachaufsicht* (substantive supervisory power) which grants the Federation a more comprehensive right of supervision (Article 85 III and IV GG) than it has been granted regarding the implementation of federal law by the *Länder,*[14] because it is not limited to the question of legality

[14] For more details, see *ibid.*, Chap. Three, 6, B.

of administrative activities but rather comprises the supervision of the expedience of the activities as well.

D. FEDERAL ADMINISTRATION (*BUNDESVERWALTUNG*)

In exceptional cases the *Grundgesetz* provides that federal law is carried out by the Federation itself. This is called *bundeseigene Verwaltung* (administration federally owned). In order to exercise these tasks laid down in the *Grundgesetz*, the Federation has the following possibilities of organisation and implementation.

(1) Federal administration under public law (*Bundesunmittelbare Verwaltung*)

First, the Federation may make use of the federal authorities. This means that it implements its administrative tasks with public authorities which are organs of the corporation "Federation". In this respect, the *Grundgesetz* provides in Article 87 GG the following three different administrative types:

(a) Federal administration can be exercised with an administrative substructure (Article 87 I 1 GG) which can comprehend a sequence of public authorities going over more than one instance. This administrative substructure, for example, has been set up with regard to the foreign services and administration of finances. The Federation administers these fields with its own public authorities and is not allowed to commission corporations under public or under private law in order to perform these tasks — the Federation must have sole responsibility for these areas.

(b) In addition, federal administration can be exercised through central offices by operation of a federal law (Article 87 I 2 GG). An administrative substructure does not exist. The federation has set up central offices like the Federal Office of Criminal Investigation and the Federal Office for the Protection of the constitution.

(c) Furthermore, federal administration can also be performed by independent federal superior authorities which are competent for the entire Federal Territory (Article 87 III 1 GG). Here, again, no administrative substructure exists. An example of such an independent federal superior authority is the Federal Cartel Office.

(2) Federal administration indirectly under federal law (*Bundesmittelbare Verwaltung*)

The Federation may perform its tasks by setting up corporations under public law, or statutory bodies; both federally owned (Article 87 II, III 1 GG). Here, the public authorities are legal entities which are federal organs acting indirectly on behalf of the Federation. Federal administration performed not by public authorities but by corporations under public law or statutory bodies has been seen in areas such as the post and telecommunications (without an administrative substructure) and employment (with an administrative substructure such as the Federal Employment Office, the *Land* Employment Office and the Employment office).

E. MIXED ADMINISTRATION (*MISCHVERWALTUNG*) AND JOINT TASKS (*GEMEINSCHAFTSAUFGABEN*)

The *Grundgesetz* pursues the fundamental principle that the Federation and the *Länder* remain separate with regard to organisation and fulfilment of tasks — although they do cooperate in the area of legislation and administration. The prohibition of mixed administration follows from this fundamental principle. Therefore, administrative forms of organisations in which participation between federation and *Länder* is carried out by consent or in which a federal authority is subordinated to a *Land* authority are inadmissible.

Nevertheless, the *Grundgesetz* provides in Article 108 IV GG one exceptional case in which the mixed administration is admissible. Under this rule cooperation between federal and regional tax authorities is possible with respect to the administration of tax — if and as long as this is a means of improving the enforcement of tax law considerably or of making the process easier.

Joint tasks which are specified in Articles 91 a and b GG constitute a further exception to this principle. Article 91 a GG restricts the term "*Gemeinschaftsaufgaben*" on three fields which are enumerated in this Article. These tasks are: building and extending institutions of higher education including university clinics, the improvement of regional economic structures and, finally, the improvement of agricultural structure and coastal preservation. These joint tasks generally remain the responsibility of the *Länder*. The Federation only participates in three respects: 1. The Federation obtains an additional legislative power (Article 91 a II GG). 2. The Federation and the *Länder* exercise a joint policy (Article 91 a III GG). 3. The

Federation has to bear at least half of the expenses and — because of this — obtains an additional financial authority (Article 91 a IV GG).

7. BASIC RIGHTS (*GRUNDRECHTE*)

A. GENERAL PRINCIPLES

The main basic rights of the German constitution are laid down in Articles 1 to 19 *Grundgesetz*. Furthermore, there are so-called "*grundrechtsgleiche Rechte*", regulations of the constitution which are not contained in the catalogue of basic rights itself, but do have the same effect and legal strength.[15] The German legislator of 1949 placed the basic rights as the first part of the then young *Grundgesetz* — this measure has to be seen as an obvious political and legal sign and as one of the results of the terrible experiences made during the twelve years of the *Drittes Reich* (Third Reich): the new constitution was designed to be dedicated to preserve and to obey human rights, and this extraordinary position is still a matter of fact today.

Basic rights are created as rules of protection for every citizen against unlawful acts or omissions of sovereign organs; moreover they ensure that each member of society is entitled to take part in the political and democratic process in Germany — the fundamental rights of freedom of speech and press (Article 5 I 1, 2 GG) are probably the best examples in this respect. But that is not the whole dimension: in certain cases *Grundrechte* give the basis of claims to a citizen against the state. For instance: Article 12 GG guarantees the Freedom of Profession — more precisely: the general freedom to select any profession and the additional safeguard that only the legislator is entitled to restrict the way one performs the profession in practice. Given this as a matter of fact, it is undisputed in German legal theory and jurisdiction that the State has the obligation to deliver a kind of "platform" which enables people to take up a certain profession. Therefore, the Federal Constitutional Court in Karlsruhe has ruled that — for instance — universities have to be equipped in an appropriate way to give young people the opportunity to study medicine, because otherwise there would be no chance at all to take up the medical profession.

---

[15] See, for instance Art. 38 GG which deals with the regulations and prepositions of democratic elections. Given the history and practical importance, this norm is equal to Arts. 1 to 19 GG. See also the further examples in Arts. 20 IV, 33, 101, 103, 104 GG.

Another very important aspect of basic rights is that these norms do not only function as *subjektive Rechte* (subjective rights) which protect the individual. Basic rights also have an objective dimension — in other words they have to be seen as an integral part of the legal system as a whole. If one takes into account that *Grundrechte* also safeguard certain legal institutions like marriage (Article 6 I GG), property (Article 14 GG) or — as we have pointed out before — Freedom of the Press (Article 5 I GG) it becomes obvious that the objective importance of basic rights for the German legal system is remarkable. The practical effect of this is that the power of the State is thereby kept in check.

Talking about the underlying principles of the system of basic rights one should not forget another distinction: there are "*Menschenrechte*", human rights, which apply to any individual — for instance Freedom of Faith (Article 4 GG) and, again, Freedom of Speech (Article 5 I 1 GG). Moreover, there are the "*Deutschenrechte*" which are rights which only German citizens are entitled to benefit from. With regard to this, Freedom of Profession (Article 12 GG) is a good example, as is Freedom of Assembly (Article 8 GG). In so far as we notice a kind of restriction which was created by the historical legislator and has to be accepted as a legislative decision. The most reasonable intention for this restriction is that the area of application of basic rights should not be over emphasised. One point is important to remember: the distinction between "*Menschenrecht*" and "*Deutschenrecht*" does not mean that foreigners are left stranded in Germany without any legal protection — anyone can still call on Article 2 GG which guarantees that one is entitled to do basically whatever one wants (as long as one does not infringe or disregard the interests and/or legal positions of other people).[16] With regard to this, Article 2 GG can be seen as the "mother" of basic rights.[17]

But the question is: who is entitled to seek protection or to build up a certain claim founded on basic right principles? First of all — as we have said before — private persons enjoy the privileges of basic rights whereas — in general — the State (and all its different organs in legislative bodies, administration or jurisdiction) never does. This is to prevent a case of confusion, because it is logically impossible to be sender of a legal norm on the one hand and addressee of its advantages on the other.

---

[16] BVerfGE 6, 32 ff. (36); BVerfGE 80, 137.

[17] German translation: "*Muttergrundrecht*" — a qualification which is often used in connection with another very general but nevertheless important basic right: Art. 1 GG — which guarantees the dignity of any individual.

There are very few exceptions to this fundamental principle: universities, for instance, are usually drawn up and organised through acts of legislation and belong to the sphere of the state. Nevertheless, universities are allowed to benefit from Article 5 III GG which safeguards the freedom of Science and the Arts.

And how about legal persons? The constitution itself gives the answer. Article 19 III GG states that "basic rights are effective for German artificial persons [*i.e.* institutions and organisations], provided it makes sense to do so". A very simple example illustrates what is meant by this legal principle: legal persons can obviously be the owner (and normally do own) of property — so Article 14 GG, which guarantees the right to possess and which protects private property, is relevant with regard to legal persons. The contrary example: by definition institutions do not have a conscience in the way an individual person has — consequently, Article 4 GG which safeguards the Freedom of Faith and Conscience, is logically not applicable.

In a different context we have already talked about the problem of the addressee of basic rights. So, who and which powers of sovereignty are bound by the legal safeguards created mostly by Articles 1 — 19 GG? Again, the answer is offered by the constitution itself. Article 1 III GG states that "the following basic rights shall bind the legislature, the executive and the judiciary as direct and enforceable law". You can see the very straightforward approach of the historical legislator, and consequently it is the undisputed opinion of jurisdiction and academic authors that Article 1 III GG contains a different dogmatic point of view than — say — the *Weimarer Reichsverfassung*. The remarkable fact is that Article 1 III GG does not present any conditions, but instead restricts the position of the State and its organs. It is the main task of the Federal Constitutional Court to ensure that basic rights are properly obeyed in practice.

Our conclusion up to this stage is that basic rights do evolve legal power in a vertical way — between the private individual and the state. And how about a horizontal effect of basic rights between individual persons? The magic formula is "*unmittelbare oder mittelbare Drittwirkung*" which means that basic rights can either have a direct or indirect power between ordinary citizens.

Due to the fact that basic rights were originally designed to protect individuals against unlawful acts of the State, in other words to function only in a vertical way, a direct effect between individuals is not accepted, whereas because of the overwhelming importance of basic rights an indirect effect is recognised as legally correct and in line with the legislative intentions laid down in the constitution. The practical result of this understanding of basic rights is that the catalogue of Articles 1 to 19 GG influences any other part of the legal system, especially private law. Private law should not be contrary to basic rights, so it is correct to talk about an *Ausstrahlungswirkung* (effect of dissemination) of basic rights to other areas of the law.

B. THE PRINCIPAL BASIC RIGHTS

(1) Human dignity (*Menschenwürde*)

The first norm of the catalogue of basic rights states that "The dignity of man shall be inviolable. To respect and to protect it shall be the duty of all state authority".

It did not happen by accident that this rule opens up the canon of Articles 1 to 19 GG. On the contrary: Article 1 III GG stands for the most relevant intention of the historical legislator which was to point out that the individual comes first, the State second. Seeing it from this pespective it is no surprise that the *Bundesverfassungsgericht* (Federal Constitutional Court) held individual dignity to be the main principle of the constitution.[18] This eminent position is underlined by the fact that due to Article 79 III GG, the *Ewigkeitsgarantie* (guarantee for eternity) of the constitution, Article 1 and Article 20 GG, are the only regulations which are definitely unchangeable — even in the case of a legitimate amendment or revision of the constitution.

Of course this is a result of the bitter experiences of the Fascist era. Article 1 GG stands for the fact that aims of the State do not have an authorisation in itself but rather have to serve the advantage of the individual. In this respect, "dignity of man" does not only describe a frontier for any act of the Government; above this, it reflects a task the State has to fulfil while dealing with its citizen.

So what is the main safeguard provided by Article 1 III GG? The Federal Constitutional Court, in its function as Keeper of the constitution, has set up a formula to explain the contents of the norm: "No person shall be handled in a way that merely degrades him to be the object of certain steps taken by the state and its organs".[19] This might sound very abstract, but becomes clear if one looks at practical examples: the principle of fair trail, for instance, is founded on Article 1 III GG,[20] and so is the

[18] BVerfGE 32, 98 (108); BVerfGE 54, 342 (357).
[19] BVerfGE 9, 89 (95); BVerfGE 57, 250 (275).
[20] BVerfGE 63, 332 (337 *et seq.*).

prohibition of torture of prisoners and the general legal principle not to harm any other person.[21]

A legally interesting aspect of Article 1 GG is the connection of this norm to other basic rights. There is a tendency amongst legal writers to enter disputes over the question of whether Article 1 GG is a basic right itself or only a kind of "entrance" to the basic rights catalogue. The argument is that Article 1 III GG states that the "following basic rights shall bind the legislature, the executive and the judiciary as directly enforceable law". With regard to the "following" basic rights — does that mean, Article 1 GG has to be excluded from the "elite club" of Articles 1 to 19 GG? Not at all; the *Bundesverfassungsgericht* has always seen this rule as part of the constitutional basic rights because of historical developments, the intention of the constitutional legislator in 1949 and its systematical position within the constitution. Nevertheless, there are more specialised basic rights than Article 1 GG: for example the Right to Life, guaranteed in Article 2 II GG, can be seen as a somehow more precise regulation. It needs no explanation that the killing of someone violates his (or her) "dignity of man". But it also violates the more specialised Article 2 II GG, and this is the reason why the *Bundesverfassungsgericht* often quotes other basic rights together with the general principle of Article 1 GG.[22]

(2) Common right of liberty (*Allgemeines Freiheitsrecht*)

This basic right specifies two main guarantees of the German constitution: the private sphere of any individual and the general guarantee of freedom of personal activities — which means the law allows one to do whatever one wants to as long as this does not hurt or disturb the equally protected rights of other people.

Article 2 I GG states:

(1) Everybody shall have the right to free development of his personality in so far as he shall not violate the rights of others or offend the constitutional order or morality.

(2) Everybody shall have the right to life and to personal integrity. The liberty of the individual shall be inviolable. Intrusion of these rights may be made only pursuant to a statute.

---

[21] See BVerfGE 45, 187 (228).
[22] BVerfGE 39, 1 (41).

We have already mentioned that the Federal Constitutional Court often refers to Article 1 GG in combination with other basic rights. The same applies with regard to Article 2 GG. The reason being that this norm is also one of the more general rules within the catalogue of basic rights, so other rules might fit predominantly in a certain case. This has to be seen as a dogmatic consequence of the rule of law that a special norm prevails when competing with a general norm. On the other side Article 2 GG is important whenever there is no other specialised basic right at hand to check whether the constitutional order is maintained. This is why judges and legal authors qualify Article 2 GG as "*Auffanggrundrecht*" — a term which cannot really be translated literally but means that any individual can claim to be hurt in a position "at least" protected by the guarantees of this certain basic right. Therefore, Article 2 GG functions as a general clause within the catalogue of Articles 1 to 19 GG. The practical consequence of this fact is that a great number of constitutional complaints are raised that are based on the allegation of an infringement of Article 2 GG.

To concentrate on the most important practical points with respect to this Article we would now like to focus the attention on the *Allgemeines Persönlichkeitsrecht* (Right of Personality) and the *Recht auf Leben* (Right to Life) which are — as we have seen — expressively laid down in Article 2 II GG.

The Right of Personality is a synonym for several protections granted by Article 2 I GG. Over the past five decades the *Bundesverfassungsgericht* has managed to build up a huge body of jurisdiction to ensure that the personal and private sphere of any individual is not infringed by others — be they private persons or organs of the State. The court has held, for instance, that it belongs to the principle of pursuit of happiness that files put together by a doctor or lawyer (and which contain personal and private information with regard to patient or client) have to be protected against misuse by unauthorised persons.[23] It has also decided that the right to have published a counter-statement in the case of a wrongful reported article in the media is part of the guarantees given by the Right of Personality in Article 2 I GG.[24] From our point of view this jurisdiction is reasonable and deserves consent, because it is quite obvious that the personal and private sphere has to be safeguarded against infringements.

Taking this as a basis it was only one further jurisdictional

---

[23] BVerfGE 32, 373 (379); BVerfGE 27, 1 (6); BVerfGE 79, 256 (268 f.).
[24] BVerfGE 63, 131; BVerfGE 72, 118 (201).

step for the judges in Karlsruhe to develop what they called "*Recht auf informationelle Selbstbestimmung*", a basic right that, as one of the guarantees of Article 2 GG — grants to any individual the authority to decide which details and which amounts of data of his private life should be made public. This is particularly significant in light of the computerised and to some extent virtual world we live in.[25] In so far (and due to the legislation of the *Bundesverfassungsgericht*) as the information protected by Article 2 GG is comprehensive: tax records are protected as well as private diaries or files referring to the divorce procedure of a couple.

(3) Equal rights principle (*Gleichheitsrecht*)

Section 1 of Article 3 GG states that "all people have to be treated equally" — a principle of equal rights which in practice is not as strict and rigorous as it may seem at first sight. Instead of this, the legal message of this very important basic right has to be understood as follows: public authorities (as addressees of the norm) are bound to treat all people in comparable situations (or cases of comparable circumstances) alike whereas others can be treated differently according to their different situations and characteristics. Article 3 GG is especially important for the work of the German legislator, because statutes have to obey the equal rights principle. Furthermore, this basic right is a remarkable sword in the hand of the judges of the *Bundesverfassungsgericht*. Due to the jurisdiction of the Court, the legislator has the freedom to decide which cases are thought of as being "alike" in the sense of Article 3 GG — however, the *Bundesverfassungsgericht* does have the power to check whether the decision taken is in accordance with the constitutional order or not. The appropriate question is whether there are *reasonable grounds* to justify the decision taken. This is obviously not the case when a ruling is described as arbitrary.

It has to be stressed that the general principle of equal rights is valid for the whole of the German legal system.[26] Therefore, this fundamental rule influences criminal law as well as tax law, labour law or even procedural law. Moreover, Article 3 GG is accompanied and completed by several other rules with regard to problems of equality. For instance: Article 3 II GG sets out that "men and women should be treated alike" — a constitutional instruction of great importance if, for instance, one

---

[25] BVerfGE 65, 1 (42) — the famous "*Volkszählungsurteil*".
[26] BVerfGE 35, 272.

thinks about the application of male and female candidates for certain positions. With regard to this, the *Bundesverfassungsgericht* has ruled that even the preference of women can be in accordance with the equal rights principle, owing to the disadvantages women have suffered in the past.[27]

In addition to this there are several other effects and legal consequences which are derived from the equal rights principle. The most important ones are as follows. The binding effect of previous decisions of courts — a principle which probably sounds familiar to the common law reader, because in fact we do see elements of the precedent system in German law. Article 3 GG guarantees, as we have pointed out, that the continuity of the application of the law is ensured; arbitrariness shall be prevented. Therefore, if the judiciary (or the legislative or executive) decides a certain case in a certain way, due to the equal rights principle one can trust in the fact that a comparable case has to be solved in the same way. Given this *conservative element* of Article 3 GG (which — by the way — works along the same lines as the precedent system), changes in the law are nevertheless possible, because changing factual circumstances lead to the need for a different legal valuation and, consequently, for a different application of the law.

Another direct effect of the equal rights principle we must mention is the principle of equal participation in the sharing of public benefits, *e.g.* the fair admission to public institutions and the guarantee of equal chances for training and school (or even university) education — regardless of the financial background of a certain candidate. This guarantee points out that *sozialstaatliche Chancengleichheit* (social equality of opportunities) is one of the main aims of German politics which strives for the best chances according to personal skills and ability. Therefore, it would infringe Article 3 GG if a capable student was not accepted onto a certain university course simply for the reason that he or she was not in a position to afford to study. To prevent cases like this, Germany has a system of loans and grants for capable students.

There is one more aspect which we would like to underline in this context. As a direct outcome of Article 3 GG, the principle of tax equity demands that tax burdens should be distributed according to the financial background and capability of the relevant taxable person. Therefore, those persons enjoying a higher private income have the duty to pay a higher percentage of their wages as tax than those who are financially not that well

---

[27] BVerfGE 74, 163 (180); BVerfGE 85, 191 (206).

off. This tax concept is quite interesting, because here we see a concept of *proportional equality* — the principles of Article 3 GG are infringed, if the legislator does not take into account certain financial circumstances which have a negative influence on the taxpayer's monetary capability.

(4) Freedom of Faith and Conscience (*Glaubens- und Gewissensfreiheit*)

The guarantee of a *Glaubens- und Gewissensfreiheit* (Freedom of Faith and Conscience) is a difficult legal question within the German constitution, because it is related to religion. In the light of the *Grundgesetz* this point has to be seen even more precisely: Article 4 GG has effect with respect to different religions, because it is common opinion that the State has to exercise a *weltanschaulich-religiöse Neutralität* — a neutral position with regard to religion and ideological belief. The best way to understand the legal status of this norm is to read the content of Articles 4 I to III GG. It is stated that the Freedom of Faith and Conscience and the Freedom of Religious and Ideological Belief are unrestrictable. Furthermore, it is guaranteed that religion can be practised without any restriction. And finally, no one can be forced to serve in the Army against his will.

From an ideological point of view, Article 4 GG is a *einheitliches Grundrecht* (uniform basic right) which is also a concrete form of the basic right of *Menschenwürde* (human dignity) as stated in Article 1 GG — with regard to the relationship between specialised and general basic rights we refer to what we have stated in the Chapter dealing with "General Principles". In addition to this it has to be mentioned that the concept of the German *Grundgesetz* is that state and church are separated from each other.

(5) Freedom of Opinion (*Meinungsfreiheit*), Freedom of the Press (*Pressefreiheit*) and Freedom of Arts and Sciences (*Freiheit der Kunst und der Wissenschaft*)

We would now like to turn your interest to one of the most important and far-reaching norms of the German constitution. Articles 5 I to III GG deal with the basic rights of communication — especially the *Meinungsfreiheit* (Freedom of Opinion), the *Pressefreiheit* (Freedom of Press) — and the Freedom of Arts and Science.

In an early decision, the *Bundesverfassungsgericht* has referred to the Freedom of Opinion as being among the *vornehmste Menschenrechte* (most dignified human rights) one can think of.[28] This value judgment of the highest German court may point out the practical relevance of Article 5 GG which is a fundamental aspect of a democratic state.

(a) We would like to begin with Freedom of Opinion and Freedom of Press: in order to understand the full legal background and capacity of Article 5 GG one should — once again — start with the wording of the rule. Due to Article 5 I GG everyone has the right to tell and to publish his opinion and also to inform himself from any source which is "*allgemein zugänglich*" (open to the general public). In addition to this, Article 5 I 2 GG states that the Freedom of Press and the Freedom of Reporting of Radio and Television are guaranteed; censorship is not allowed.

The term *Meinung* (opinion) has to be understood in a very extensive way that includes *Werturteile* (value judgments) and *Tatsachenbehauptungen* (statement of facts). This makes sense if one takes into account that at the time of the enactment of the constitution it was the intention of the legislator to implement a comprehensive safeguard.

Obviously a free press is vital in a democratic society, because journalists have the important task of informing people about the political situation and developments. Therefore, a free and unrestricted press is a legal institution which is protected by the constitution — and the *Bundesverfassungsgericht* which has defended the Freedom of Opinion against attempts to restrict this eminent basic right in many cases.

Protection is granted to anyone who claims to exercise his right to constitutional freedom, be they journalist or common citizen. With regard to journalistic work there is no difference between the varied forms of reporting — in other words: newspaper journalists enjoy the same privileges as television or radio journalists. In addition to this, we would like to mention *Zeugnisverweigerungsrechte* (right to refuse to give evidence) in connection with journalistic work as one of the practically most relevant advantages that journalists can demand with regard to Article 5 GG. Furthermore, it is forbidden for state organs to exercise a *Durchsuchung* (search) within editorial offices. Both elements — *Zeugnisverweigerungsrecht* and restricted *Durchsuchung* — are key points to ensure the Freedom of the Press.

(b) Now to the Freedom of Arts and Science — another very important basic right is laid down in Article 5 III 1 GG:

---

[28] BVerfGE 7, 198 — the famous *Lüthruteil*; BVerfG BB 1958, 168.

"*Kunst und Wissenschaft, Forschung und Lehre sind frei*" (arts and science, academic research and scientific teaching are free). Compared with Article 5 I GG this section is *lex specialis* — in other words a more specialised norm. The intention of the legislator was to safeguard an unrestricted development of arts, science, research and teaching as an expression of a democratic and liberal state. It is worth noting that the term "arts" has to be interpreted quite extensively, in order to avoid any kind of "official" understanding of what art is or should be. The other aspects of Article 5 III GG speak for themselves: Freedom of Science, Academic Research and Teaching has to be guaranteed in order to talk about the democratic organisation of the state.

(6) Freedom of Assembly (*Versammlungsfreiheit*)

If you take a look at Article 8 GG you will also find a key norm and further basic right of practical importance. This rule states that:

"*Alle Deutschen haben das Recht, sich ohne Anmeldung oder Erlaubnis friedlich und ohne Waffen zu versammeln*" (All Germans have the right to form a peaceful and unarmed assembly without a prior application).

As you can imagine, this basic right has done a lot to secure the democratic development in Germany, because it basically protects political assemblies which are important for citizens to participate in the political process by announcing their opinion and by forming demonstrations. Details with regard to Article 8 GG are regulated in the *Versammlungsgesetz* (Law concerning Assemblies and Processions). Moreover it has to be added that *Versammlungen unter freiem Himmel* (assemblies outside closed rooms) can be restricted whenever a registration might be necessary in order to comply with the law.

(7) Freedom of Occupation (*Berufsfreiheit*)

Article 12 I GG states that:

"*Alle Deutschen haben das Recht, Beruf, Arbeitsplatz und Ausbildungsstätte frei zu wählen*" (All Germans have the right to choose their profession, place of employment and place of practical and academic education freely).

With regard to the scope of this book — which is restricted to providing a general overview of the legal system and not the substantive law — we only have space to introduce you to the importance of this norm. To go through the interesting details of the basic rights (and Article 12 GG in particular) would definitely take a book of its own.

But to come back at least to the basics of this basic right: Article 12 GG shows that the German legislator implemented another rule into the constitution that fulfils the task to create a truly democratic surrounding in the state. Everybody shall have the chance to take up the profession he or she is qualified and educated for. Therefore, restrictions with regard to this should be kept to a minimum.

Nevertheless, certain rules with regard to professions are necessary and in line with the constitution. For instance it is stated in Article 12 I 2 GG that "*Die Berufsausübung kann durch Gesetz oder aufgrund eines Gesetzes geregelt werden*". This means that the practical way of how to do a certain job is subject to statutory regulation. To give you an example: the lawyer's profession is regulated by the *Berufsordung der Rechtsanwälte* (rules of profession). These regulations are necessary in order to organise a profession (and all its rights and duties) properly.

(8) Guarantee of Property and Succession (*Eigentumsgarantie und Erbrecht*)

The basic right we would like to mention (at least in detail) is the *Grundrecht auf Eigentum und Erbrecht* (Guarantee of Property and Succession) which is laid down in Article 14 GG. This norm simply states that:

"*Das Eigentum und das Erbrecht werden gewährleistet*".

The *Bundesverfassungsgericht* has ruled that this norm is an "elementary basic right" and a decision of the historical legislator which is of a special importance. This interpretation makes sense and becomes clear if one takes into account the theoretical opposite: a state which does not give a guarantee to its citizens with regard to private property and succession can hardly claim to be democratic. So, with respect to this, Article 14 GG safeguards the possibility to act freely in one's own personal sphere and to act unrestricted with one's own property — even with regard to the next generation, because the State is not allowed to influence the decision of who will be the entitled *Rechtsnachfolger* (legal successor).

Obviously, the guarantee of property and succession has another impact with regard to trials of state organs to expropriate private people. It is stated that "*Eine Enteignung ist nur zulässig zum Wohle der Allgemeinheit*" — which can be translated as "an expropriation is only justifiable if it is to the advantage of the society as a whole". It is quite clear that this is a wide and difficult section to interpret. Therefore, the legal theories and jurisdiction with regard to this part of Article 14 GG do fill libraries and keep legal writers busy.

(9) Further basic rights laid down in Articles 1 to 19 GG

We do not want to close this Chapter without introducing you to the other basic rights we have not explained in-depth. Again we have to point out that this does not mean that the other Articles are of a minor rank or importance, but due to the scope of this book we have to restrict ourselves.

If you study the German constitution you will have to take a look at Article 6 GG which deals with *Ehe und Familie* (marriage and family) and provides a certain protection for these institutions. The same applies for Article 7 GG which safeguards the *Schulwesen*, the system of education at school level. Article 9 GG deals with the *Vereinigungs- und Koalitionsfreiheit*, the freedom to found and to join societies and associations. This norm is of an eminent practical importance, because it also contains the legal questions arising from *Tarifverträge* (collective agreements) und *Arbeitskämpfe* (strikes) — in other words: Article 9 III GG deals with the Freedom to Organise Strikes.

Also important is Article 10 GG which contains the *Brief-, Post- und Fernmeldegeheimnis*, the secrecy of letters, post and telecommunications. Article 11 GG regulates the *Freizügigkeit*, the Freedom of Unrestricted Mobility, whereas Article 12 a GG deals with the *Wehrdienst und Ersatzdienst* — in other words the constitutional situation with regard to military service and the refusal to serve in the armed forces.

We would also like to mention Article 13 GG which guarantees the *Unverletzlichkeit der Wohnung*, the protection of the private residential space. Article 15 GG contains a special legal position which should be read in association with Article 14 GG. As we have already said, there is the Guarantee of Property as a general rule — Article 15 GG is the exception to this, because it regulates the possibility of an *Überführung in Gemeinwirtschaft* — the transfer of certain goods and/or real estate into the social economy. To do so in a legally acceptable form, a certain statute is necessary which also regulates the compensation that has to be paid for the loss of property.

Furthermore, we have to point out Articles 16, 16a GG and Article 17 GG. These basic rights deal with the *Schutz vor Ausbürgerung und Auslieferung* (protection against expatriation and extradition), the *Asylrecht* and the right of asylum. Article 17 GG contains the *Petitionsrecht* (Right of Petition).

Finally, you should study Articles 17a, 18 and 19 of the constitution. Article 17a GG introduces you to certain *Grundrechtseinschränkungen zu Verteidigungszwecken* (restrictions of basic rights) which might enter into force in the unlikely event of a national defence in military conflicts. Article 18 GG deals with the *Verwirkung von Grundrechten* (forfeiture of basic rights), and, finally, Article 19 GG regulates and explains restrictions to basic rights, *Grundrechtsträger* (entitlement with regard to basic rights) and *Rechtsschutz* (questions of legal protection). The latter is set out in more detail in Chapter Five.

8. JURISDICTION (*RECHTSPRECHUNG*)

It is stated in Article 92 GG that judicial power is entirely entrusted to judges and is exercised by federal courts, courts of the *Länder* and by the *Bundesverfassungsgericht* (Federal Constitutional Court).

The judges — irrespective of which court they hear cases in — hold the *Rechtsprechungsmonopol* (judicial monopoly). The *Grundgesetz* puts particular stress upon this third judicial power. Its position is constitutionally safeguarded: above all, the crucial importance of judicial power flows from the allotted powers of the *Bundesverfassungsgericht*, the guarantee of legal protection (Article 19 IV GG), the independent and autonomous position of the judges (Article 97 GG) and the various constitutional guarantees for the operation of judiciary (*e.g.* Articles 101 to 104 GG).[29] This section intends to give you a broad overview of the position and tasks of the *Bundesverfassungsgericht* in Germany.

A. FEDERAL CONSTITUTIONAL COURT (*BUNDESVERFASSUNGSGERICHT*)

As outlined before — the position of the *Bundesverfassungsgericht* can be regarded as exceptional. It is not only the highest body of administration of justice and jurisdiction but also a constitutional organ and, due to this, its position is

---

[29] For more details, see *ibid.*, Chap. Five, 1, and Chap. Seven, 3, A.

independent and autonomous among the remaining federal constitutional organs. This is stated in § 1 BVerfGG (*Bundesverfassungsgerichtsgesetz* — Code of the Federal Constitutional Court) which is the act governing the organisation and powers of the *Bundesverfassungsgericht*.

The *Bundesverfassungsgericht* is regarded and known as the "*Hüter der Verfassung*" (guardian of the constitution). Its rulings are binding for all constitutional organs of the Federation and the *Länder* just as for all courts and public authorities (§ 31 I BVerfGG). In some cases, which are enumerated in § 31 II BVerfGG, its judicial decisions may also enter into law.

The *Bundesverfassungsgericht* consists of two senates each of them being composed of eight professional judges (§ 2 BVerfGG). These judges are elected by the *Bundestag* and the *Bundesrat*.[30] The powers of each senate hearing a case are specified in § 14 BVerfGG. Thereby, the 1st senate is primarily competent for legal disputes concerning basic constitutional rights and the 2nd senate for all legal disputes referring to the law of the constitutional organs.

B. POWERS AND TYPES OF PROCEEDINGS

With regard to the powers of the *Bundesverfassungsgericht*, the *Enumerationsprinzip* (principle of enumeration) applies. This means that the court does not have jurisdiction for all legal disputes raising a constitutional question but only by operation of law. The question of jurisdiction is partly governed in Article 93 GG, and beyond this, the powers are scattered all over the *Grundgesetz*. An overview of the powers of the *Bundesverfassungsgericht* is provided in § 13 BVerfGG; these provisions finally enumerate in numbers 1 to 15 any proceeding to be adjudicated by this court. Each of these proceedings presupposes for its success that certain requirements be satisfied. But in detail that depends on which kind of proceedings have been initiated. As a general rule: the application has to be admissible and well founded. Again the scope of this book prohibits examining this subject in greater detail.

(1) Court proceedings between administrative bodies (*Organstreitverfahren*)

To begin with, there is the *Organstreitverfahren* which is governed under Article 93 I No. 1 GG, and §§ 13 No. 5 and

---

[30] For more details, see *ibid.*, Chap. Four, 2, A.

63 to 67 BVerfGG. The subject matter of these proceedings are disputes between constitutional organs, and the clarification of their mutual rights and duties; for instance, a parliamentary group of the *Bundestag* might intend to change the composition of a certain parliamentary committee, or the *Bundesrat* might demand participation in the law-making process.

In order to be successful, an initiated application has to be admissible which means the procedural requirement governed under §§ 63 to 67 BVerGG must be satisfied. At first, the law restricts the persons and bodies who might be a party to these proceedings: only the *Bundespräsident*, *Bundestag*, *Bundesrat*, can be parties to these proceedings as well as Federal Government and parts of the other constitutional organs, provided that they have been vested with their own rights in the *Grundgesetz* or Standard Orders of the *Bundestag* or *Bundesrat* (*e.g.* committees of either the *Bundestag* and *-rat*, Members of the Federal Government, parliamentary groups, Members and political parties of the *Bundestag*, as far as the dispute concerns their own constitutional status).

The applicant initiating proceedings must be an entitled person or organ for filing this application. This is called *Antragsbefugnis* (legal ability to institute proceedings). An applicant has to assert that he has been infringed or that he expects to be endangered in his rights and duties under the *Grundgesetz* by a measure or an omission of the respondent. The Article of the *Grundgesetz* which — due to the applicant's opinion — is infringed by the measure or omission under appeal must be specified as well. In addition, it is demanded that an application is filed within six months of the challenged measure or the omission has been made public.

As far as the admissibility of such an application initiating the *Organstreitverfahren* can be confirmed, its legal justification is reviewed by the *Bundesverfassungsgericht* in a second step of the process. The case will be examined as to whether the challenged measure or omission has infringed an Article of the *Grundgesetz* and, therefore, has infringed applicant's rights and duties.

(2) Judicial review of the constitutionality of laws (*Normenkontrolle*)

Constitutional law provides for different types of proceedings reviewing the constitutionality of laws: one is called *abstrakte Normenkontrolle* (abstract judicial review of the constitutionality of laws) and the other type of proceedings is the *konkrete*

Normenkontrolle (concrete judicial review of the constitutionality of laws).

(a) We would like to begin with the abstract judicial proceedings on the constitutionality of laws. This type of proceeding is laid down in Article 93 No. 2 GG, §§ 13 No. 6 and 76 to 79 BVerfGG. With respect to these proceedings, the *Bundesverfassungsgericht* is concerned with questions like whether federal law or regional law is compatible with the *Grundgesetz* or whether regional law is compatible with other federal law. As a rule, there are doubts or disagreements in opinion upon the validity of a rule of law. For the application's admissibility, it is required in § 76 BVerfGG that the applicant regards the law norm as:

- void; or
- as having legal force after a court, a public authority or another state organ has not made use of the legal provision as being inconsistent with the *Grundgesetz* or federal law.

The organs entitled to file such an application are restricted; only the Federal Government, the Government of a region or one third of the parliamentary members of the *Bundestag* can initiate this *Normenkontrollverfahren*. A peculiarity of these proceedings is that there is no respondent.

An application is legally justified if the legal rule is not in accordance with the constitution. In such a case, the *Bundesverfassungsgericht* generally declares the respective legal provision as void or merely confines itself to stating its incompatibility with the *Grundgesetz*.

(b) As mentioned, the *Grundgesetz* provides so-called concrete judicial proceedings on the constitutionality of laws as well. This procedure is outlined in Article 100 GG and § 13 No. 11 BVerfGG. It is the judicial review of all Acts legislated by the Parliament after the *Grundgesetz* came into force on May 24, 1949 (excluded statutory instruments and byelaws are excluded) and all Acts legislated prior to 1949 but which have been taken up by the legislator in the laws passed after 1949.

Only courts are entitled to file an application in order to review the constitutionality of this kind of law. A court may submit a case to the *Bundesverfassungsgericht* for decision on condition that it is convinced of the unconstitutionality of a rule of law which is material for the decision in the pending trial to be decided by this court.

Such an application lodged by a court is legally justified as far as the legal rule in question is not in accordance with the *Grundgesetz*. Again if this is the case, the *Bundesverfassungsgericht* may declare the respective rule of law as void or confine itself merely to stating its incompatibility with the *Grundgesetz*.

(3) Disputes between Federation and *Länder* (*Bund-Länder-Streitigkeiten*)

The *Bund-Länder-Streitigkeiten* are governed under Articles 93 I No. 3 and 4 GG and §§ 13 No. 7 and No. 8, 68 to 72 BVerfGG. As the name of this procedure suggests, the parties of the proceedings are on the one hand the Federation and on the other hand the *Länder*. Matters in controversy are constitutional rights and duties between the Federation and the *Länder* (for instance the extent or legality of Federal Government supervision pursuant to Article 84 IV GG) and other legal disputes under public law between the Federation and the *Länder* provided that no other recourse to the courts is at hand. The Federal Government is entitled to file such an application on behalf of the Federation, and the Regional Government on behalf of the region. With regard to the further procedural prerequisites, proceedings are conducted like the *Organstreitverfahren* which has been outlined above and to which we would like to refer.

If an application is admissible, the *Bundesverfassungsgericht* has to review its legal justification. An application is well founded if the claimed constitutional right is in existence or the disputed right does not exist, and the challenged measure or omission of the respondent, therefore, is a breach of the *Grundgesetz*.

(4) Constitutional Complaint (*Verfassungsbeschwerde*)

The *Verfassungsbeschwerde* is governed under Articles 93 I No. 4 a GG and §§ 13 No. 8 a, 90 to 95 BVerfGG and is a complaint against an Act of the State infringing basic rights of another person.

At first, this complaint has to involve an "*Akt der öffentlichen Gewalt*" (act of the public power) which includes any *Hoheitsakte* (Acts of the State) of German public authority being relevant in law. The legal possibility of instituting proceedings is possessed by anyone who can assert that an Act of the State infringes his fundamental rights enumerated either in Articles 1 to 19 GG or in Articles 20 IV, 33 38, 101 and 104 GG. The appellant has to plead that he has been infringed in *his* basic rights — the allegation of the possibility of an infringement of a basic right would not be sufficient. The appellant must be the holder of the infringed basic right, and the Act of State must relate to him — from a legal point of view — not only indirectly but rather directly and also immediately. The requirement of a present infringement of a basic right which must be pleaded makes clear that the appellant must be prejudiced by it at the moment of filing the complaint; the possibility of an infringement of a basic right in the (near) future does not entitle a person to file a *Verfassungsbeschwerde.* And finally, the appellant must also have the capacity to sue and be sued and, due to this, be able to plead his basic rights.

In the application, the infringed basic rights and the act or omission of an organ or public authority infringing basic rights must be specified. Such an application, then, has to be filed within one month after the challenged measure is served or has been communicated to the appellant. As far as the measure under appeal is a law or an Act of the State which has no recourse to law, the time limit amounts to one year after the Act came into force or after the Act of the State has been issued. Furthermore, a constitutional complaint can only be filed in cases of a given *Rechtswegerschöpfung* which means that due process of law has been exhausted. As a result, the constitutional complaint is subsidiary in relation to judicial remedies which can be obtained by special courts.

A *Verfassungsbeschwerde* which is admissible has to be legally justified in order to be successful. The *Bundesverfassungsgericht* reviews the case and decides whether in fact the appellant has been infringed in his basic rights through an Act of the State. This demands that the scope of protection of the respective basic right is infringed by the Act of the State, and, above all, that the Act of the State is unlawful too.

(5) Constitutional complaint of the local authority (*Kommunalverfassungsbeschwerde*)

The *Kommunalverfassungsbeschwerde* is set forth in Article 93 No. 4 b GG and § 91 BVerfGG and is the constitutional complaint of local authorities. The subject matter of this complaint is an Act of the State which affects the legal position of a local authority guaranteed in Article 28 I GG. It is a special constitutional complaint in which only an infringement of Article 28 GG can be pleaded.

A local authority is entitled to file a constitutional complaint if an infringement of Article 28 I GG can be asserted. Article 28 I GG provides a basic right, and the holders of this right are exclusively local authorities. This basic right guarantees — for the benefit of local communities — self-government with regard to all affairs and administrative tasks in their respective territory. A local authority filing such a complaint must plead that they have been infringed in the right of local government — and that has to be also, immediately and at present. The *Bundesverfassungsgericht* only hears cases in which an infringement of the right of Article 28 I GG is asserted by federal law: due to this, the *Bundesverfassungsgericht* does not hear cases in which Article 28 I GG is not breached by federal law but by *Land* law. Then, only the respective *Landesverfassungsgericht* (Constitutional Court of a *Land*) is competent to hear the case. Regarding the further requirements, we may refer to the constitutional complaint as outlined before because both complaints have similar conditions which must be satisfied in order to be successful.

(6) Provisional order (*Einstweilige Anordnung*)

If there are urgent reasons for the issue of a provisional order, the *Bundesverfassungsgericht* can issue such an order in accordance with § 32 BVerfGG. The court may do so with respect to any type of proceedings. But nevertheless the law sets a high standard to be met for the issue of a provisional order, and the *Bundesverfassungsgericht* has to weigh up the pros and cons of the issue of a provisional order and then balance the different interests.

9. ADMINISTRATION OF FINANCES

Questions of finance are of material importance for the Federal order so that the main principles of the apportionment of pecuniary resources and costs are regulated by the *Grundgesetz* itself (Articles 104 a *et seq.* GG). The distribution of costs between the Federation and the *Länder* is governed under Article 104 a GG. This norm states that the Federation and the *Länder* generally have to bear the costs which arise during and from the performance of their administrative tasks. In certain cases, which are laid down in Article 104 a II to IV GG, this established principle is breached; for instance a region acting on commission by the Federation does not have to bear the costs, these are borne by the Federation as the party ordering (Article 104 a II GG).

The question of who holds the legislative power in financial matters is set forth in Article 105 GG. The federation has exclusive legislative power in matters concerning customs and revenue-producing monopolies. The remaining taxes are subject to concurrent legislative power provided that the revenue from taxation is due or partly due to the Federation or that the conditions of Article 72 II GG — which we have already outlined[31] apply. The further question of how to distribute the revenue of taxation between the Federation and the *Länder* is answered in Article 106 GG.

The *Grundgesetz* also regulates the main features of the budgetary law (Articles 109 *et seq.* GG). Under these provisions, the Federation and the *Länder* have to establish their budget in every financial year which is reviewed by the *Bundesrechnunghof* (Federal Audit Office). Besides the *Grundgesetz* further details concerning the *Haushaltsplan* (budget) are provided in the *Bundeshaushaltsordnung* (Federal Budgetary Regulation).

[31] For more details, see *ibid.*, Chap. Three, 5, A, 2.

Schedule 1: Legislative Procedure

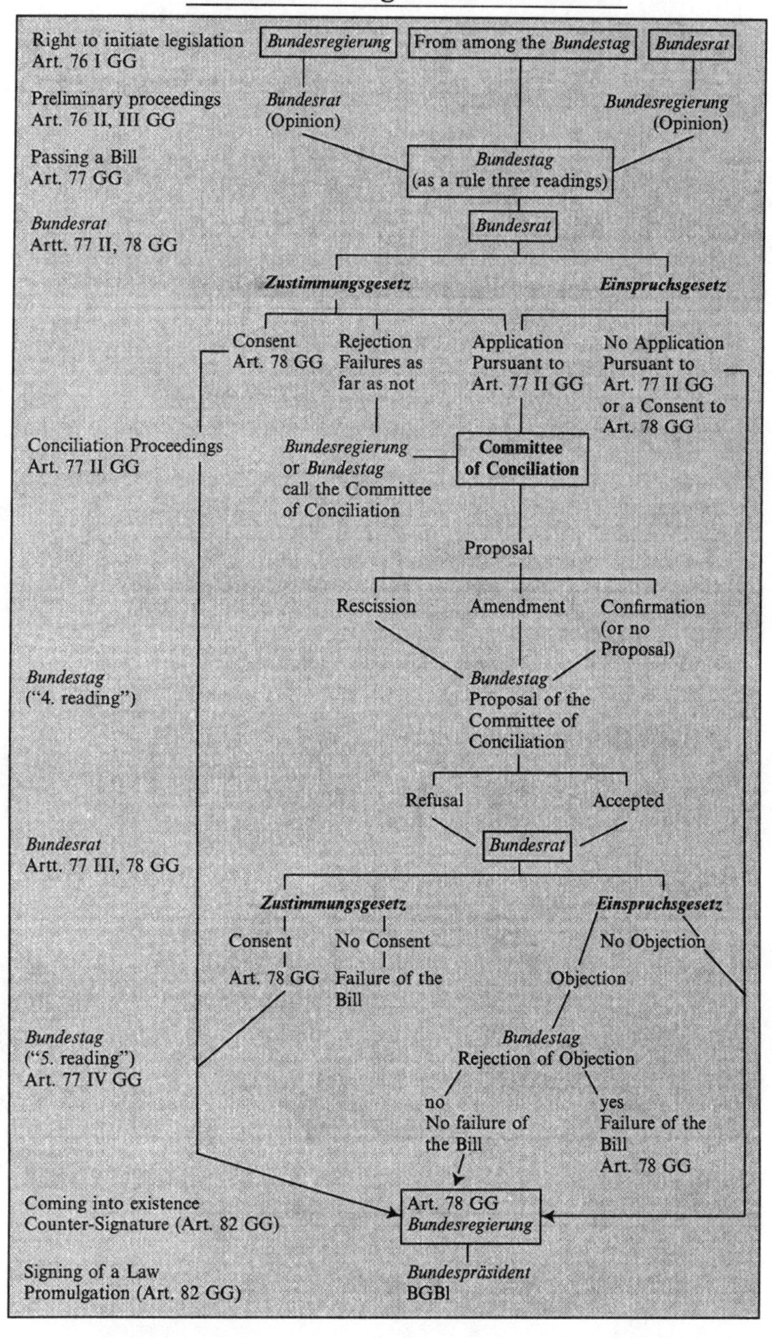

SELECTED BIBLIOGRAPHY

I. Commentaries

Jarass, Pieroth, *Grundgesetz für die Bundesrepublik Deutschland* (4th ed. 1997).
Leibholz, Rinck, Hesselberger, *Grundgesetz für die Bundesrepublik Deutschland* (7th ed. 1997).
Maunz, Dürig, *Grundgesetz* (7th ed. 1996).
Von Münch, Kunig, *Grundgesetz-Kommentar*: Vol. 1 (Präambel bis Articles 20) (4th ed. 1992); Vol. 2 (Articles 21 bis 69) (3rd ed. 1995); Vol. 3 (Articles 70 bis 146 und Gesamtregister) (3rd ed. 1996).

II. Textbooks

Bleckmann, *Staatsrecht I — Staatsorganisationsrecht* (1993).
Bleckmann, *Staatsrecht II — Die Grundrechte* (4th ed. 1997).
Degenhart, *Staatsrecht I* (14th ed. 1998).
Herzog, *Das Bundesverfassungsgericht und die Anwendung einfachen Rechts* (1991).
Maunz, Zippelius, *Deutsches Staatsrecht* (29th ed. 1994).
Pestalozza, *Verfassungsprozeßrecht* (3rd ed. 1991).
Pieroth/Schlink, *Grundrechte — Staatsrecht II* (14th ed. 1998).
Richter, Schuppert, *Casebook Verfassungsrecht* (3rd ed. 1996).
Schlaich, *Das Bundesverfassungsgericht* (4th ed. 1997).
Zippelius, *Allgemeine Staatslehre* (12th ed. 1994).

Chapter Four
The Legal Profession

1. Legal education

The way in which *Juristen* (lawyers) are trained and educated helps considerably to influence and form the legal culture of a country. In Germany, the training pattern is standardised and, therefore, basically the same for any lawyer irrespective of which part of the legal profession the trainee intends to work. Due to this, the qualification for judicial office enables the holder of such a qualification to become a judge, public prosecutor, counsel or notary. Even individuals who wish to work in a legal capacity in administrative authorities have to be qualified in the ordinary way.

Given this, the picture of a lawyer in Germany is determined by the idea of an *Einheitsjurist*. This term is difficult to be translated literally, but means that after passing the exams a graduate should be capable of entering any legal profession. A further aim of legal education is that any lawyer should be able to make himself completely familiar with all the components of a certain legal field which may have been unknown to him before and do this, in theory, within a reasonable time limit.

The training of a lawyer is composed of two state examinations set by professors of the respective university, judges of the *Land* and officials from the Education and Justice Ministries. The first set of exams is taken after graduating from university and the second concludes the practical training. The *Deutsches Richtergesetz* (German Law of Judiciary) supplied by certain regulations of the *Länder* contains details of the university instructions, practical training and examination. Moreover, it has to be noted that the training of lawyers may vary from *Land* to *Land*.

A. The first state examination

First of all — and that is important to English readers — there are no university entrance exams in Germany. Anybody graduating from *Gymnasium* (grammar school) may apply for admission to university. The school leaving certificate is called *Abitur* which is the equivalent to the English "A"

Level. Normally, it takes 13 years for a candidate to obtain this certificate and become qualified to attend university. Women are usually 19 years old when they enter university, whereas men tend to be older because they have to undertake National Service in the forces or service in a civil occupation before taking up their studies.

Graduates intending to study law have to apply for a university place at the *Zentralstelle für die Vergabe von Studienplätze* (Central Office for the Allocation of Places in Higher Education). This central office allots university places, and by far the majority of applicants will normally be accepted by the law faculties. In Germany the faculties have no right to refuse an applicant as long as a certain ceiling figure fixed by state regulations has not been reached. In the last two centuries, the maximum capacity of the faculties has far been exceeded and courses with 400 to 500 students at some faculties are not rare. As a result, some faculties have set up barriers for applicants and demand a certain standard in the *Abitur* — a *quota* or *numerus clausus.* But such a *numerus clausus* has been quashed on the basis that it appeared to infringe the basic right of university entrance which is guaranteed in Article 12 GG and includes the right to choose certain training and education.[1]

Once a candidate has been admitted to a law faculty, he[2] has to go to university for at least seven semesters (three and a half years) before he may pass the first state exam. But, the practice is different — it used to take not less than nine or more semesters before most candidates took examinations. However, this is changing. The different *Länder* have now amended the legislation and do allow the so-called *Freischuß* (free-go).[3] This is an attempt to cut the overall time people need to complete their studies. The extra go is likely to encourage students to pass the exam as soon as possible. On the other hand this procedure adds some extra pressure to the students and does lead to stronger competition among them. It is difficult for young lawyers to find a job after becoming qualified. Therefore, employers look very closely at results scored in the exams — and the time that has been taken to pass them.

Any law faculty operates in accordance with its own model of *curricula* — but these plans do not really differ from each other in a significant way. Before a law student is admitted to the first

---

1 For more details, see *ibid.*, Chap. Three, 7, B, (7).
2 Referring to males includes, as well as females.
3 Which has the pleasant effect that candidates who fail to pass the *Freischuß*, will still have two further attempts to pass the exam.

exam, it is required that he will obtain (usually) six or seven so-called *Scheine* (certificates) which are composed of written tests and research papers. Apart from these strict requirements, students are free to organise their studies, choose their courses and decide when to finish.

In Germany, university studies are not concluded by obtaining a university degree but by passing the *Erstes juristisches Staatsexamen* or *Referendarexamen* (first state exam). The exam is administered by the relevant Court of Appeal. It starts with written tests which are composed of up to eight five-hour exams within a period of just two weeks. The subjects of the exams are private, criminal and public law along with another topic of choice (the so-called *Wahlfach*).[4] As a matter of principle, the candidates are presented with a set of hypothetical facts, and the task is to provide a reasoned legal opinion and solution of the given case. In order to find such a reasoned legal opinion, the students are only allowed to use the statute texts — commentaries or other legal books cannot be used. Any exam paper is graded by one professor and one practitioner. Any candidate whose aggregated grade reaches the necessary minimum level is admitted to the final oral exam. The oral exam takes place before a panel composed of two practitioners and two professors. Usually four to six candidates at a time are examined for about four to six hours. The subjects to be examined are private, criminal and public law and the elective subject. Directly after the oral exam the panel pronounces its ruling, and each candidate receives a final aggregate grade.

B. THE SECOND STATE EXAMINATION

After students have successfully passed the first exam, they usually start the second part of their training — the *Referendardienst* (preparatory service or practical legal training). The State runs the *Referendardienst* and, as a result of this, the trainees known as *Referendare* enjoy (in most of the *Länder*) the status of civil servants on a temporary basis. They receive a (modest) salary from the State.

---

[4] The subject matter of the first state exam is set out in the various legal training regulations of the *Länder*. The hard core is private law (like obligations, property, family law and succession, fundamental features of commercial law, company law and labour law), criminal law and public law (constitutional and administrative law with its general principles and special areas), together with the respective rules of procedural law. In addition, each student has to choose a certain topic in which he wishes to specialise — subjects range from legal history to criminology or to antitrust and competition law.

The practical training consists of a number of compulsory *Stationen* (placements) on a three and four month basis; only a few of these placements may be chosen. During traineeship, the trainees are placed, for instance, as legal assistants with a court division of a civil, criminal and administrative court, a public prosecutor, an administrative body, a lawyer's office, or they get to know other types of legal practice. This training is intended to introduce them to the various legal professions, and to teach certain legal skills which are needed in practical legal life. The *Referendare* learn, for instance, to write judgments, draft administrative acts, draw up pleadings or notarial documents. In addition to their placements, the trainees have to attend *Arbeitsgemeinschaften* which are practical legal training courses run either by judges or civil servants in which the trainees are taught in the field of law in accordance with their respective placement.

After two years of this kind of practical training, the *Referendare* have to pass the *Zweite juristische Staatsprüfung* (second state examination) whose pattern is similar to the first state exam. But with regard to its form and content this exam varies much more between the different *Länder* than the first state exam. It consists of up to 12 written papers which usually last five hours and in which the candidates have to draft judgments, court orders or decisions of public prosecutors or public authorities. After the written exam has been graded, candidates — reaching the minimum grade — have to sit the oral exam. Candidates who have succeeded in that exam, are allowed to use the title *Assessor* or *Volljurist* (fully-qualified lawyer). They are now free to choose their branch of the legal profession, and may try to secure an appointment as a judge, notary, public prosecutor or as a private practitioner.

C. CURRENT CRITICISMS

The method of training lawyers has been the subject of continuing discussion among German academics, legal practitioners and, of course, politicians. Far-reaching reforms were demanded in the early 1970s and most recently in the 1990s. These calls for reform especially concern the fact that the training pattern is standardised, namely, that any student who wishes to become a lawyer has to follow legal training set forth in the German Law of the Judiciary — an act which is especially designed and shaped for the requirements of becoming a judge, irrespective of the fact that less than 20 per cent of the candidates will opt for a career as a judge — or have the chance to do so.

Moreover, the legal training has also been criticised in that many students — in order to prepare for their exams — feel forced to visit private crammer tutorials (*Repetitorien*) for up to 18 months because they think that this is the only way to pass the exam. In other words: there is a widely spread feeling among students that legal education at universities does not prepare them sufficiently for the exams. The law faculties, however, may see their primary function as preparing their students for the final state exam. Unfortunately, in practice they fail to do so because in times of low public expenditure universities are not ideally equipped to attain this aim.

A further subject of steady criticism is that legal training in Germany lasts for too long; moreover it is said that law students are not really educated and prepared for the practical tasks of a lawyer — a very serious criticism because by far the majority of newly qualified *Juristen* wants to (or — due to difficulties in getting different employment: is forced to) practice as a *Rechtsanwalt* (lawyer). Obviously it is in the public interest that people who act as lawyers are well-qualified, able to advise their clients properly and that they meet high professional standards. Therefore, from our point of view the critical voices certainly do have a point to make. But irrespective of the call for reforms, the training pattern outlined above has proved to be largely resistant to changes.

2. LEGAL PERSONNEL (*JURISTISCHE BERUFE*)

A. JUDGE (*RICHTER*)

It is said in the first sentence of Article 92 GG that "The judicial power is entrusted in the judges". In other words, only individuals in judicial office are allowed to perform and exercise the administration of justice. In Germany, there are different 'types' of judges. For instance, there are judges who hold a professional capacity and are specialists in law because they have successfully passed the two state examinations. In addition, there are honorary judges holding a lay capacity because they have not received university training in law or passed any law exams; their main task being to assist professional judges who have to administer the law. A further difference is that there are federal judges and *Land* judges who either work with federal courts or courts of the *Länder*.

(1) Professional judge

The legal position and functions of (professional) judges are laid down in the *Grundgesetz* and in the *Deutsche Richtergesetz*

(DRiG) as well. As outlined below, justice operates by independent judges (Article 97 II GG).[5] In particular, because of this specific function, judges do not hold the legal position of a civil servant because such a legal status would not be compatible with their required independence and judicial functions. Given this, judges are not employed on terms as civil servants but appointed in a particular judicial relationship. Their employment is regulated under public law — especially in the German Law of the Judiciary — which includes, for instance, a particular (and very intense) duty of loyalty for judges working at a Federal Court to the Federation and for judges working at a court of a certain *Land* to the respective *Land.*

As a matter of principle, lawyers who have successfully passed the two state examinations always have the ability to move to the bench. They then might enter directly after passing the second state exam into the judiciary which in Germany is a separate career. This is the theory — in practice, entry into the judiciary is only really open to those with exceptionally good grades in the second state exam. Besides this fact, the respective candidate for judgeship has to be qualified for holding a certain judicial office, namely, to have passed two judicial state examinations. The respective person has also to be a German citizen, and must guarantee to stand up for the *freiheitliche demokratische Grundordnung* (liberal democratic constitutional order). In general, requirements for the appointment to judgeship are enumerated in § 9 DRiG.

The arrangements for appointing judges vary between the different *Länder*, but appointments and promotions are usually made by the Minister of Justice of the respective *Land* and additionally, in some regions, with the consent of the *Richterwahlausschluß* (Committee on Judicial Appointments) which is composed of members of the *Land* Parliament, judges and attorneys. Judges are appointed at ceremonies in which they receive the certificate of appointment and swear an oath. By delivering the oath, the appointed person confirms to exercise the judicial duties with respect to the German *Grundgesetz* and the law, to pass rulings in accordance with their best knowledge, and with the conscience to serve justice and truth.

Appointment for a judgeship takes place for the first time after three years of judicial practice (§ 10 DRiG); during these three years each candidate holds the position of a judge on probation (§ 12 DRiG). Judges are usually appointed for life, and before reaching the retiring age, they cannot be dismissed

[5] For more details, see *ibid.*, Chap. Five, 1, C.

from office against their will (Article 97 II GG). Only in exceptional circumstances may judges be removed from office on the basis of a decision of the Judicial Service Court. To achieve this, certain statutory conditions which are laid down in the *Deutsche Richtergesetz,* have to be fulfilled. As a matter of principle, all judges must retire at the age of 65, except for the judges at the Federal Constitutional Court — they may remain in office until the age of 68. A minimum age to move to the bench is not prescribed in the law. But the law does prescribe a minimum age for judges sitting in the Federal Constitutional Court of 40 years; furthermore, to become a judge at one of the highest federal courts, the candidate has to be at least 35 years old.

Judges will only be promoted to higher courts after 10 years service in a Court of First instance. As with any other career service, promotion is not automatic and depends to a large degree on good service and seniority. In higher positions, such as president of a division or senate of the Court of Appeal, a further aspect becomes decisive — political opinion. This aspect is quite important because the Ministers may prefer to appoint those candidates who appear to be politically sympathetic and suitable. This may be criticised as weakening judicial independence but it makes the electoral process more arguable than, perhaps, in England. Finally, it has to be pointed out that the career hierarchy of the Federal Constitutional Court is not a part of the ordinary career path of the judiciary. In fact, federal judges and occasionally judges from the courts of the *Länder* might be appointed to this court. But, unlike appointments to other courts, half of the judges are appointed by the *Bundestag* and the other half by the *Bundesrat.*

(2) Honorary judge

Honorary judges are lay judges, and their main function is to assist professional judges. Honorary judges have full voting rights and work with professional judges by virtue of special statutory provisions. As a matter of principle, honorary judges have a non-professional capacity — except for the honorary judges sitting in discipline courts for the legal profession because they are fully-qualified lawyers. The combination of professional and honorary judges is most common, for instance, in criminal courts and in the commercial division of the Regional Courts, in the labour, social, administrative and finance jurisdiction, and in service and disciplinary courts.

The main reason for installing honorary judges in the courts is that they create a link between the judiciary and the people, and, due to this, ensure that justice is exercised in a generally comprehensible way and manner. Honorary judges are regarded as representatives of the general public and contribute their specific knowledge about society and their ability to assert particular interests. It is intended that social views and experiences of the honorary judges find an expression in the ruling of the courts. Moreover, professional judges are required to explain their legal arguments and assessments in a simple and comprehensive way which honorary judges — just as the ordinary people — will understand. This is a further check before the judgment is rendered.

Finally, the position of judges in German society is quite different to their position in England, the judiciary in Germany is not an occupation which often catches the public eye. Judges rarely become famous nor do they enjoy a comparable social status within society as an English judge usually does. A further difference is that German judges do not tend to have a comparable level of experience or reputation as English judges have when they start working as a judge. Furthermore, it is worth noting that there are far more judges in Germany than in England. Therefore, their outstanding importance in social and public life is difficult to compare in general terms.

B. LAWYER OR COUNSEL (*RECHTSANWALT*)

(1) General introduction

Unlike in Great Britain German law does not recognise the difference between a solicitor and a barrister. There is one legal profession of *Rechtsanwalt* (lawyer) which nowadays forms the largest part of the profession with 90,000 people competing for clients and retainers. Therefore, "*Anwaltsschwemme*" — which is probably best translated as "flood of lawyers" — is a popular quotation to describe the recent developments in this sector of the legal market. In point of fact most of the young trainee lawyers who pass the second state exam want to or simply have to search for a seat in a lawyers office — be it because the profession in general is quite popular, or because of the fact that these applicants are not qualified enough to get a job as judge, civil servant or in the industry. As we mentioned before, a pretty high score in the state exams is necessary to take up, for instance, a career path as judge.

In recent years, just after the German Reunification in 1989, there was an obvious need for lawyers to sort out legal problems arising from Unification. Basically there was no free advocacy in the former *Deutsche Demokratische Republik* (German

Democratic Republic — GDR), so for the first half of the 90s West German lawyers practising in the *Neuen Länder* (which used to be the former GDR) had the chance to build up substantial practices. But this buoyant period seems to be over now, and it is easy to predict that in the near future even more applicants will practice as a *Rechtsanwalt* — and, therefore, flood the profession even more.

(2) Tasks and legal basis

(a) The ideal concept: "freedom of advocacy"

The legal basis which describes the view of the historical legislator is laid down in not more than three paragraphs which are key norms to understanding the position of the lawyer within the German legal system. Due to § 1 *Bundesrechtsanwaltsordnung* (Federal Statute on Attorneys — BRAO) the lawyer is a court officer and an independent agent of the administration of justice as well. In addition to this, § 2 BRAO states that a lawyer works as *Freiberufler* — which means freelance and in private practice. Given this, a lawyer does not have a trade or business (see § 2 II 2 BRAO for details). Finally, the *Rechtsanwalt* is the chosen and independent adviser and representative in any legal question of his client. The privilege to retain the lawyer one wants to have is unrestrictable as long as it is in line with the law. Basically, the empowered lawyer is entitled to represent his client in court — as well as in *Schiedsgerichte* (courts of arbitration) — and in legal disputes with *Behörden* (public authorities).

If one reflects on this concept, it becomes clear that the ideal of a *Rechtsanwalt* is that of a freely-acting, independent and not restricted legal adviser. However, it has to be said that "freedom of advocacy" means a lack of restrictions from pressures of state organs. A totally different question is whether the *Rechtsanwalt* is independent from his client (or even his senior partners). But this is a point which should not be discussed in-depth at this stage, because obviously it is difficult for any legal adviser to keep a distance from the person who pays his fees.

(b) Admission as a lawyer

Due to § 4 BRAO anyone who has successfully passed the second state exam can begin practising as a *Rechtsanwalt*. The admission is not restricted to the *Bundesland* in which the applicant has sat the exam — for instance a Bavarian lawyer can decide to practice in Saxony and vice versa. Furthermore, any applicant from a Member State of the European Union can be admitted in Germany, provided he or she manages to pass the *Eignungsprüfung* — a written and oral test which is demanded by the German legislator and is intended to find out whether the candidate has a certain knowledge of German law and the legal system. Obviously this is an important factor for our non-German readership, and it shows that the integration of legal systems in Europe is on the way. The legal background is laid down in §§ 206 and 207 BRAO.

There are several restrictions which might prevent their admission as a lawyer. § 7 BRAO for instance contains a catalogue of reasons such as a conviction for criminal deeds or other circumstances which are not suitable for a lawyer who has to be a trustworthy person.

(3) Main aspects of professional practice

(a) Rights of audience

Lawyers in Germany enjoy a decent monopoly, because representation in court by an attorney is required by law in any higher court. Due to § 78 *Zivilprozeßordnung* (Code of Civil Procedure) there is no obligation to retain a *Rechtsanwalt* in the court of first instance in local ordinary, tax, labour, administrative and social courts — but in practice people obviously tend to engage a lawyer whenever they feel the need for professional legal advice.

(b) Advertising

There have been quite remarkable changes in the German legal system with respect to the possibility of advertising by legal firms and lawyers. Today, the key norm is § 43 b BRAO which states that advertising is not restricted as long as the information is about the concrete form of profession, objective with regard to form and content and not designed to achieve a certain retainer. This obviously very liberal interpretation of the law was intended by the legislator to open up competition within the legal profession to a modern level — and to give as much information as possible to the citizen who needs to find "Mr (or Mrs) Right" among many lawyers. There is basically no restriction with regard to time, reason and placement of a certain advertisement. In other words: a lawyer can choose any form of advertisement that he favours — for instance newspapers, magazines, radio programmes, television and, of course, the internet. But again, the forms of advertising just mentioned are only lawful provided the advertising is in line with the requirements of § 43 b BRAO.

As we mentioned before, once this hurdle is overcome, the lawyer is free to advertise, for instance, the fees he charges for certain legal work or advice; he can also stress which *Interessen* — or *Tätigkeitsschwerpunkte* (areas of law he specialises in or particular areas of expertise) he has. Obviously, on the one hand, this is very helpful for a citizen seeking advice, because one gets better information about the lawyer one really needs in a given case. On the other hand there is the danger that lawyers might be tempted to mislead people by wrongfully claiming to be an expert in a field of law. Nevertheless, this danger is acceptable, because at the end of the day the powers of the market will regulate a fraud like this. In other words, a lawyer who promises more than he can perform in court or as legal adviser is not likely to be retained again in the future. And, above this, a bad reputation, is probably one of the things a lawyer would most want to avoid.

(c) Fees

Not less than 133 paragraphs are necessary to answer the questions arising from lawyers' fees which are controlled by the *Bundesrechtsanwaltsgebührenordnung* (Statute on Attorneys' Fees — BRAGO). In this practically important statute the legislator has laid down rules for criminal matters — which are regulated by fee guidelines — and for civil work as well. The renumeration for the latter principally depends on the *Gegenstandswert* (value of the subject matter). Details with respect to this are set out in § 7 BRAGO. Also important are §§ 20 to 30 BRAGO which contain certain common rules with regard to lawyers' fees. Due to § 21 BRAGO for instance, the remuneration for expert opinions worked out by a lawyer on a given legal problem has to be *angemessen* (adequate) — which basically means fair in comparison with the time needed and the difficulty of the legal topic. There are also certain rules which deal with fees for a *Vergleich* (settlement, see § 23 BRAGO) or *Geschäftsreisen* (business trips) in connection with a mandate (see § 28 BRAGO for further details).

Apart from fees charged on the basis of the *Bundesrechtsanwaltsgebührenordnung* there is the possibility of a *Gebührenvereinbarung* (fee agreement) between lawyer and client. This form of remuneration — which has to be in written form (§ 3 BRAGO) — is quite common in law firms who advise business clients in company and tax law questions, whereas it is probably less widespread in the ordinary practice of a highstreet lawyer. Fee agreements in general work on the basis of fixed *Stundensätze* (hourly rates) for the work of an attorney; the rate charged in a case obviously depends on the experience and reputation of the lawyer, the difficulty of the legal problems in question and the fee level demanded by the law firm.

(d) Specialised lawyer (*Fachanwalt*)

The growing specialisation of lawyers is a general trend which we have observed over the past 10 to 15 years. Several reasons explain this trend. The most obvious ones being the (already mentioned) *Anwaltsschwemme* ("flood of lawyers") and, resulting from this, the stronger competition within the profession as well as the complexity of the law leads to the fact that lawyers have to specialise in their work in order to find a professional niche and to meet the increasing demands of the clients.

The practical importance of *Fachanwaltschaften* should not be underestimated. Today there are six different areas of specialisation: labour and social law, tax law, administrative law and — the most recent supplements — family and criminal law. As of January 1, 1997 6.5 per cent of all lawyers have achieved the title *Fachanwalt*. Surveys indicate that the average income of specialised lawyers is substantially higher compared with "ordinary" colleagues. Therefore, it is not difficult to predict that there will be further fields of specialisation in the future. European law and constitutional law seem to be the most likely "candidates" if one takes into account their growing practical importance.

The legal basis for specialised lawyers is § 43 c BRAO (further details are laid down in the *Fachanwaltsordnung*, specialised lawyers' order — FAO) which states that a lawyer is allowed to call himself (and, therefore, to promote his work as) a *Fachanwalt* provided he has gained "*besondere Kenntnisse und Erfahrungen in einem Rechtsgebiet*" (specialised knowledge in a certain field of the law). The local *Rechtsanwaltskammer* (Law Society) is responsible for checking whether the requirements of the *Bundesrechtsanwaltsordnung* and the *Fachanwaltsordnung* are fulfilled.

In practice, specialisation is a useful indicator of the quality of work one can expect from the lawyer, because the applicant has to show theoretical and practical knowledge in his field of law and has to be admitted to the bar for a period of at least three years. Due to § 4 FAO it is necessary to take a course of at least 120 hours of teaching in order to reach the standard of acceptable theoretical knowledge. § 5 FAO demands in addition to this that any applicant can prove that he/she was responsible for handling a certain amount of cases related to their area of specialisation in court.

(e) Professional cooperation

Lawyers typically used to work as sole practitioners or organised in a *Sozietät* (professional partnership), which from a legal point of view is a *Gesellschaft des Bürgerlichen Rechts* (partnership under the Civil Code). In recent years, the German legislator has opened up the door to different forms of cooperation. As of July 25, 1994 the *Partnerschaftsgesellschaftsgesetz* (Statute on Societies of Professional Partnership) is in force. This code is meant to link the partnership under the Civil Code and commercial partnerships such as the *Offene Handelsgesellschaft* (general partnership). Due to § 1 PartGG only *Freiberufler* (members of a profession in private practice) can join the newly created form of a partnership. This means, that besides lawyers medical doctors, dentists and journalists can demand to be registered as *Partnerschaftsgesellschaft*.

Another interesting fact is that after a long legal struggle it is now possible for lawyers to organise their practice in the legal form of a *Gesellschaft mit beschränkter Haftung* (limited liability company). It remains to be seen in which direction the legal profession will head, although this form of practice is likely to become more common.

(4) Other forms of lawyer's practice

In order to provide a complete overview of the profession of attorneys we would like to mention the *Notar* (notary), the *Patentanwalt* (patent lawyer) and the *Syndikusanwalt* (in-house lawyer or staff lawyer).

The profession of notaries is regulated in the *Bundesnotarordnung* (Federal Law on Notaries, BNotO). Due to § 1 BNotO, a notary is personally independent and fulfils a public office. His main task is the *Beurkundung* (recording in an official document) of contracts or other important legal issues. Furthermore, a notary plays an important role, for instance, in the process of drafting *Gesellschaftsverträge* (partnership agreements) or *Eheverträge* (matrimonial property agreements). The professional profile of a *Notar* is quite different in the northern and southern part of Germany. In the northern *Bundesländer* the tasks of a notary are fulfilled by a specialised *Rechtsanwalt*, whereas in the south the profession of the *Notar* is a career path of its own: there the *Amtsnotar* is either a civil servant or self-employed.

A *Patentanwalt* (patent agent) is a very specialised attorney who deals — as the title indicates — with questions of *Patentrecht* (patent law). He is a legal adviser as well as a court lawyer acting in the *Patentamt* (patent office) and the *Patentgericht* (patent court). The law of patent agents is regulated in the *Patentanwaltsordnung* (patent lawyers' order). The professional education is unusual, because in order to practice as a patent agent, a candidate has to have a university degree in scientific or technical studies, certain legal knowledge and practical experience in his area of work.

Finally, a *Syndikusanwalt* is a legal adviser within a company who only acts for this firm. An in-house lawyer is not allowed to handle cases in court as *Rechtsanwalt*, because he is not independent from instructions. Nevertheless, his work is at least similar to that of a typical lawyer. Therefore, a *Syndikusanwalt* can be admitted provided that his contract leaves the organisation of the working day entirely to him — without any restrictions given by the company (for details see § 7 BRAO).

C. PUBLIC PROSECUTOR (*STAATSANWALT*)

A Public Prosecutor holds a legal position as a civil servant and has to be qualified for judicial office; the detailed requirements are outlined below. The *Staatsanwaltschaft* (public prosecutor's office) is an organ of judicial administration and, due to this, is part of the power of the executive. Along with judges, public prosecutors ensure that there is justice in criminal and regulatory matters — they assist criminal judges in producing a fair judgment.

Nevertheless, the office of a public prosecutor is independent from the court (§ 150 GVG). They are installed by the State.

In Germany, prosecutions are only carried out by the public prosecutor's offices. Their organisation functions in criminal proceedings and the way to prosecute a case is set forth in the *Gerichtsverfassungsgesetz* (Judicature Act — §§ 141–152 GVG) and the *Strafprozeßordnung* (Code of Criminal Procedure). Due to § 141 GVG, there should be a public prosecutor's office at any court which should have its own hierarchy and organisation.

(a) The highest office is the *Bundesstaatsanwaltschaft* (Federal Prosecutor's Office) which is attached to the *Bundesgerichtshof* (Federal Supreme Court of Justice — § 142 I No. 1 GVG) and headed by the *Generalbundesanwalt* (Federal Public Prosecutor).

(b) The middle-ranking office is called *Generalstaatsanwaltschaft* (Chief Prosecutor's Office) which is attached to any *Oberlandesgericht* (Regional Appeal Court — § 142 I

No. 2 GVG). This office is presided over by a *Generalstaatsanwalt* (Chief Public Prosecutor) — the further prosecutors are called *Staatsanwälte* (public prosecutors).

(c) The *Staatsanwaltschaft,* as the office of the lowest level, is attached to the *Landgerichte* (Regional Courts — § 142 I No. 2 GVG) and is headed by the *Leitender Oberstaatsanwalt* (Senior Public Prosecutor). These offices are also responsible for the *Amtsgerichte* (County Courts).

Public prosecutors participate in criminal proceedings from the beginning to the end. They conduct the investigations, investigate a crime, arrest a suspect and exercise searches. They may call on the police to assist them to investigate the offences. In addition, they bring charges and take part at oral hearings as representatives of the public interest. Once a judgment has become final and conclusive, it is the task of the public prosecutors to ensure that the judgment is executed by the punitive measures prescribed in it, such as the implementation of a prison sentence or specific disciplinary measures. As mentioned above public prosecutors are civil servants, because of this, they are obliged to comply with official instructions from their superiors and are bound by these instructions as far as they are lawful.

D. ALTERNATIVE LEGAL PROFESSIONS

Apart from the "classic" and typical branches of the legal profession mentioned above, there are other legal careers employing large numbers of legally qualified lawyers. For instance, there is the profession of the *Landesanwälte* (public authority attorneys) as specialised legal representatives of the regional authorities. Their role and task is to represent the public authority in administrative trials before the administrative courts. They should ensure that the public interest is taken into account and finds its expression in those public law trials.

Qualified lawyers also play an important role in public administration. Here there is a great demand for lawyers. They may fill a place in the municipal, regional or federal public authorities, and this career might lead to promotion as a state secretary. These lawyers enjoy the legal status of civil servants with all the associated benefits.

Moreover, qualified lawyers may also work in the bureaucracies of international organisations, such as the European Community or the UNO.

Of course, lawyers who follow the described career routes outside the "ordinary" branches of the legal profession are outnumbered by the many applicants who fulfil legal tasks in commerce and industry. They may collaborate in legal departments of big firms, have full-time employment as *Syndikusanwälte* (in-house lawyers) of a company, or they may work as legal advisers of unions or confederations. Sometimes the lawyers working in these areas leave a legal career path and work in management — however, in this area they have to compete with economists who are also qualified to take up those positions.

Finally, if we talk about statistics for the legal profession — only a few lawyers opt for a career as a professor at a German University. More precisely, only a few have the chance to take up this path, because a Chair at a German University is only within the reach of those candidates with excellent grades in the state examinations. To become a professor, it is required to write a *Promotion* (the equivalent to an English PhD) and a *Habilitation* (a further in-depth and outstanding piece of academic work). This is the formal path to academic lecturing. Furthermore, the prospective professor has to spend several years as *Wissenschaftlicher Assistent* (academic assistant) to a professor in charge.

SELECTED BIBLIOGRAPHY

I. Commentaries

Claussen, Janzen, *Bundesdisziplinarordnung* (8th ed., 1996).
Hartung, Holl, *Anwaltliche Berufsordnung* (1997).
Henssler, Pütting, Bundesrechtsanwaltsordnung (1997).
Kleine-Cosack, *Bundesrechtsanwaltsordnung* (3rd ed., 1997).

II. Textbooks

Baumann, *Einführung in die Rechtswissenschaft* (8th ed., 1989).
Baur/Walter *Einführung in das Recht der Bundesrepublik Deutschland* (6th ed., 1992).
Bohrer, *Das Berufsrecht der Notare* (1991).
Borgmann, Haug, *Anwaltshaftung* (3rd ed., 1995).
European Law Students' Association (ELSA), *Guide to Legal Studies in Europe 1996–1997* (1996).
Endrös, Waltl, *Der Wirtschaftsanwalt* (1995).
Flesch, *Beamtenrecht* (1991).
Gleiss, *Soll ich Rechtsanwalt werden*? (3rd ed., 1992).
Gramm, *Jura erfolgreich studieren* (2nd ed., 1997).
Kaiser, Bellstedt, *Die Anwaltssozietät* (2nd ed., 1993).
Little, *Cross Border Practice Compendium* (1993).
Robbers, *Einführung in das deutsche Recht* (1994).
Teubner, *Die Bestellung zum Berufsrichter in Bund und Ländern* (1994).
Wegerich, "The qualified lawyers transfer test" *EuZW* (1994), pp. 275–278.

Chapter Five
Jurisdiction

This chapter aims to give a broad overview of the main principles and the organisation of the *Gerichtsbarkeit* (jurisdiction) in Germany. The administration of justice is mainly governed in the *Grundgesetz.* The principle rules are laid down in Article 20 III GG and Articles 92 *et seq.* GG which govern the constitutional principles for the operation of the judiciary. Further details can be found in the *Gerichtsverfassungsgesetz* (Judicature Act) and in various codes of procedure which contain legal rules regarding the organisation, constitution and responsibilities of courts as well as court proceedings. The most important ones are the *Zivilprozeßordnung* (Code of Civil Procedure), the *Strafprozeßordnung* (Code of Criminal Procedure), the *Verwaltungsgerichtsordnung* (Rules of the Administrative Courts), the *Finanzgerichtsordnung* (Rules of Procedure of the Tax Court), and the *Sozialgerichtsgesetz* (Law concerning Social Courts and its Procedure).

1. Common Structure and Principles

Irrespective of the particular branch of jurisdiction, there are common principles applying to any trial before German courts. These are constitutional guarantees for the operation of the judiciary and general principles for the operation of judicial proceedings.

A. The Guarantee of Legal Protection (*Rechtsschutzgarantie*)

The fundamental guarantee of legal protection is laid down in Article 19 IV GG. There it states that "where rights are violated by a public authority the person affected shall be permitted to have recourse to the courts". This norm enjoys the privileged status of a basic right. Thereafter, acts of public authorities are subject to full judicial review on both points of fact and law. But public authority in the sense of this norm only means the executive and not the judiciary or the legislature. The reason for this is simply that — for instance with regard to the judiciary — Article 19 IV GG is designed to safeguard legal protection through the judiciary but not against the judiciary.

The *Grundgesetz* takes a fundamental decision because it guarantees access to the courts, proceedings before the courts and decisions by the courts. This only implies state courts whose organisational position and composition meet the requirements set forth in Article 92 and Article 97 GG. With regard to this, the *Grundgesetz* recognises various branches of jurisdiction[1] (Articles 95 and 96 GG) and establishes a few of the powers of ordinary courts (Article 14 III 4 and Article 34 GG).

However, such a guarantee of legal protection in Article 19 IV GG must be practicable and workable. To become effective, the codes of judicial procedure impose formal requirements on recourse to the courts, such as compulsory and proper representation, deadlines or rules regarding costs.

Nevertheless, a central element of the rule of law principle is that any citizen should be encouraged to bring his private dispute before a state court — instead of trying to enforce the law on his own. Disputes should be settled without resorting to violence, but in accordance with structured proceedings and by means of a binding judicial decision.

B. THE JUDGE

No one including the Parliament, the Government or any other agency — should be able to influence or obstruct the work of a judge, prevent a judge from hearing a particular case, or select and appoint a specific judge to hear a certain case. For this purpose, the *Grundgesetz* provides specific guarantees on the judiciary which are especially designed to secure that the jurisdiction of a judge to hear a case and to pass judgment is determined in advance.

Given this, in the second sentence of Article 101 I GG it states that "Nobody may be removed from the jurisdiction of his lawful judge". With regard to this, a judge is the one (and only) person who is competent to hear and deliver a ruling in a particular case. The judge is subject to a provision of legality, that is to say, only the law is able to chase the judge in any case. Therefore, to determine the judge in a specific case, it has to be stated at the outset — in accordance with the Judicature Act and the various Codes of Procedure — the due process of law

---

[1] For more details, see *ibid.*, Chap. Five, 2.

(*e.g.* ordinary or administrative courts) and the competent court[2] (*e.g.* county court or regional courts). The particular judge handling the specific case is not determined in these Acts but in the *Geschäftsverteilungplan* (work schedule) of the court. This schedule lays down which panel of judges (*e.g.* 1st senate or 2nd senate) and which judges of this panel (*e.g.* judge A, B or C. of the 1st senate) is the judge in the case in question.

One year in advance, each court has to draw up and issue its own *Geschäftsverteilungsplan*. It sets out the judges comprising each adjudicating body and allocates the various fields of law or types of action to the adjudicating bodies (§§ 21e ff. GVG). The allocation of duties and tasks set up in the schedule is binding and can be changed only because of a (very restricted) canon of reasons enumerated in § 21 III GVG. This binding effect is a consequence of the concept of the legally competent judge. The competent judge has to be definitely appointed in advance in order to prevent him being vulnerable to manipulation when hearing a certain case. The work schedules of the Federal Constitutional Court and the five highest courts of the Federation are annually announced in the *Bundesanzeiger* (Federal Gazette) which is organised by the Federal Ministry of Justice.

C. JUDICIAL INDEPENDENCE (*RICHTERLICHE UNABHÄNGIGKEIT*)

The *Grundgesetz* guarantees judicial independence in Article 97 GG. The independence of judges is one of the fundamental principles of the constitutional state and belongs to the central achievements of the modern democratic state. The German *Grundgesetz* attaches particular importance to the creation of a strong guarantee to protect the constitutional order which requires independent judges. Article 97 I GG sets out that "Judges shall be independent and subject only to the law". That means: the judiciary is independent from the influences of any other organ of the executive and legislative power, and judicial independence also means independence with regard to the case and the person.

Factual independence signifies that the judge has to adjudicate upon a case merely in accordance with his own conviction and the law. Due to this, it is forbidden to advise him about a particular case. It is also forbidden for him to accept advice. Given this fact, a government or administration cannot dictate the legal decision of a judge. Moreover — and this might sound strange to an English lawyer or law student — judges

---

[2] For more details, see *ibid.*, Chap. Five, 2.

in Germany are generally *not bound* by precedents, except for those cases which — at the end of the day — have prejudice (for instance because of the outstanding importance of a certain case). But, in practice, courts tend to comply with a certain supreme court practice.

A judge's factual independence may not be sufficient to guarantee his complete impartiality. This means that any judge has also to be personally independent — a logical consequence which is guaranteed in Article 97 II GG. This norm states that:

"Judges appointed to full-time and permanent posts cannot, against their will, be dismissed or permanently or temporarily suspended or transferred or retired before the expiration of their term of office except by virtue of a judicial decision and only on the grounds and in the form provided for by law. Legislation may set age limits for the retirement of judges appointed for life. In the event of changes in the structure of their districts judges may be transferred to another court or removed from office, but only on full salary."

This norm means that during their term of office, judges in Germany cannot be removed or transferred at all. They are not subject to dismissal — which, if you think about it — is a privilege that leads to an (at least almost) perfect personal and factual independence from outside pressures. The legal status of judges — and the question of how judicial independence can be achieved, is set out in the *Richterdienstgesetz* (German Law of Judiciary), which is of great general significance to the administration of justice in Germany.[3]

D. GENERAL PRINCIPLES FOR JUDICIAL PROCEEDINGS

As mentioned above, any trial in Germany is governed by general principles. One of these principles is the right of a fair trial — due to German legal theory everyone is entitled to have the chance of a fair trial. This principle is not expressively spelt out in the *Grundgesetz*, but is the logical extension of the rule of law principle, and is one of the most important principles of lawful court proceedings which means that courts always have to conduct proceedings correctly and fairly.

The court has to give the participating parties the opportunity to be heard when it considers an individual case with the view of delivering a ruling at the end of the day. This common

[3] For more details, see *ibid.*, Chap. Four, 2, A.

constitutional principle is called *Grundsatz des rechtlichen Gehörs* (principle of the right of audience) and is laid down in the German Constitution (Article 103 I GG) as well as in Article 6 I of the *Menschenrechtskonvention* (MRK — Human Rights Convention). Article 103 I GG declares that "In the courts everybody shall be entitled to a hearing in accordance with the law". Due to this, all parties involved have the right to express their view on the circumstances that have occasioned them before any decision is taken. The parties have the right of audience before any decision affecting their rights is taken.

Moreover, the court is, as a rule, required to conduct oral hearings before it may deliver a ruling. This is the principle of orality which means that only those facts of the case which have been part of the oral hearing may form the basis for a judgment or order. The principle of orality does not require oral submissions only. However, the parties may prepare all oral hearings by written pleadings in which they brief the court about the points they wish to make, submit these pleadings in court and simply refer to them in the actual hearing. The content of these pleadings, then, has the same status as oral submissions.

Closely connected to the principle of orality is a further principle, according to which procedure must be conducted in public. This so-called *Grundsatz der Öffentlichkeit* (principle of public trial) is governed in §§ 169 *et seq*. GVG and also in Article 6 MRK. This principle intends that judicial proceedings be attended by the public in order to guarantee the due process of the law, while the community performs a controlling and protecting role. After all, one should bear in mind that judgments are given "*Im Namen des Volkes*" ("In the Name of the People"). Publicity in this context means that the actual place of negotiation must ensure free admission to hearings for the public. Individuals who are unconnected with the parties must be able to watch, listen and (hopefully) understand what goes on in court. The public has to be able to observe courts in operation. But it has to be pointed out quite clearly at this point that the public nature of oral hearings does not mean that radio or television recordings of proceedings have to be made available to the public. In Germany the opposite is the case, recordings of proceedings in court rooms are banned at least during the actual court hearing. This is because cameras and microphones influence the parties to the proceedings and, therefore, directly or indirectly the outcome of the proceedings themselves. Moreover, the principle of public proceedings is limited. The Judicature Act (§§ 169 *et seq*. GVG) enumerates certain cases, in which the public can be excluded from court, for instance to protect a participating party (*e.g.* family law cases) or for reasons of national security.

2. Branches of Jurisdiction

Germany's third power, jurisdiction, is guaranteed in the *Grundgesetz*. Article 92 GG declares that judicial power is entrusted to judges and only exercised by the *Bundesverfassungsgericht* (Federal Constitutional Court), the *Bundesgerichte* (Federal Courts) and the courts of the *Länder*. This is known as the *Rechtsprechungsmonopol* (judicial monopoly). The division into these types of courts may be regarded as the product of the federal nature of Germany, its historical development and the codification of German law.[4]

In addition, judicial power is composed of different independent jurisdictions. In the main, adjudication is allotted to "five jurisdictions" which may be put in order with the legal fields enumerated in Article 95 I GG as follows: *ordentliche Gerichtsbarkeit* (ordinary jurisdiction), *Arbeitsgerichtsbarkeit* (jurisdiction in labour matters), *Verwaltungsgerichtsbarkeit* (administrative jurisdiction), *Sozialgerichtsbarkeit* (jurisdiction of the social courts) and the *Finanzgerichtsbarkeit* (jurisdiction of the tax courts). Each of these jurisdictions is headed by a Federal Court as the highest court of the Federation and as the court of last resort. Their main duties are to act as final appeal courts for the courts of the *Länder* and to ensure a uniform interpretation and development of the law. In addition to the vertical separation of the "five jurisdictions", there is a horizontal, hierarchical court structure as well. As a matter of principle, court procedures start at a lower court and can be brought to a higher court by filing rights of appeal — such as appeals on points of facts and/or appeals on points of law. Each *Land* has set up its own individual court structure in accordance with the general model prescribed in the *Grundgesetz*, and is responsible for its own administration of justice, jurisdiction and procedure.

Moreover, in Germany there is a highly specialised *Verfassungsgerichtsbarkeit* (constitutional jurisdiction) which is handled by the Federal Constitutional Court in Karlsruhe and the different constitutional courts of the *Länder*. Constitutional jurisdiction is laid down in different specialised procedural codes such as the *Bundesverfassungsgerichtsgesetz* (Code of Procedure of the Federal Constitutional Court) on national

[4] For more details, see *ibid.*, Chap. One.

level and comparable codes for the relevant *Länder*. Nevertheless, an all embracing Supreme Court — such as the Supreme Court of the United States or the *Bundesgericht* in Switzerland — does not exist at all.

In addition to these federal courts at the head of each of the "five" hierarchies, the Federation has set up further Federal Courts which have jurisdiction to pass judgments in particular affairs and have an exclusive jurisdiction (Article 96 GG), such as the *Truppendienstgericht* (Federal Military Court) in disciplinary affairs of soldiers, the *Bundesdisziplinarhof* (Supreme Federal Disciplinary Tribunal) in disciplinary cases of federal officials; the *Richterdienstgericht* (Disciplinary Court for judges) in disciplinary affairs of Federal judges and the *Bundespatentgericht* (Federal Patent Tribunal) in patent cases.

As outlined above, specialisation is a characteristic feature of the court system in Germany. The advantage of the division reflecting major parts of legal fields is that the judges have specialist knowledge and experience, and, therefore, should be able to produce a better quality of judicial application for the individual. Irrespective of this positive factor there is a disadvantage as well, namely the problem of choosing the correct division in cases where the legal matter may overlap between the jurisdictions of two or more court hierarchies.

Having said that, the question arises as to what happens if the courts of two jurisdictions disagree on which of them is responsible for hearing a particular case. The answer is as simple as this, whenever a court from one jurisdiction has taken a binding decision on its capacity (or lack of capacity) to hear a certain case, this ruling is binding on the courts of the remaining jurisdictions as well. If the court comes to the conclusion that it has no competence to hear the case at all, it refers the case — upon application by the plaintiff — to the first instance court of the jurisdiction which it considers as the competent court (see § 17 a GVG). This court, then, is bound by the referral.

The division into different branches of jurisdiction may sometimes lead to a different evaluation of single legal questions or to a contradiction in the adjudication of two or more different jurisdictions. To avoid this unsatisfactory result, the *Gemeinsamer Senat der obersten Gerichtshöfe des Bundes* (General Senate of the Highest Federal Courts of Justice) can be called upon to clear up the contradiction in adjudication and to pass a corresponding decision (Article 95 III GG).

A. ORDINARY JURISDICTION

Ordinary jurisdiction[5] in the sense of § 13 GVG has to be understood as the *Zivilgerichtsbarkeit* (civil jurisdiction)[6] which is responsible for civil cases, and the *Strafgerichtsbarkeit* (criminal jurisdiction)[7] which by definition is competent to decide criminal cases and regulatory offences. The hierarchy of both, civil and criminal jurisdiction, is structured in the same way. The pyramid of these "ordinary" courts starts with the *Amtsgerichte* (County Courts) at the bottom, which are followed by the *Landgerichte* (Regional Courts) and then by the *Oberlandesgerichte* (Regional Appeal Courts); the court of last resort is the *Bundesgerichtshof* (Federal Supreme Court of Justice), which is based in Karlsruhe. The Federal Supreme Court of Justice as the highest Federal Court has jurisdiction for the entire Federal Republic of Germany. The Regional Appeal Courts are courts of the *Länder* and are competent as the regional courts in their *Bundesland* — each *Bundesland* has at least one Regional Appeal Court.

In addition to the ordinary courts outlined above, there are further courts which are attached to the ordinary jurisdiction. First we would like to draw your attention to the Federal Patent Tribunal in Munich. From a systematic point of view, this court belongs to the ordinary jurisdiction division, although it is not a part of its hierarchy — it only appears at the level of the federation as mentioned above. The *Patentgesetz* (Patent Act) regulates the organisation, powers and procedure of this court. The Federal Patent Tribunal hears cases for the withdrawal or cancellation of patents and licences. Its judgment may be appealed on points of law and the decision under appeal is reviewed by the Federal Supreme Court of Justice. In addition, a number of specialised courts are installed to hear cases arising from public service matters. These professional courts deal especially with civil servants and the army, as well as questions of service and discipline in the legal profession and other professions. Finally, there are *Schiedsgerichte* (arbitration tribunals) for the private resolution of legal disputes, which are used

---

[5] This odd term "*ordentliche Grichtsbarkeit*" is based on the fact that in 1877 (the time when the statute came into force) only ordinary courts — such as civil and criminal courts — were independent courts whereas administrative and tax courts were incorporated within the administration. Today all branches of the judiciary — for instance ordinary jurisdiction, jurisdiction of administrative courts, fiscal court jurisdiction, jurisdiction of labour courts and for social security litigation — are independent (Article 95 GG).

[6] For more details, see *ibid.*, Chap. Six.

[7] For more details, see *ibid.*, Chap. Seven.

extensively in commercial law. The tribunals are subject to the provisions of the *Zivilprozeßordnung* (Civil Code of Procedure) and to judicial review of the legality of their decision (see §§ 1027 *et seq.* ZPO).

B. JURISDICTION IN LABOUR MATTERS

Next to the ordinary jurisdiction stands the jurisdiction in labour matters. Labour law disputes arise out of the contractual relationship between employers and employees, and include, for instance, complaints from employees about payment of wages, disputes about holiday entitlements or about dismissal or redundancy — these are the disputes on which labour law courts spend most of their time. A further area of labour matters involves, for instance, disputes between the unions and (individuals or groups of) employers; such a dispute might be, for example, the extent or the interpretation of a collective bargaining agreement.

Labour jurisdiction is an autonomous branch of the judiciary and organised on three levels. At first instance, all litigation is dealt with by the *Arbeitsgerichte* (Labour Courts); the second instance is formed by the *Landesarbeitsgerichte* (Higher Labour Courts) — each *Land* has at least one Higher Labour Court. The *Bundesarbeitsgericht* (Federal Labour Court) is the court of last resort which today is situated in the city of Kassel — but will be moved to the formerly East German city of Erfurt as a tribute to the social implications of the Reunification. Jurisdiction, organisation and proceedings of Labour Courts are governed in the *Arbeitsgerichtsgesetz* (Labour Courts Act). In general terms, labour court procedure corresponds to that in ordinary civil proceedings. A number of special provisions, however, try to meet the necessities of a labour law trial. For instance the parties can choose to conduct litigation themselves or to have a representative of their trade union or employer's association appearing on their behalf. Only parties in proceedings before the Higher Labour Court have to be represented by counsel or someone from their trade unions or employer's associations — in other words: representation by counsel is mandatory at a higher court level. Another special feature of labour court proceedings which should be mentioned is that any trial starts with *Güteverhandlung* (conciliation proceedings). These are proceedings before the presiding judge of the Labour Court which aim to achieve a settlement without further dispute. Only if such a settlement is out of reach, are proceedings finally set down for hearing.

C. ADMINISTRATIVE JURISDICTION

A further branch of jurisdiction is administrative jurisdiction which is designed to protect citizens against measures taken by public authorities. The administrative courts adjudicate upon all public law disputes, as far as these cases are not specially allocated to a particular system of administrative courts by federal law. Those cases may be assigned either to social courts or tax courts — both of these will be outlined below.

The structure, powers and procedural rules of the Administrative Courts are laid down in the Rules of Administrative Courts,[8] the common system of these courts is organised on three levels. Decisions are taken at first by the *Verwaltungsgerichte* (Administrative Courts), at second instance by the *Oberverwaltungsgerichte* (Higher Administrative Courts) and at final instance by the *Bundesverwaltungsgericht* (Supreme Federal Administrative Tribunal), which — for historical reasons — has its seat in Berlin and Munich. But this court will soon move to a formerly East German city as well, Leipzig, which belongs to the State of Saxony, will regain its place as one of the most eminent German cities with regard to legal institutions.

D. JURISDICTION OF THE SOCIAL COURTS

As outlined above, social jurisdiction is a special and autonomous branch of administrative jurisdiction which operates in specific legal fields of public administration. The legal basis is the *Sozialgesetzbuch* (Social Courts Act) regulating its structure, organisation and proceedings. This kind of jurisdiction is organised on three levels as well. There are the *Sozialgerichte* (Social Security Tribunals) as courts of first instance and the *Landessozialgerichte* (Regional Social Appeal Tribunals) as courts of second instance; the final instance is the *Bundessozialgericht* (Federal Social Court), which is based in Kassel.

Social jurisdiction deals primarily with decisions on entitlement to social benefits affecting people's livelihood. It involves, for instance, public law litigation in areas like social or unemployment insurance, war pensions or the law on panel doctors. In general terms, its procedure corresponds to that in the administrative proceedings. Nevertheless, there are a few specific procedural features — for instance, proceedings before social courts are generally free of charge; moreover, the participants can appear unassisted before courts or choose to be represented by an employee of the trade unions, employers'

---

[8] For more details, see *ibid.*, Chap. Eight.

associations, war victims' associations or by lawyers. A party before a Federal Social Court also has to be represented by one of the persons just mentioned.

E. JURISDICTION OF THE TAX COURTS

Fiscal jurisdiction is — just as social jurisdiction — a special but independent branch of administrative jurisdiction. This jurisdiction deals merely with all public law disputes arising from disagreements of an individual (or a company) with decisions of the tax authorities. The legal basis is the *Finanzgerichtsordnung* (Tax Court Code). It has to be underlined that fiscal jurisdiction — unlike other branches of the judiciary — operates on just two levels. Decisions at first instance are taken by the *Finanzgericht* (Fiscal Court); the second and also final instance is the *Bundesfinanzhof* (Federal Fiscal Court), which is situated in Munich.

The fiscal courts are first and foremost concerned with tax cases, for instance, the courts have to adjudicate on the legality of a tax demand or upon the collection of levies imposed under European Union rules on the importation of particular goods. Procedure before the Fiscal Courts closely resembles that operated (and pointed out above) by the administrative courts. The participants may choose whether to conduct litigation themselves or to be represented by a third party which might be their accountant, lawyer or auditor. In a fiscal court, the representation by counsel or any other professional assistant — such as an accountant or auditor — is not mandatory. But again, when appearing in the Federal Fiscal Court, one has to have the professional assistance of a legal or fiscal adviser.

F. JURISDICTION ON CONSTITUTIONAL QUESTIONS

A particular position within the court system belongs to the jurisdiction on constitutional questions at *Land* and federal level. In Germany, any *Bundesland* has a *Verfassungsgerichtshof* (Supreme Constitutional Court) — which in some of the *Länder* is also called *Staatsgerichtshof* (State Tribunal). These constitutional courts render findings upon legal disputes, which have their legal basis in the respective *Land* constitution.

The jurisdiction on constitutional questions at federal level is exercised by the *Bundesverfassungsgericht* (Federal Constitutional Court) in Karlsruhe.[9] This court — which was created

---

[9] For more details, see *ibid.*, Chap. Three, 8.

in 1951 — is of outstanding importance within the legal system in Germany. It is the highest German court and belongs to one of the most highly respected and powerful institutions of the Federal Republic of Germany. The Federal Constitutional Court renders its judgments solely upon questions concerning the *Grundgesetz* and, then, only within the certain procedural types enumerated in the *Grundgesetz* (*e.g.* Articles 93 and 100 GG). Its exclusive task is to render decisions on questions of constitutional law; its interpretations of the text of the *Grundgesetz* are final and binding. In addition, its adjudication influences the entire legal system because the *Grundgesetz* is the highest legal source within the legal system and may have implications on any field of the law.

Irrespective of the undisputed reputation of the Federal Constitutional Court it has to be underlined that the jurisprudence of the European Community Court — the *Gerichtshof der Europäischen Gemeinschaft* (European Court of Justice) — is of steadily growing importance. Of course, this effect can be recognised in any of the Member States of the European Union. The future will tell us to what extent European Law will influence, change and transform the legal system in Germany as a whole. At this stage, those cases dealing with questions of European Law — such as interlocutory decisions, where courts of the Member States submit cases containing doubts on the interpretation of European Law — are of particular importance.

SELECTED BIBLIOGRAPHY

I. Commentaries

Baumbach, Lauterbach, Albers, Hartmann, *Zivilprozeßordnung* (56th ed., 1997).
Germelmann, Matthes, Pütting, *Arbeitsgerichtsgesetz* (2nd ed., 1995).
Gräber, *Finanzgerichtsordnung* (4th ed., 1997).
Jarass, Pieroth, *Grundgesetz für die Bundesrepublik Deutschland* (4th ed., 1997).
Kleinknecht, Meyer-Goßner, *Strafprozeßordnung* (42nd ed., 1997).
Kopp, *Verwaltungsgerichtsordnung* (10th ed., 1994).
Maunz, Dürig, *Grundgesetz* (7th ed., 1996).

II. Textbooks

Bleckmann, *Staatsrecht II — Die Grundrechte* (4th ed., 1997).
Erlenkämpfer, Fichte, *Sozialrecht* (2nd ed., 1996).
Maunz, Zippelius, *Deutsches Staatsrecht* (29th ed., 1994).
Schenke, *Verwaltungsprozeßrecht* (6th ed., 1998).
Schlaich, *Das Bundesverfassungsgericht* (4th ed., 1997).
Zippelius, *Allgemeine Staatslehre* (12th ed., 1994).

Chapter Six
Civil Court Structure and Procedure

The *Zivilverfahren* (civil procedure) as a public institution regulates conflicts between private parties. It is operated by the state courts. Given this, civil procedure may be defined as nationally ordered and ruled proceedings before civil courts whose purpose is to enforce individual rights.

Civil procedure is governed by the *Zivilprozeßordnung* (Civil Code of Procedure) and can be divided into two parts. It starts with the *Erkenntnisverfahren* (contentious proceedings) which leads to a decision and is the judicial review of the alleged rights and claims in the lawsuit. The relevant provisions from the filing of an action to the legally binding decision are laid down in the first to seventh books of the ZPO. The second part of civil proceedings is the *Zwangsvollstreckungsverfahren* (execution proceedings) which enforces the rights or claims determined in the judicial decision. These proceedings are largely governed in the eighth book of the ZPO and — as far as compulsory auction of landed property or judicial sequestration is concerned — in the *Zwangsversteigerungsgesetz* (Compulsory Auction of Immovable Property Act) as part of the Code of Civil Procedure (§ 869 ZPO).

1. Civil Jurisdiction (*Zivilgerichtsbarkeit*)

As outlined above — civil jurisdiction is a part of ordinary jurisdiction.[1] Any *bürgerliche Rechtsstreitigkeit* (civil case), non-contentious proceedings[2] and those cases which are specifically assigned to civil jurisdiction[3] belong to this jurisdiction (§ 13

[1] For more details, see *ibid.*, Chap. Five, 2, A.

[2] This is laid down in the *Gesetz über die freiwillige Gerichtsbarkeit* (German *Ex-Parte* Jurisdiction Act). These proceedings are applicable in those fields of law which must be governed by public authority intervention such as cases concerning guardianship — or curatorships or the task of keeping registers (*e.g.* Land Registry, commercial register). The civil courts perform these tasks.

[3] For more details, see *ibid.*, Chap. Eight, 4, A.

GVG). As a rule, civil cases include any dispute involving the conduct of individuals in their private lives and have to be distinguished from public law disputes before the administrative courts.[4]

A. CIVIL COURTS (*ZIVILGERICHTE*)

Civil courts responsible for hearing civil cases are — as outlined above — courts of the *Länder* such as *Amtsgerichte* (County Courts), *Landgerichte* (Regional Courts), *Oberlandesgerichte* (Regional Appeal Courts) and the *Bundesgerichtshof* (Federal Supreme Court of Justice) as the civil court of the Federation. The constitution, organisation and jurisdiction of these courts is set forth in the Judicature Act — the *Gerichtsver-fassungsgesgesetz* (GVG).

— The highest German civil court is the *Bundesgerichtshof* which is located in Karlsruhe. Its panel of judges are *Senate* (senators) which are composed of four associate judges and one presiding judge (§ 139 GVG).

— The *Oberlandesgericht* is the highest civil court of the *Länder*. Its panel of judges is also called a *Senate* and sits with two associate judges and one presiding judge (§ 122 GVG).

— *Landgerichte* are attached to a *Oberlandesgericht* within a certain *Land.* Their panel of judges are the *Kammern* (chambers) which consist of two associate judges and one presiding judge (§ 75 GVG). Each *Landgericht* also has *Handelskammern* (chambers of commerce) which are competent to hear commercial cases only (§§ 93 *et seq.* GVG). These chambers are composed of one (professional) presiding judge and two non-professional judges. These lay judges may be either members of the board of directors of a company or businessmen; they are appointed by the chamber of industry and commerce for a period of three years.

— *Amtsgerichte* are placed under the respective *Landgericht* and consist of *Einzelrichter* (single judges) only (§ 22 I GVG).

B. JURISDICTION

Each court has to review *ex officio* whether it is competent to hear the submitted case. A court lacking jurisdiction has to transfer the case to the competent court upon application by

[4] For more details, see *ibid.*, Chap. Eight, 4, A.

the plaintiff (§ 281 I ZPO). Otherwise the action will be inadmissible. The jurisdiction of civil courts is mainly governed in the Code of Civil Procedure and the Judicature Act. The law provides different types of jurisdictions.

There is, for example, *internationale Zuständigkeit* (international jurisdiction) which regulates the competence of German courts to hear cases involving foreign affairs. Special provisions are contained in bilateral international treaties or conventions such as the *Europäisches Gerichtsstands- und Vollstreckungsabkommen* (European Convention on Jurisdiction and Enforcement of Judgments in Civil and Criminal Matters). German domestic rules are subsidiary to these treaties and conventions. In the remaining cases, the international jurisdiction of German courts is governed by the rules of local jurisdiction set forth in §§ 12 *et seq.* ZPO and in §§ 606 a and 640 a II ZPO as rules for only a few specific cases.

The *örtliche Zuständigkeit* (venue or local jurisdiction) is specified in §§ 12 to 37 ZPO and prescribes the place of the competent court where the plaintiff has to file his suit. The ZPO provides places of general, special and exclusive jurisdiction. As a matter of principle, all actions against natural persons, legal entities or public authorities may be brought at the *allgemeiner Gerichtsstand* (place of general jurisdiction) which may be, for example, the defendant's domicile or registered office when the defendant is a legal entity or public authority. However the general place of jurisdiction applies only as far as the law gives no reason for another special venue. Other venues for hearing special cases could be the *besonderer Gerichtsstand* (place of special jurisdiction) such as place of inheritance, place of performance or place of tort. Finally, there is the *ausschließlicher Gerichtsstand* (exclusive jurisdiction) which is, for instance, the *in rem* jurisdiction and the jurisdiction in tenant cases. A lawsuit has to be filed at the court having an exclusive jurisdiction. If an action does not fall in an exclusive jurisdiction, the plaintiff may choose between the various places as far as different jurisdictional venues are at hand (§ 35 ZPO).

Moreover, there is the *sachliche Zuständigkeit* (jurisdiction over the subject matter). It determines which court within the pyramid of civil courts is competent to hear the case in the original instance — the *Amtsgericht* or *Landgericht* — and as Court of Appeal. As a rule, *Amtsgerichte* are responsible for cases of minor importance whereas *Landgerichte* hear considerably larger cases.

(a) Thus, in any pecuniary case with the value in dispute up to DM10.000, disputes between landlords and tenants and matrimonial, paternity and maintenance cases belong to the *Amtsgerichte* as courts of first instance (§§ 23 No. 2, 23 and 23 b GVG). Judgments of the *Amtsgericht* are heard by the *Landgericht* on appeal (§ 72 GVG; see Schedule 2). There is no resort to a higher court or authority against these appeal judgments of the *Landgericht*. A particular rule applies to parent and child cases or family law cases: appeals against the judgments of the *Amtsgericht* in these cases are not heard by the *Landgericht* but by the *Oberlandesgericht* where a specified panel of judges (called family senate) will preside (§ 119 I No. 1 and II GVG; see Schedule 2). Then, these judgments of the *Oberlandesgericht* can be appealed to the *Bundesgerichtshof* as the court of last instance (§ 133 GVG; see Schedule 2 and 3).

(b) *Landgerichte* can act as courts of both first and second instance. As a rule, *Landgerichte* - including the chambers of commerce — hear any cases at first instance which are not allocated to the *Amtsgerichte* (§ 71 I GVG). Hence, they are competent for pecuniary disputes with a value in dispute of up to DM10.000, all non-pecuniary disputes, claims against the revenue authorities founding on the Civil Services Act and cases involving any breach of official duty (§ 71 II GVG). The chamber of commerce hears all cases dealing with commercial activities such as disputes under company law, relating to competition, stock exchange, cheques or trademarks.

Appeals against judgments of the *Landgericht* have to be lodged at the *Oberlandesgericht* (§ 119 I No. 3 GVG). Appeals against these appeal judgments are heard by the *Bundesgerichtshof* at last instance when — in pecuniary disputes — the value of litigation of up to DM60.000 is reached or — in non-pecuniary disputes — the *Oberlandesgericht* has granted leave to appeal because of the case's fundamental importance (§ 133 No. 1 GVG and § 546 I ZPO). With the consent of the opponent, an appeal on points of law against the judgment of the *Landgericht* of first instance may also be filed directly at the *Bundesgerichtshof* under the requirements set forth in § 566 a ZPO; this, then, is called *Sprungrevision* (leap-frog appeal; see Schedule 3).

The *funktionelle Zuständigkeit* (limited jurisdiction with regard to the type of case) regulates the allocation of powers between the bodies of civil administration of justice. It deals, for instance, with the question of who is competent to decide an opposition in the execution proceedings: the judge or judicial officer.

As a matter of principle, stipulations as to venue are forbidden under the Code of Civil Procedure, except for cases laid down in §§ 38 to 40 ZPO. As far as the requirements of the aforementioned legal norms are met, a venue deviating from the statutory jurisdiction may be agreed. For instance, special parties — such as merchants — may set up such a stipulation as to the venue (§ 38 I ZPO). Next, such a stipulation may be made by any party after the accrual of a legal dispute (§ 38 III ZPO). In addition, parties which have no place of general jurisdiction in Germany may also conclude a stipulation as to venue (§ 38 II ZPO, Article 17 EuGVÜ). Last but not least, after filing a suit, the jurisdictional venue deviating from the statutory one may also be established in as far as the defendant pleads to the merits of the case without raising the jurisdictional plea (§ 39 ZPO).

2. PRINCIPLES OF PROCEDURE

Civil law procedure is governed by certain procedural principles outlined below. These principles give civil proceedings their characteristic features. In addition, the general fundamental principles already mentioned such as the principle of right of audience, of orality and of public trial[5] also influence civil proceedings to a great extent.

A. PRINCIPLE OF PARTY DISPOSITION

One very important principle of civil proceedings is the *Dispositionsmaxime* (principle of party disposition) which says that the parties are the masters of civil procedure. Due to this principle, only the parties determine the subject matter of proceedings of which they can choose freely. It is also their decision whether to file actions, motions or appeals. Moreover, the parties determine the extent both of judicial review and the judgment through their pleadings (§§ 308, 536, 559 ZPO). Thus, the court cannot award more or differently than has been applied for (*ne eat judex ultra petita partium*); but the court, of course, may grant less than demanded if the action is partly unfounded. The parties hold the disposing power over the subject matter during trial and, therefore, may either change the object at issue by an amendment of action or terminate the lawsuit, for instance, by withdrawal, settlement, acceptance of the claim or waiver of the action.[6]

---

[5] For more details, see *ibid.*, Chap. Five, 1.
[6] For more details, see *ibid.*, Chap. Six, 8.

B. PRINCIPLE OF PARTY PRESENTATION

A further important procedural principle is the *Verhandlungsgrundsatz* (principle of party presentation) which requires and demands that all facts of the case on which the court may base the judgment have been provided beforehand by the participating parties. Therefore, the parties themselves decide which facts to introduce at trial, whether and which kind of evidence they present. The court itself cannot introduce facts in trial and adduce evidence.

The Code of Civil Procedure provides a few exceptions to the principle of party representation. For instance, courts are obliged to review *ex officio* the admissibility of lawsuits, rights of appeals and other legal remedies (§§ 56, 88 II, 341, 519 b and 554 a ZPO). Courts examine whether the facts delivered by the parties may found the action's or appeal's admissibility and, in some cases, indicate their doubts. Moreover, the parties are obliged to be truthful in pleadings (§ 138 ZPO), and the court does not take into account an allegation of facts known to be untrue. A further limitation of this principle is that courts must provide clarification, are obliged to warn or put questions to the parties whenever they are needed in order, for instance, to clarify an unanswered question or to give proper directions to pleadings. The parties, however, are free to follow the court's suggestion and advice.

In specific civil proceedings — concerning family cases or parent and child cases — the principle of party presentation is not in force but rather (and exceptionally) the *Untersuchungsgrundsatz* (principle of investigation). The reason for this exception is that the subject matter of these trials demands that all true facts of the respective case be stated and established. As a result, the court is obliged to investigate all facts of the case.

C. PRINCIPLE OF CONCENTRATION

In civil procedure it is intended that the trial be concluded in one comprehensive date of hearing which means that the trial can be conducted at one stage; this procedural principle is called *Konzentrationsgrundsatz* (principle of concentration). As a result of this, courts are obliged to provide clarification, to explain, to put questions (§ 139 ZPO) and order specific measures to prepare the hearing (§ 273 II ZPO). An important way of speeding up the trial is that courts can request that the parties deliver their pleadings within a given period and — as far as they fail to meet the deadline — can declare the delayed pleadings as being out of time (§ 296 ZPO).

D. PRINCIPLE OF DIRECTNESS

The *Grundsatz der Unmittelbarkeit* (principle of directness) requires that the hearing has to take place before a trial court because the court which has to deliver the ruling must — due to this principle — obtain the most direct impression of the case. Therefore, only judges who have attended the hearing are allowed to take part in the adjudicative process (§§ 128, 309 ZPO).

3. PARTICIPANTS IN THE PROCESS

A. CIVIL JUDGE

As mentioned before — the legal position of civil judges is largely governed in the German constitution and Law of the Judiciary.[7] In addition, the Code of Civil Procedure provides certain rules to exclude or reject a judge, on the grounds listed in §§ 41 to 48 ZPO, *e.g.* if he is a close relative of one of the litigants or is involved in the case in some way or is suspected of partiality.

Civil judges participate in the process and their judicial tasks are different according to the case as to which position and function they have to administer justice. They may act as *Einzelrichter* (single judge) at the *Amtsgericht* or may sit in a chamber or *Senate* of a higher civil court. Naturally, their judicial practice as single judges or panel members of a chamber or *Senate* is very different. For instance, the single judge conducts proceedings and gives his ruling as the trial court; before the chamber or senate might render their judgments, a secret deliberation on the case has to take place and every panel member has to take his vote on the case. In contrast to the position in English law a dissenting judgment of one of the participating judges of a panel is unknown in German civil procedure; a judge who advocates a dissenting opinion has to step back behind the majority opinion of the panel. In addition, his dissenting judgment does not become public.

Single judges may act as trial court at the *Amtsgericht* but the Code of Civil Procedure recognises a further *Einzelrichter* with a different function. Single judges are also known in the adjudicative process in chambers or senates. Although chambers of the *Landgericht* and senates of the *Oberlandesgericht* generally hear cases as a panel of judges, they may transfer a particular task to one of their panel members. For instance, the chamber

---

[7] For more details, see *ibid.*, Chap. Four, 2, A.

at the *Landgericht* at first instance should transfer a case to one of its members as far as the case does not contain a specific difficulty on points of fact or law and is not of fundamental importance (§ 348 ZPO). In this case the single judge gives his ruling on the case,[8] not the chamber.

The *beauftragter Richter* (commissioned judge) can be distinguished from a judge acting as a single judge. A panel of judges may transfer a case to one member of the panel who then acts as the commissioned judge. Contrary to the single judge, he will deal only with specific parts of proceedings, for instance the taking of evidence (§§ 355 I, 375 I ZPO) or the attempt at reconciliation (§ 279 I 2 ZPO). Beyond this assigned task, he is not allowed to give a ruling.

Finally, a judge may also act as an *ersuchter Richter* (requested judge) who is requested for a certain task by another court. The following example explains the details: a court in Munich has to examine a witness living in Hamburg who, as a rule, is obliged to appear in the trial court in Munich. Obviously, this would produce unnecessary costs like travelling expenses and loss of earnings. In cases like this, the trial court may demand the requested judge for judicial assistance (here the *Amtsgericht* in Hamburg), to examine the witness. The requested judge, then, interrogates the witness.

B. CLERK OF THE COURT'S OFFICE

Another participant who indirectly participates in the process is the *Urkundsbeamte der Geschäftsstelle* (clerk of the court's office) whose legal position and tasks are set forth in § 153 ZPO just as in federal and *Land* law. These clerks are court officials sitting in any court office. Their task entails numerous occupations, for instance, they are clerical officers responsible for keeping files or authenticators responsible for keeping minutes of judicial hearings.

C. JUDICIAL OFFICER

The task of the *Rechtspfleger* (judicial officer) as another court official is governed in the *Rechtspflegergesetz* (Act concerning the office of *Rechtspfleger*). Judicial officers are civil

---

[8] In appeal procedure before the *Land-* and *Oberlandesgericht*, the panel of judges may transfer specific tasks to one of its panel members such as to prepare court's finding or to progress a case so that it may be settled in full court (§ 524 I and II ZPO). Single judges in appeal procedure may give ruling in the enumerated canon of cases in § 524 III ZPO.

servants of an executive class. In order to qualify they must pass a three-year period of preparation. Judicial officers are an independent body whose legal position may be seen as being somewhere between judges and clerks of the court's office. They carry out minor judicial functions which entail no judicial power; this only being entrusted to judges (Article 92 GG). Judicial officers are independent in exercising their task but this independence is subject to more restrictions than that of a judge. Like judges, judicial officers may also be excluded and rejected for reasons as mentioned above (§ 10 RPflG and §§ 41 to 48 ZPO).

D. LAWYER

The position of *Rechtsanwälte* (lawyers) in civil trials is important because to a large extent they influence the way that civil proceedings are conducted — this is one of the consequences of the procedural principles which have been explained above. In all courts, starting in hierarchy from the *Landgericht*, and in important cases in family courts, there is the principle of mandatory representation by a lawyer. Thus, the parties have to engage the service of a lawyer for their representation in civil courts.[9] The legal position of lawyers is governed in the *Bundesrechtsanwaltsordnung* (Rules and Regulations for the German Bar) which *inter alia* says that lawyers are an independent body of justice (§ 1 BRAO). They are obliged to look after their client's interest and must also conduct the case properly and take care that the client fulfils the duty to tell the truth.

4. SKETCH OF PROCEDURE

Civil proceedings are started by filing the action. The service of process to the defendant is initiated by the courts. In addition, the defendant is asked to commission a lawyer admitted to the bar if the action is pending at a court where the mandatory representation of a lawyer is required.

Next, the trial court has to prepare the process and has to have in mind that the legal dispute has to be dealt with in one comprehensive and prepared main hearing. In lawsuits before the *Landgericht*, the presiding judge may choose: he may order either a so-called *frühen ersten Termin zur mündlichen*

---

[9] For more details, see *ibid.*, Chap. Four, 2, B.

Verhandlung (preliminary hearing for trial) and fix a date for hearing in which the case will be discussed with the parties at an early stage (§§ 272 II, 275 ZPO); or he may order a *schriftliches Vorverfahren* (written pre-trial process) in which the parties have to submit their written pleadings (§§ 272 II, 276 ZPO). Which course the judge may choose is entirely a discretionary matter. However, in order to speed up trial, in every case the judge will fix a deadline for submission of the *Klageerwiderung* (defendant's statement) as well as the plaintiff's response. The legal consequence of the failure to observe such a deadline is that the respective party will be precluded from presenting the pleading in question (§ 296 I ZPO).

Civil trial begins with the calling of the case. The court introduces the matter in issue to the parties and discusses the case with them (§ 278 ZPO). The main hearing may be regarded as an adversarial procedure: the parties put their opposed applications, the plaintiff demanding a judgment and the defendant applying for dismissal of action. During proceedings the court is obliged to consider the possibility of settling the case at any stage of the process (§ 279 ZPO).

In order to determine whether an action is successful, the court reviews the admissibility and legal justification of the action. This review has to be conducted in a special sequence because only when an action's admissibility is confirmed, can the court start to examine the action's justification. If the court has no reason to dismiss the case on procedural grounds, it adjudicates upon the merits. In order to check whether an action is well founded the court has to first review the plaintiff's presented statement of facts. Starting from these facts — assuming their truth — the court must deduce the legal consequence being asserted by the plaintiff. If the complaining party failed to state the claim, the action is not conclusive and can be dismissed on the merits. But, as far as the statement of claim is conclusive, the court looks at the statement of defence, considers and reviews the arguments of the defence with regard to relevance and substance. In case of an irrelevant answer to a claim, the court gives a ruling on the merits of the case.

Otherwise, the court must consider which of the facts submitted by one party and denied by the other will be material to the decision and need to be proved. If there are matters to be proved, the evidence will be heard. Sometimes evidence can show that the fact to be proved can neither be proved nor refuted — this is called *non liquet*. In this case, the court will deliver a decision nevertheless while using the concept of burden of proof. In this case the party on which the onus of proof rests must bear the legal consequence that sufficient evidence was not furnished to discharge this burden. The lack of proof counts against this party and the unproved facts are considered as not existing.

In any case, the first instance concludes with the pronounced judgment. As far as no appeal is filed against this judgment it becomes final and absolute. The contentious proceedings are terminated, and the judgment may be enforced in the execution proceedings.

5. ACTION (*KLAGE*)

A. TYPES OF ACTION (*KLAGEARTEN*)

(1) Action for performance (*Leistungsklage*)

The German Civil Procedural Law provides different forms of civil actions. At first, there is the *Leistungsklage* (action for performance). By filing such a suit the plaintiff is demanding a court order to the effect that the defendant has to perform or refrain from a certain act. It is the correct action if the complaining party claims, for example, the performance of a contractual or statutory duty such as payment of a certain amount of money or delivery of personal or real property. The judgment, which obliges a party to perform or refrain from a certain act, may be enforced against the defendant in the execution proceedings.

(2) Action for a declaratory judgment (*Feststellungsklage*)

Another form of action is the *Feststellungsklage* (action for a declaratory judgment) which means that the plaintiff demands a declaration given by a court that a legal relationship between the litigant parties *inter se* or between one participant and personal or real property does or does not exist (§ 256 ZPO). The matter of controversy is the legal relationship which may be based on contract, statute or an absolute right such as the right of property or the use of a name. The plaintiff who files such a suit must show that he has an existing legal interest to seek a declaratory judgment — this is called *Feststellungsinteresse* — which has to be denied, for instance, if the complaining party lodges an action for performance in order to reach his aim. Actions for a declaratory judgment are subsidiary. Moreover, contrary to an action for performance, actions for a declaratory judgment cannot be enforced — apart from the ruling as to the costs.

A further type of declaratory action is the *Zwischenfeststellungsklage* (petition for an interlocutory judgment — § 256 II ZPO). It is the correct action if the declaration of a claim during trial becomes material and requires its interlocutory declaration in the form of a judgment.

(3) Action requesting a change of a legal right or status (*Gestaltungsklage*)

The *Gestaltungsklage* (action requesting a change of a legal right or status) can be distinguished from all actions outlined above because this action immediately induces a direct change in law with the legal force of the judgment. A judgment changing a legal right or status, therefore, requires no enforcement. A plaintiff filing such an action wants to terminate, modify or resolve a legal situation by judgment. This presupposes that — due to a statutory regulation — a dissolution, destruction or change of a legal relationship is carried out only by judgment. Examples are:

(a) under family law the petition for divorce (§ 1564 BGB) and denial of legitimacy of a child (§ 1599 BGB);

(b) under commercial law the petition for dissolution of a company, exclusion of a partner, revocation of the power to conduct business, revocation of the power of attorney (§§ 117, 127, 131 No. 6, 133, 140, 142, 161 II HGB), the denial of a general meeting's resolution and the nullity of a joint-stock company (§§ 243, 275 AktG); and

(c) under procedural law the action to oppose execution (§ 767 ZPO), third-party action against execution (§ 771 ZPO) and petition to modify a judgment (§ 323 ZPO).

B. FORM AND CONTENT OF THE STATEMENT OF CLAIM (*KLAGESCHRIFT*)

The plaintiff has to file the statement of claim in written form or let his claim be recorded in the court office by a clerk — the latter is only possible in proceedings before the *Amtsgerichte*. There is a duty to help citizens in drafting the statement of claim because the parties do not always have to be represented by a lawyer.

The required content of the statement of claim is laid down in § 253 II ZPO. Every statement of claim must specify the respective court and the litigant parties. In addition, the cause of action and subject matter in dispute has to be presented and specified, and the plaintiff must state in detail the facts of the case from which, in his opinion, the desired legal consequences may be derived. These presented facts should, in his opinion, provide the legal basis of his claim. Furthermore, the statement of claim has to contain a clear and definite *Antrag* (declaration of intent) which is important because only then can it be enforced in later execution proceedings. Moreover, the declaration of intent determines both the scope of the judicial examination and judgment.[10]

As mentioned before, the statement of claim must contain a declaration of intent but this is not possible in every case. An exception is made with regard to actions for the recovery of money when — at this stage of proceedings — the plaintiff is unable to quantify the demanded amount of money; this might be the case in actions for damages due to physical pain and suffering. In those lawsuits the plaintiff will — for the initial claim — obtain all information to quantify the loss or damage during trial. Then, a non-enumerated action for the recovery of money can be filed but the plaintiff must provide all facts which, in his opinion, are relevant for the computation of damage and has to indicate a rough estimate of the extent of his demand. The action must be the basis for the determination and appraisal of the damage. In these cases, the *Stufenklage* (action by stages — § 254 ZPO) is the correct form of action in which issues arising at various stages are tried separately. This action demands with its first stage, for instance, the required information and with the second stage the payments which — at this stage — cannot be numbered. The latter is at first a non-enumerated demand for relief which will be specified after the defendant has given the information required with the demand for relief on the first stage.

C. PROCEDURAL PREREQUISITES (*PROZEẞVORAUSSETZUNGEN*)

In order to be successful, any action has to meet certain procedural requirements which may be classified in three different groups. One of these groups are the *"echte" Prozeßvoraussetzungen* ("true" procedural prerequisites) to which an effective commencement of the statement of claim and German jurisdiction belongs. In cases of its absence, the

[10] Parties must not file applications with regard to costs orders (§ 308 II ZPO) or orders of the provisional enforceability. The court judges upon them *ex officio*.

statement of claim will not be served upon the defendant, no date of hearing will be fixed and therefore no trial arises. It has to be noted that these will be absent only if the action contains grave faults.

The *Sachurteilsvoraussetzungen* are a further group of procedural prerequisites but are quite different from the others mentioned previously — lawsuits failing to meet these requirements initiate proceedings anyway. A date of the hearing is fixed and the statement of claim is served upon the defendant. The missing procedural prerequisites can then be carried out before the oral hearing. If the plaintiff fails to do so, the action will be dismissed on procedural grounds. This group of procedural prerequisites includes, for instance, a correctly filed action (§ 253 ZPO), parties who are able to participate in trial (§§ 50 to 52 ZPO), a court having jurisdiction, a legitimate interest to take legal action, no other final judgment with the same object at issue and no other action pending with the same matter in controversy (§ 261 III No. 1 ZPO).

The *Prozeßhindernisse* (impediments to an action) are another group of procedural prerequisites which are the presence of an arbitration agreement, for example (§ 1027 a ZPO), the lack of reimbursement of costs of litigation (§ 269 IV ZPO) and the lack of security for costs of action (§ 110 ZPO). Their non-existence is necessary for a successful action. But, contrary to the procedural prerequisites mentioned before, courts do not consider *ex officio* impediments to an action. Only if a party has raised the plea that there are impediments to an action, is the court obliged to investigate their presence.

D. MATTER IN DISPUTE (*STREITGEGENSTAND*)

The matter in dispute is specified in the statement of claim. The application to be filed and the submitted facts of the case which provide the legal basis for the claim specify in detail the matter in dispute. Due to this, a change of both the declaration of intent or the factual situation (after the suit has been filed) is regarded as an amendment of the original matter in dispute and such an amendment of an action has to meet specific procedural requirements in order to become effective.[11]

The matter in dispute plays an important role in civil procedure. As a result, it is very important to specify and find out the subject matter of action in any case, which highlights the following examples: a joinder of action dealing with

[11] For more details, see *ibid.*, Chap. Six, 5, E.

more than one matter in dispute may be filed, and the court may order a severance of action with the consequence that any matter in dispute is prosecuted in a separate trial; this then presumes to state the matters in controversy beforehand. In addition, while the action is pending, a new action with the same matter in dispute is inadmissible (§ 261 III No. 1 ZPO); material finality (or *res judicata*) prohibits the filing of a new action and the rendering of a further judgment with the same object at issue — such an action will be dismissed.

E. EFFECTS OF THE COMMENCEMENT OF AN ACTION (*KLAGEERHEBUNG*)

The commencement of an action establishes its *Rechtshängigkeit* (pendency of a suit or *lis pendence*) which presupposes that an action has been filed with the court and, in addition, served to the defendant (§ 261 ZPO). The pendency of a claim must be distinguished from an action's *Anhängigkeit* (pending litigation or *lis pendens*) which has already arisen with the filing of a suit. The pendency of a suit, however, presupposes that the service of an action to the defendant, and only the pendency of a suit produces the following legal consequences. It especially has an influence on the position of a creditor or debtor, for instance it may lead to strict liability (§§ 292, 989 BGB), an interruption of the period of limitation (§ 209 BGB) or to an extension of rights (§ 291 BGB). In addition to this, the pendency of a suit also has procedural effects. It is an impediment for filing a lawsuit with the same object of issue; such an action filed is dismissed *ex officio* because of another action pending (§ 261 III No. 1 ZPO). This is true even if its suppositions are dismissed during the course of proceedings (*perpetuatio fori*, § 261 III No. 2 ZPO).

Besides the *Rechtshängigkeit*, the commencing of an action has further effects. For instance, it prohibits, as a rule, amendments once the action is filed. The reason is that the defendant should be able to prepare his statement of defence after the action is served upon him and responding to an action would be quite impossible if a suit could be amended at any time. Nevertheless, in certain cases an amendment of action is admissible because it may lead to the conclusion of a trial and, therefore, stands in the interest of procedural economy. Due to §§ 263 *et seq.* ZPO, an amendment of action — which may be defined as the change of the matter in dispute after pendency — is admissible in the following circumstances: the law enumerates in § 264 ZPO certain cases which, under law, are not regarded as an amendment of an action and, therefore, do not need to fulfil the requirements of § 263 ZPO (outlined below). Examples are to add or correct the legal or factual statements presented in the suit, to extend or restrict the main declaration of intent or the incidental claim, or to change the original demanded object or interest because of an event which occurred later. The remaining cases are regarded as an amendment of action under law (§ 263 ZPO). Because of this the plaintiff can only amend his action with the consent of the defendant or upon the court's approval which is given as far as its expediency may be confirmed; the latter is the case as far as it effects a final settlement of the legal dispute.

Finally, the commencement of action affects the alienation of property which is the subject matter of the litigation during the course of proceedings. The provision of § 265 I ZPO makes clear that pendency of action does not exclude parties' rights to transfer property in litigation and, as a matter of principle, such a transfer does not influence the lawsuit. Litigant parties will continue to conduct the case. But the party alienating the property in litigation will loose its legitimacy as the proper party of proceedings. As a result, the party will conduct proceedings in *Prozeßstandschaft* (capacity to sue or be sued in one's own name without being directly involved in the subject matter of the action) on behalf of the newly entitled or obligated party. This requires two things: the property in dispute must indeed be subject to litigation and the party's legitimacy must rest on a legal relationship towards the property involved. In this case, the plaintiff is obliged to change the declaration of intent while he now demands performance not towards him but towards his legal successor. Only then will the rendered judgment become effective towards and against the legal successor (§ 325 ZPO).

6. PARTIES

A. THE RIGHT TO PARTICIPATE IN PROCEEDINGS

In order to take part in proceedings effectively, every party has to meet specific requirements. At first, parties must be *parteifähig* (right to be a party in a lawsuit) which is anyone possessing the legal capacity in the sense of § 1 BGB such as every human being and legal entity (§ 50 I ZPO).[12] The right to

[12] Although general mercantile partnerships, incorporated associations, trade unions and political parties have no legal capacity, it is acknowleged by law that societies like this may sue and be sued.

be a party in a lawsuit, therefore, is nothing more than the procedural side of the legal capacity laid down in § 1 BGB. The idea behind this is that one who is the subject of rights and duties should be able both to enforce rights and to be held liable for the duties.

Nevertheless, the right to be a party to legal proceedings only means being capable of being a party in a lawsuit and not whether this person is able to stand up in court. This capability is set forth in § 51 ZPO and is called *Prozeßfähigkeit* (capacity to sue and be sued). It is the ability to stand up in court and carry out actions and steps in proceedings in his own right and name. A person legally incapable of conducting proceedings is allowed to authorise another person to represent his legal interest in court.

The capacity to sue and be sued has nothing in common with the mandatory representation by lawyers — the *Postulationsfähigkeit* (right of audience). This is the capacity to conduct a case in special courts in which the mandatory representation by lawyers exists such as in *Landgerichte*, *Oberlandesgerichte* and *Bundesgerichtshof* (§§ 78, 79 ZPO). A party who intends to conduct proceedings in such a court must instruct a lawyer admitted to the bar.

Finally, there is the *Prozeßführungsbefugnis* (right of action or *locus standi*) which is the litigation of a third party in his own name but on behalf of another. It requires a certain authority to conduct a case granted to a third party. Such an authority may rest on the strength of a law such as an executor's or receiver's authority (§ 6 II KO and § 152 ZVG). It may also be based on an agreement in which the entitled party transfers the authority to conduct the case to a third party, and the third party must show his own legal interest in the case.

B. Joint parties

A litigant party in civil proceedings is the one by and against whom judicial relief is demanded. The lawsuit may be subdivided into a two-party relationship whereas on both sides further people may participate. The main parties — such as plaintiff and defendant — are from a formal point of view on the same footing, owning the same rights and duties. The principle of equal opportunities governs civil trials. Sometimes more than one party either on the plaintiff's side or on the defendant's side participates in a lawsuit. With regard to the need of joint parties to take part in a trial, Civil Procedure provides the following rules:

Several parties may jointly sue or be sued as *Streitgenossen* (joint parties as plaintiff or defendant) if they have either a unity interest with regard to the matter in dispute or are jointly entitled or obliged on factual or legal grounds. The simple joinder of parties is governed in §§ 59 to 61 ZPO and is the summing up of several independent proceedings — as a matter of convenience — into one procedure in which, as a rule, each party keeps its legal independence. In addition, the law provides compulsory joinder resting on procedural or substantive grounds which is set forth in § 62 ZPO. In this case only a uniform judgment may be rendered towards any compulsory joinder — a different judgment may be delivered towards simple joinders.

Also a third party may take part in a trial as an intervening party. Due to §§ 66 to 71 ZPO, the *Nebenintervention* (intervention of a third party in support of a plaintiff or defendant) is the support of one of the litigants by the intervening party who must only show the legal interest in this support. An important legal consequence of the intervention is called the intervening effect, that is to say, the intervening party may not object in a later legal dispute that the initial judgment was wrong or that the main party had wrongly conducted the case — such a plea is precluded (§ 68 ZPO). The intervening party, however, does not become a party participating in the process.

Also the main parties — such as the plaintiff or defendant — may include a third party in the process and may serve a third party notice on the respective party. This is called *Streitverkündung* (third party notice) and governed in §§ 72 to 74 ZPO. A litigant party can give notice to a third party against whom — in his opinion — he may claim or who may file a suit against him if he loooses the case. It is then advisable for him to give notice to the third party in question. The third party has the opportunity to choose. He may enter proceedings as a *Streithelfer* (party intervening on the side of a litigant), take part in the trial, influence it and obtain the legal position of an intervening party in proceedings; the advantage is that the afore-mentioned intervening effect of § 68 ZPO applies. The third party may also refuse to enter proceedings with the result that the trial continues to proceed without him and is concluded by judgment. Then an action is filed against the third party, the judgment is introduced and the intervening effect of § 68 ZPO comes into force as well. The third party is then precluded from objections like wrongful conduct of the former case. A judgment which has, as a rule, only a binding effect between the main participating parties can, in this way, establish a legally binding effect towards a third party who has not taken part in the initial trial.

C. CHANGE OF PARTIES AND THEIR ENTRY TO PROCEEDINGS

A *Parteienwechsel* (change of parties) may become necessary during the course of proceedings. It is admissible under the Code of Civil Procedure to continue the trial without its repetition after a change of parties. A change of parties may become necessary, for instance if one of the litigants dies (see § 239 ZPO). In addition, a change of party may be necessary if the plaintiff has sued the wrong defendant. With regard to such a situation, the Code of Civil Procedure has no equivalent provisions. But as specified by the courts[13] the change of parties is legally regarded and dealt with as an amendment of action and, due to this, the provisions of §§ 263 *et seq.* ZPO apply. Therefore, a change of parties requires the consent of the new party (either on the defendant's or plaintiff's side) or the court's approval.[14] A change of defendant in a trial of second instance always requires the defendant's consent because he will enter trial and must proceed in the process as it stands at second instance. His consent may only become dispensible if the refusal to enter proceedings is regarded as an abuse of law.

A party may also enter proceedings as a further plaintiff or defendant. This is called *Parteienbeitritt* (entry to proceedings) which is not regulated in the Code of Civil Procedure but is specified by the courts[15]: it is treated as a change of action (§§ 263 *et seq.* ZPO) and, therefore, an entry into proceedings on the defendant's side requires the consent of the new defendant which is only dispensible as far as the refusal is an abuse of law.

7. DEFENDANT'S DEFENCE

The defendant may reply to an action filed against him in different ways. At first he may be inactive which is — as a rule — admissible behaviour because the defendant is not obliged to respond. He has no duty to appear in court, to participate in trial or to submit a statement of defence — he is free to ignore the served action and the fixed-date summons. But his failure to act and appear in court leads to a judgment by default[16] which is a judgment on the merits and may be executed. However inactivity can also be an effective defence — because the arisen

---

[13] BGH NJW 1962, 347; BGH NJW 1989, 3225; BGHZ 40, 185, 189.
[14] For more details, see *ibid.*, Chap. Six, 5, E.
[15] BGHZ 40, 185, 189; 56, 73, 75; 65, 246, 268; For more details, see *ibid.*, Chap. Six, 5, E.
[16] For more details, see *ibid.*, Chap. Six, 12, B.

legal costs are reduced in this case — when the defendant has nothing to plead as an effective answer to the action.

The defendant may also acknowledge the claim of the plaintiff with the consequence that — by a declaration of intent of the plaintiff — a judgment based on the defendant's acknowledgement is given (§ 307 ZPO). The advantage is that if the defendant makes an immediate admission of the plaintiff's claim, he can reduce the legal costs to be borne by him. Moreover, if he has given no cause for action, the plaintiff has to bear the costs of litigation (§ 93 ZPO).

The defendant may also concentrate on the procedural requirements of the action and strives for the dismissal of action on procedural grounds. In most cases, however, the defendant attempts to get a dismissal simply on the merits of the case because only then can this action not be commenced against him again. Such a defence presupposes that the defendant answers and expresses his opinion on the claim. With regard to this, he has various possibilities.

(a) He may accept a matter of fact alleged by the plaintiff with the result that the court has to treat these facts as true. Such an admission refers only to facts and is binding in all instances (§§ 288 to 290 and § 532 ZPO).[17]

Facts which he has failed to deny or he has insufficiently denied are dealt with as if he had admitted them (§ 138 III ZPO). Such a fictitious admission is just as binding as an explicit admission but — contrary to the latter — the defendant is free to contest it at a later stage during the course of proceedings.

(b) The defendant may also plea in demurrer while he contests the founding facts of the claim (simple denial) or set forth new allegations deviating from those of the plaintiff's claim (substantive denial). If a plea in demurrer is relevant against a conclusive action, the taking of evidence becomes necessary.

(c) Moreover, the defendant may also raise an *Einrede* (defence). Defences are new allegations particularising another legal argument in order to defeat the plaintiff's claim. To achieve this, the defendant may put forward various defences: the plea in law (for instance judicial incapacity under § 105 BGB or immorality under § 138

---

[17] An admission may only be revocated as far as proof may be furnished that the admitted fact is untrue and that the admission has been caused by mistake.

BGB), the preemptory plea (such as performance under §§ 362 and 364 BGB or repudiation of contract under § 346 BGB) or the dilatory exception (for example limitation of action under § 222 BGB).

(d) The defendant may also take an active role in proceedings and take up his defence while he raises the *Aufrechnung* (set-off) and pleads that the claim of the plaintiff becomes extinct by the set-off claim. Similar to the concept of set-off in Anglo-American law, the *Aufrechnung* in Germany is governed by substantive law. Due to this, the set-off is a substantive legal transaction whose effectiveness has to comply with §§ 389 *et seq.* BGB. However, the notice of the set-off — namely that the plaintiff's claim has been redeemed by the set-off — has to be declared in court. Given this, a set-off declared in court has a double legal nature: it is a substantive transaction governed under the BGB — the Civil Code — and is also a step in proceedings whose effectiveness must comply with the ZPO — the Code of Civil Procedure.

(e) The defendant may also attack the action by bringing an independent action against the plaintiff which is called *Widerklage* (counterclaim — § 33 ZPO). The counterclaim is a "normal" action which must meet the procedural prerequisites of any other civil action. In addition, a few particularities have to be met, the original action must be pending, the counterclaim has to contain an independent matter in dispute which is different from that of the action and a factual connection between action and counterclaim is required as well.

8. DISCONTINUANCE OF A TRIAL

The normal course of proceedings is that parties introduce their declarations of intent and pleading and after reviewing the case, the court gives a ruling on the merits. However the parties may discontinue a trial in such a way that the court can no longer come to a decision on the merits. The act exercised in court to conclude proceedings is called *Prozeßhandlung* (steps of proceedings). As a rule, all acts of the litigants — and not only those terminating a trial — carried out in order to start, continue or terminate a trial are steps in proceedings. Parties which bring about these acts must be capable of being a party in a lawsuit, to sue and be sued and — in case of representation —

have power of agency and rights of audience. Steps in proceedings have to be exercised in a clear, definite and unequivocal way and are non-appealable.

A. WITHDRAWAL OF AN ACTION (*KLAGERÜCKNAHME*)

The plaintiff is free to withdraw the action as long as the legal dispute is pending and not concluded by a final judgment (§ 269 ZPO). But after the defendant has pleaded on the main issue, the plaintiff can withdraw the action only with the consent of the defendant. An effective withdrawal of an action retrospectively removes the action's pendency and, due to this, no ruling on the merits is given by the court; and the plaintiff is free to bring the same suit again. A further legal consequence is that the plaintiff bears all legal costs including those of the defendant.

B. WAIVER OF AN ACTION (*KLAGEVERZICHT*)

The waiver of an action is another means of discontinuing trial (§ 306 ZPO). In this case, the plaintiff declares in court that he no longer demands action and waives the asserted claim. The court passes — on motion of the defendant — a judgment for the defendant without examining the case. As a legal consequence, the plaintiff cannot file the same suit again because of the final force and effect of this judgment. The plaintiff has to bear all costs of the lawsuit (§ 91 ZPO).

C. ACKNOWLEDGEMENT (*ANERKENNTNIS*)

The defendant may accept and acknowledge the claim of the plaintiff while he gives a respective notice in court. The acknowledgement puts an end to the trial (§ 307 ZPO); a judgment based on a defendant's acknowledgement is rendered on motion of the plaintiff. The court delivers a finding for the plaintiff which exclusively rests on the defendant's acknowledgement of the claim and not on a judicial review of the case.

D. TERMINATION OF THE SUBSTANTIVE DISPUTE (*ERLEDIGUNG DER HAUPTSACHE*)

During the course of proceedings, the lawsuit may be disposed of when a disposing event occurs such as a payment of the amount sued or a destruction of the object whose delivery has caused the dispute. In this case, parties may declare the substantive dispute as finally disposed of and leave the issue of costs to be decided by the court (§ 91 a ZPO). The court is bound by such a declaration. It puts an end to the pendency of action, and the court is not allowed to examine whether the substantive dispute is in fact finally terminated. The court issues a cost order in consideration of the case's position at the time of its conclusion; the party who would presumably have lost the case will bear the legal costs of the lawsuit.

The one-sided termination of the substantive dispute is not laid down in the Code of Civil Procedure but is generally accepted. If only one litigant (such as the plaintiff) declares that the lawsuit has been discontinued, it does not put an end to the lawsuit. The pendency of action continues to exist and the plaintiff has to amend his original motion for judgment into a motion for judgment declaring the dispute as terminated. In this case, the court examines whether the action was admissible and well founded, and whether the action has been disposed of after its pendency. If these requirements can be confirmed, a decree will be delivered declaring the termination of the lawsuit. The defeated party has to bear the legal costs (§ 91a ZPO).

E. COURT SETTLEMENT (*PROZEẞVERGLEICH*)

Finally, a trial may be amicably settled in court (§ 794 I No. 1 ZPO); courts are legally encouraged to propose such settlements (§ 279 ZPO). A court settlement is a mutual settlement governed in § 779 BGB in which parties settle their relationships in a comprehensive way, such as including claims beyond the lawsuit. The settlement has to be concluded in court and recorded in the court report. An effective court settlement puts an end to the lawsuit and is a judicially enforceable instrument. Court settlements have a dual nature of substantive legal transaction and procedural act.

9. TAKING OF EVIDENCE (*BEWEISAUFNAHME*)

After the case has been discussed, the court considers which of the facts alleged by one party and denied by the other party will be material to the decision. The court must find out which facts are necessary to be proved in order to state whether the *Beweisaufnahme* (taking of evidence) must be conducted and, also upon which facts evidence has to be taken. Only facts in dispute which are also of direct relevance and material for decision are subject to the calling of evidence. Facts not denied or admitted, obvious facts or facts of which the court has judicial knowledge do not have to be proved. These facts have to be accepted without further review. Examples of facts beyond dispute are obvious facts (§ 291 ZPO), *i.e.* facts subject to a statutory (§ 292 ZPO) or factual (prima facie evidence) presumption.

In civil proceedings, there are different kinds of evidence. To begin with, there is *Strengbeweis* (stringent evidence). The hearing and consideration of stringent evidence has to follow the formal rules set forth in §§ 355 *et seq.* ZPO and it is required in any proceedings striving for the rendering of a decision on the merits. It is intended to establish the truth of an allegation. Only the following evidence is admissible: visual inspection by the court (§§ 371 *et seq.* ZPO), witnesses (§§ 373 *et seq.* ZPO), experts (§ 402 *et seq.* ZPO), documents (§§ 415 *et seq.* ZPO) and interrogations of parties (§§ 445 *et seq.* ZPO). Moreover, there is the *Glaubhaftmachung* (furnishing prima facie evidence) which is laid down in § 294 ZPO. This evidence is only admissible in proceedings in which it is prescribed in law such as in summary proceedings like arrest (§ 920 II ZPO) or interlocutory injunctions (§ 936 ZPO). Furnishing prima facie evidence involves a lesser burden of proof which is satisfied by showing a probability; the *Versicherung an Eides statt* (affirmation in lieu of an oath) is admissible proof in this regard. The difference in comparison to stringent evidence already mentioned is the lesser burden of proof to be established. Finally, there is *Freibeweis* (informal evidence) which does not have to be furnished with admissible proof of stringent evidence and is admissible, for example, in proceedings of legal aid (§§ 114 *et seq.* ZPO). In these proceedings, hearing of evidence, taking of evidence and means of proof are left to the court's discretion.

After the court has stated the facts in dispute as being decisive for the decision-making and are therefore necessary to be proved, the court looks to the party's offers to produce evidence. With the *Beweisantritt* (offer of proof), a party introduces in trial the evidence for a particular allegation. It is left to the parties — and not to the court — to offer evidence. Only that evidence which has been offered by the participating parties in advance is heard in court, as a rule. The party bearing the burden of proof must tender evidence. As a matter of principle, parties bear the burden of proof for the existence of all facts beneficial to them. The plaintiff has to prove all facts founding his claim whereas the defendant bears the burden of proof upon all facts denying the claim. This principle is perforated if particular rules shift or reverse the burden of proof for the benefit of one party (*e.g.* §§ 179 I, 282, 345, 442, 2336 III BGB and presumptions of law or facts).

The court orders to hear the evidence on a fixed date in court and issues a *Beweisbeschluß* (order to take evidence). Then, all witnesses and experts are examined by the court (not by the parties or their counsel), inspection is carried out by the court for instance by vision, hearing, touching, tasting or smelling. Next, the court reviews the results of evidence and states whether the proof is furnished, namely, if the allegation upon which evidence has been taken, is proved. This judicial task is called *Beweiswürdigung* (consideration of evidence) and the principle of free evaluation of the evidence (§ 286 I ZPO) governs the German civil trial.

With a few statutory exceptions, the admission and weighting of evidence, including, for instance, hearsay or lies within the discretion of the court. The court adjudicates upon the case in consideration of all circumstances, such as the whole trial and the result of the hearing of evidence. An allegation is proved to be true as far as the court is convinced of its truth. The court has to specify the grounds for the evaluation of evidence in detail in the reasons for the decision. There might be cases in which the court is neither convinced of the allegations' truth or of its falsehood. Such a failure to prove an allegation — which is called "*non liquet*" — will then work to the detriment of the party bearing the burden of proof. Therefore, the burden of proof will decide who loses the trial.

The Code of Civil Proceedings provides in §§ 485 *et seq.* ZPO a *selbständiges Beweisverfahren* (independent proceedings for the introduction of evidence) which is started by a motion and runs independently beside the trial. These proceedings are for the preservation of evidence which can be initiated either with the consent of the opponent or if there is a concern that the evidence may either get lost during trial or may be produced under aggravating circumstances.

10. JUDICIAL DECISIONS

During the course of proceedings, the court renders different judicial decisions, and any issue is terminated by such a decision. One of these decisions is the *Urteil* (judgment). As a matter of principle, a lawsuit is concluded by judgment as soon as it is ready for a decision. The Code of Civil Procedure contains various judgments which are distinguished from each other with regard to:

— the scope of judgments such as *Prozeßurteile* (judgments on procedural grounds) and *Sachurteile* (judgments on the merits of the case);

— the content of their operative part such as *Leistungsurteile* (judgments which oblige a party to perform or refrain from a certain act), *Feststellungsurteile* (declaratory judgments) and *Gestaltungsurteile* (judgments changing a legal right or status);
— the position of the judgment in the trial such as *Endurteile* (judgments completing the case at trial court — § 300 ZPO), *Teilurteile* (part-judgments — § 301 ZPO), *Zwischenurteile* (interlocutory judgments adjudicating only a matter in dispute) and *Grundurteile* (judgments on the basis of the cause of action reserving the amount to a later decision — § 304 ZPO).

Judgments are judicial decisions which have to have a particular content. They are headed by a *Rubrum* (recitals), the heading of the case, which gives a detailed description of the participating parties, panel of judges and date of the hearing (§ 313 I No. 1–3 ZPO). This is followed by the *Urteilstenor* (operative part of the judgment) as the judgment, verdict or sentence (§ 313 No. 4 ZPO). The *Tatbestand* (findings of fact) of a judgment then presents the asserted claims, parties' motions and offensive or defensive means (§ 313 I No. 5, III ZPO). Finally, the *Urteilsbegründung* (reasons for the judgment) contains the findings of law of the judgment (§ 313 I No. 6, II ZPO).

Any judgment is rendered on the strength of a court hearing and pronounced "*Im Namen des Volkes*" ("In the Name of the People"). Once a judgment is pronounced, it is unchangeable. Only corrections and supplements — such as corrections of small typographical errors or mistakes concerning the facts of the case are possible after the pronouncement of the judgment pursuant to §§ 319, 320 and 321 ZPO.

Any judgment not being appealed becomes *Rechtskraft* (*res judicata*), that is to say that once decided, an issue may not be litigated again except in the way provided by law. In this regard, a difference has to be made between *formelle Rechtskraft* (formal *res judicata* or unappealability of a judgment) and *materielle Rechtskraft* (substantial *res judicata* or force of a final judgment). *Formelle Rechtskraft* (§ 705 ZPO) means that a decision can no longer be challenged and therefore it stands for the unappealability of a decision. The unappealability of decisions may be established by the expiry of the period to appeal, with a waiver to lodge an appeal and with a last-instance judgment becoming final. The *materielle Rechtskraft* is the force of a final judgment and binds the courts and the participating parties in a later trial dealing with the same matter in controversy or only with aspects of it which are decisive for the new trial. But the force of a final judgment is limited as follows: it exists only between the participating parties ("*inter partes*", § 325 I ZPO); a decision may become final and absolute as far as an asserted claim has been adjudicated (§ 322 I ZPO); and the legal force concerns only facts of the case which have been present in the last hearing. As a matter of principle, a final and absolute judgment cannot be repealed unless one of the exceptions laid down in law is given such as the restoration (§§ 233 *et seq.* ZPO). Examples of this are the petition to modify a judgment (§ 323 ZPO) and the reopening of an appeal (§§ 578 *et seq.* ZPO).

The *Verfügung* (order), as another judicial decision, is an instruction to conduct proceedings such as the setting down for trial (§ 216 I ZPO) or the order of written pre-trial (§ 272 ZPO). In contrast to judgments, orders are not final and absolute but can be changed at any time. A further measure to influence a suit is the *Beschluß* (court order or ruling or decision) which is a decision delivered by a court without a court hearing (except for § 91 a ZPO). Unlike a judgment the *Beschluß* is not subject to the formal requirements of judgments listed in § 313 ZPO and does not bind a trial court.

11. RIGHT OF APPEAL (*RECHTSMITTEL*)

Under the Code of Civil Procedure, a judicial decision can be challenged by filing a right of appeal. Typical features of rights of appeal are that the next highest court gives a ruling on the appeal (devolutive effect) and, that the appeal postpones the entry of the unappealability of the challenged judgment (suspensive effect). These features are decisive in order to distinguish rights of appeal from so-called *Rechtsbehelfe* (legal redress) — such as notice of objection to a judgment of default (§ 338 ZPO) — because legal addresses have no devolutive effect: the same court decides appeal.

The Code of Civil Procedure contains three different kinds of rights of appeal: the *Berufung* (appeal), the *Revision* (appeal on points of law) and the *Beschwerde* (request for relief from a court order): in order to be successful, rights of appeal have to be admissible and well-founded. The decision of the court to be challenged must be appealable and the appeal must be lodged in due form and time. The party may only lodge a right of appeal as far as he is aggrieved by the decision under appeal. The decision appealed from can only be amended as it has been applied for and, in addition, applying for a harsher judgment under appeal against the appellant is forbidden by the principle of *reformatio in peius* if only one party has lodged the appeal (§§ 536, 559 ZPO).

A. Appeal (*Berufung*)

A right of appeal is the *Berufung* which takes place against final judgments of first instance (§§ 511 to 544 ZPO). Therefore, only final judgments of first instance are appealable — for example those rendered by *Amtsgerichte* or *Landgerichte*; the sum involved having to be more than DM1.500. The appeal has to be lodged in due form and time by counsel, namely, within one month after the judgment has been served or — as far as no service of judgment has taken place — within five months after judgment has been pronounced (§ 516 ZPO). For the submitting of the statement of grounds for appeal, there is another month time limit (§ 519 ZPO).

The appeal is heard by the Court of Appeal which may be either the *Landgericht* competent for judgments rendered by the *Amtsgericht*, or *Oberlandesgericht* competent for judgments of the *Landgericht* (see Schedules 2 and 3).[18] The court of appeal reviews the whole case and the case will be reheard on both points of facts and law. The parties may submit new allegations, facts and offers of evidence.

An appeal is well-founded as far as the judgment under appeal has been issued contrary to law. In this case the judgment under appeal will be quashed, and the Court of Appeal gives its own ruling on the case. Alternatively, the case can also be referred to the lower court which will then render its decision (but this is quite seldom). An inadmissible appeal is dismissed on procedural grounds.

B. Appeal on points of law (*Revision*)

An appeal on points of law takes place in the court of third instance after an appeal has been unsuccessful (§§ 545 to 566a ZPO). Only judgments of the Court of Appeal which — as a rule — are the judgments of the *Oberlandesgericht* are subject to appeal. The sum involved has to be more than DM60.000. In the remaining cases, the Court of Appeal must expressly grant a particular leave for appeal which may be granted because of the fundamental importance of the lawsuit or a deviation by the appellate judgment from the adjudication of the *Bundesgerichts-*

---

[18] For more details, see *ibid.*, Chap. Six, 1, B.

hof. The appeal on points of law has to be lodged by counsel with the *Bundesgerichtshof* within one month after judgment has been served or — if judgment has not been served — within five months after the judgment has been pronounced. There is another month time limit for filing the *Revisionsbegründungsschrift* (statement of grounds for appeal). In this statement, counsel must specify to what extent the judgment under appeal will be challenged and set forth the grounds of appeal which may only be a violation of substantive law, so that the infringed rule of law has to be named, or a violation of procedural law, so that the facts founding this violation must be submitted and specified.

The court of last resort — the *Bundesgerichtshof* — hears and reviews the case but only on points of law. The appeal on points of law is well founded as far as a *Revisionsgrund* (ground for appeal) is at hand. If this is the case, the court of last resort may remand the case to the Court of Appeal which will render a decision while it takes into consideration the legal view of the court of last resort. Such a remand to the appellate court will be carried out, if an investigation of the facts of the case becomes necessary before a judgment may be rendered. If the appellate judgment contains only a mistake in applying the law, the court of last resort will render its own decision.

C. Request for relief from a court order (*Beschwerde*)

The request for relief from a court order is a further right of appeal (§§ 567 to 577 ZPO). This request for relief is not a reversal of a judgment like the rights of appeal mentioned above but a reversal of intermediate court orders (like *Beschlüsse*, *Verfügungen*[19]). The request for relief is admissible and available in cases prescribed by law. There is for instance the *einfache Beschwerde* (ordinary appeal from a court order) which is an appeal not subject to a time limit, or the *sofortige Beschwerde* (immediate appeal from a court order) which must be filed within the statutory two-week period. The request for relief is heard by the court of next instance. The court order will be reviewed on points of facts and law. It is not prescribed by law to conduct a court hearing. The appellate court will give a ruling by court order which can only be appealed with the *weitere Beschwerde* (further appeal on points of law) if new reasons for complaint can be presented.

---

[19] For more details, see *ibid.*, Chap. Six, 10.

12. SPECIAL PROCEEDINGS

A. PROCEDURE BEFORE THE LOCAL COURT (*AMTSGERICHTE*)

The Code of Civil Procedure sets forth a few procedural particularities in order to simplify the process before the *Amtsgerichte.* Due to this aim, in these courts no mandatory representation by lawyers is generally necessary — unless certain child and family cases have to be dealt with (§ 78 I ZPO) — because it is presumed by law that cases with a low value in dispute are generally more simple and can be conducted by the parties without counsel. A further simplification in proceedings before the *Amtsgericht* is that in cases with a value in dispute below DM1.200 it is left to the discretion of the court how to conduct proceedings (§ 495 a I ZPO); a court can order a written trial and only has to hear the case on application.

B. DEFAULT PROCEEDINGS (*VERSÄUMNISVERFAHREN*)

The *Versäumnisverfahren* (default proceedings) are governed under §§ 330 *et seq.* ZPO as an exception from the principle of orality. The default proceedings deal with the legal situation when a party fails to appear in court and rests on the idea that a legal dispute has to be concluded in case one litigant fails to cooperate in the trial. If a party fails to appear in court, a *Versäumnisurteil* (judgment by default) is rendered — on application by the remaining party.[20] In case of the plaintiff's non-attendance, action is dismissed and, if the defendant fails to appear, the statement of claim is regarded as admitted and the defendant suffers a judgment by default for the plaintiff. But the latter presupposes that the action is conclusive and that none of the grounds enumerated in §§ 335 and 337 ZPO are present precluding the rendering of the judgment by default; such a ground is, for instance, that the summons to appear has not been duly served upon the defendant.

The party who has failed to appear may lodge the *Einspruch* (objection) against the judgment by default. The objection has to be lodged within a two-week period after the judgment has been served. An inadmissible objection is overruled. An admissible objection puts the trial back to the legal situation

---

[20] A judgment by defaut is rendered in a written pre-trial (§ 331 III ZPO), if the defendant fails to show his intention of defence within the time period (§ 276 I, II ZPO).

before the entry of the default judgment. The legal dispute then continues to proceed.

C. TRIAL BY RECORD (*URKUNDENPROZEß*), SUMMARY BILL-ENFORCEMENT PROCEDURE (*WECHSELPROZEß*) AND CHEQUE PROCEEDINGS (*SCHECKPROZEß*)

The Code of Civil Procedure provides summary proceedings for claims, the requirements of which may be proved by records in order to obtain a (provisional) title for execution within a short period of time. One such proceeding is the *Urkundenprozeß* (trial by record). The trial by record is governed under §§ 592 to 600 ZPO and is a summary procedure available for claims for a specified sum or quantity where the plaintiff relies entirely on documentary evidence. In practice, a quite important form of the trial by record is the summary bill-enforcement procedure (§§ 602 to 604 ZPO) and the cheque proceedings (§ 605a ZPO) which — except for a few particularies (like short periods for serving the summons) — are generally conducted like the trial by record the principles of which are outlined below.

In addition to the general procedural requirements to be met by any civil suit, an action in the trial by record can exclusively be a claim for a specified sum or quantity, and the facts founding the claim in favour of the plaintiff must be entirely provable by documents or party's interrogation (§ 592 ZPO); this restriction applies as well to the statement of the defendant. Counterclaims are excluded (§ 595 I ZPO). The restriction to these means of evidence is designed to speed up the procedure. Because of these limitations only a provisional judgment — the *Vorbehaltsurteil* — is rendered which, nevertheless, is already an enforceable instrument. Subsequent to this trial — in cases where the defendant has reserved his rights — the *Nachverfahren* (subsequent proceedings) will follow which is an ordinary procedure without restriction on any evidence. The case is re-heard and the asserted claim is reviewed under considerations of all offered evidence.

D. SUMMARY PROCEEDINGS FOR AN ORDER TO PAY DEBTS (*MAHNVERFAHREN*)

The summary proceedings for an order to pay debts are laid down in §§ 688 to 703d ZPO. It is a quick, cheap and simple way for the plaintiff in undisputed claims to obtain, without a court hearing, a title for execution. These kind of proceedings are only available for pecuniary claims of a monetary debt or a definite amount of money. Proceedings are set in motion with the filing of a *Mahnantrag* (application for a default summons) with the *Amtsgericht* irrespective of the sum involved. The court will only review the application with regard to whether the asserted claim is reasonably determined, can be distinguished from other claims and whether there is a probability that the claim exists. As far as these requirements can be confirmed, the court will issue the *Mahnbescheid* (default summons); otherwise the application will be dismissed.

The default summons can be appealed by the respondent. He can challenge the default summons by lodging a *Widerspruch* (protest or objection) within two weeks after it has been serviced (§ 694 ZPO). A timely lodged protest will transfer the legal affair to trial court. Then the legal dispute becomes pending in court and will be conducted like any normal litigious procedure.

If a protest has not been lodged in due time, the court will, on the applicant's motion, issue the *Vollstreckungsbescheid* (writ of execution). The writ of execution can be appealed by an *Einspruch* (objection) filed within two weeks after the writ of execution has been serviced (§ 700 III ZPO). With the objection, the matter in dispute becomes pending and an ordinary litigation procedure will now be conducted. As far as no protest has been lodged in due time, the writ of execution becomes non-appealable and is a title for execution.

E. Proceedings in family law cases

The Code of Civil Procedure governs proceedings in family law cases as well as an ordinary procedure unless the described particularities of §§ 606 to 638 ZPO apply. In law, family law cases are regarded as matrimonial cases — such as divorce suits, actions for a judicial declaration on the existence or non-existence of a marriage — and the other family law areas such as parental care and custody. These cases are only heard by family courts which have an exclusive jurisdiction. The *Familiengericht* (family court) at the *Amtsgericht* will deal with such a case on first instance. Its judgment under appeal will be heard by the *Familiensenat* (family law panel) at the *Oberlandesgericht* (see Schedules 2 and 3).[21]

As an exception to the general principle outlined above, in the family courts at the *Amtsgericht* the participating parties have to be represented by a lawyer admitted to practice before the

[21] For more details, see *ibid.*, Chap. Six, 1, B.

respective court (§ 78 II ZPO). A further particularity is that the public is excluded; family law proceedings have to be conducted in private (§ 170 GVG). Moreover, the principle of party presentation is restricted with the result that the court is not bound by parties' statements, pleadings and offers of evidence. The principle of party disposition applies in a restricted way too; for instance, in divorce proceedings the court *ex officio* will investigate the case. Further particularities are that divorce proceedings are started with the submission of an *Antragsschrift* (written application), and both the divorce dispute at first instance and further pending family cases in this matter will be united in one proceeding. All family cases within this union are called *Folgesachen* (ancillary proceedings in divorce cases). The purpose behind this is to obtain one judgment which contains the divorce dispute and the ancillary proceedings in divorce cases.

F. PROCEEDINGS IN PARENT AND CHILD CASES

For proceedings in parent and child cases — such as actions for declaration of the parent-child relationship, actions to establish paternity (§ 641 ZPO) or actions for the denial of legitimacy (§§ 1593 *et seq.* ZPO), the general rules of the Code of Civil Procedure apply. The *Amtsgericht* not the family court hears parent and child cases; with the *Oberlandesgericht* competent to decide appeals (see Schedules 2 and 3). Proceedings are not open to the public (§ 170 GVG). Contrary to family law cases — the participating parties need not be represented by a lawyer admitted to the bar. Proceedings will be conducted as any ordinary litigation as far as no procedural particularities of the family law cases — as outlined below — apply.

G. ARBITRATION PROCEEDINGS (*SCHIEDSGERICHTSVERFAHREN*)

The *Schiedsgerichtsverfahren* (arbitration proceedings) are governed by §§ 1025 *et seq.* ZPO and take place before the courts of arbitration which are not national but private courts. Instead of calling the national court, parties may agree to settle their disputes before a court of arbitration. In practice, this is quite common in disputes between shareholders or disputes concerning commercial affairs. Parties may set up a *Schiedsvertrag* (arbitration treaty) in which they can regulate in detail, for instance, the procedural rules and determine the arbitrator in advance. Arbitration proceedings are terminated by a *Schiedsspruch* (arbitration award) which has the same effect as a final judgment. An arbitration award can be enforced after a national court has stated it to be an enforceable instrument.

H. LAW CONCERNING COSTS

Obviously judicial proceedings are not free of charge. The State demands *Gerichtskosten* (court fees) for the activity of the courts; these fees should recover the expenses of administering justice as far as possible. In addition, the instructed lawyer demands remuneration for his activity which is called *Rechtsanwaltsgebühr* (lawyer's fee).[22]

With the commencement of an action or appeal, court fees must be paid by the plaintiff or appellant; otherwise no service of action or appeal will take place. After proceedings have been concluded, the court will impose the duty to bear the costs on the party which has lost the case (§ 91 ZPO). In other words: the unsuccessful party will be the party primarily liable for all legal costs. Court fees are *Gebühren* and *Auslagen* (expenses). Fees are flat rates, irrespective of the actual amount of work done. Their individual amount depends on the sum involved, and its calculation is carried out in accordance with the rules laid down in §§ 3 to 9 ZPO and §§ 12 *et seq.* GKG. The *Kostenverzeichnis* (costs schedule) determines how many fees have arisen.

The remuneration of a lawyer is laid down in the *Bundesrechtsanwaltsgebührenordnung* (Attorney's Fees Act). Lawyer's fees are flat rates, independent from the actual amount of work done. Fees are ascertained according to the procedure carried out, such as a *Verfahrensgebühr* (court fees of proceedings), a *Beweisgebühr* (court fee for evidence — §§ 31 *et seq.* BRAGO). Their individual amount acts in accordance with the respective sum involved. Nevertheless, parties are free to agree a remuneration deviating from the Attorney's Fees Act (§ 3 BRAGO), such as a remuneration according to an agreed hourly rate; a payment by result, however, is inadmissible.

In any suit the court renders a cost order *ex officio* (§§ 91 *et seq.* ZPO) in the operative part of the judgment and — as a rule — a cost order can only be appealed together with the judgment. The cost order states which party has to bear court and lawyer's fees as well as the expenses. As a matter of principle, the loosing party has to bear any legal costs (§ 91 ZPO). But the costs will be split as far as both parties have partly succeeded and are partly defeated, namely, each side has to bear half the court costs and its own lawyer's fees and expenses (§ 92 ZPO). If the

---

[22] For more details, see *ibid.*, Chap. Four, 2, B.

defendant has not given any cause for the commencement of action and has accepted the claim at once, the costs are imposed on the plaintiff (§ 93 ZPO). Finally, if a party unsuccessfully appeals a decision, the court imposes the arisen legal costs on this party (§ 97 I ZPO). After the court has given ruling as to the costs, the *Kostenerstattungsanspruch* (entitlement to costs) is furnished. The successful party may claim its legal costs from the losing party. But before he may claim the costs, the court must determine them. The arisen costs will be determined — on application — by an order of determining the costs (§ 104 ZPO). Such an order is a title for execution.

I. CIVIL LEGAL AID (*PROZEßKOSTENHILFE*)

With regard to high legal costs arising in civil proceedings, there are people who are not able to conduct legal proceedings because they cannot afford to pay the costs and, due to this, a justified prosecution or defence of a case would have been left undone. The *Prozeßkostenhilfe* which is laid down in §§ 114 to 127 ZPO is a compromise between the striving for an improved individual protection of the law and the economic possibilities of the State.

The grant of civil legal aid for the benefit of a party has certain requirements to be met. The intended prosecution of the case must have a reasonable prospect of success and not seem to be mischievous. The party's personal and financial relations as they stand at the time of passing the resolution are relevant. The proceedings are instituted by a motion for legal aid with the trial court. The trial court enters a decision by order. In every instance, the grant of legal aid is separately decided. Legal aid covers the entire cost of proceedings. The respective party, however, has to use his property in order to pay the legal costs provided that it can still be regarded as reasonable. In this case, a special schedule will be set up which determines up to which amount a party itself has to bear the costs of an action. Otherwise, the State pays the arisen costs.

13. EXECUTION ENFORCEMENT (*ZWANGSVOLLSTRECKUNG*)

A. PREREQUISITES

Execution proceedings are laid down in the eighth book of the Code of Civil procedure. Its first part (§§ 704 to 802 ZPO) prescribes the general requirements for the enforcement and determines judicial remedies; the second part (§§ 803 to 898

ZPO) governs in detail the different measures to levy execution. Execution proceedings are initiated by one creditor (party holding a legally enforceable claim) and an object of the property of the debtor is liable for execution. This procedure has to be distinguished from bankruptcy proceedings which is intended to satisfy all creditors of a debtor and, due to this, the entire property of the creditor is subject to execution and will be realised. Bankruptcy proceedings are still regulated in the *Konkursordnung* (Bankruptcy Act), *Vergleichsordnung* (Law on Composition Proceedings) and the *Gesamtvollstreckungsordnung* (Law on Universal Execution) but will be replaced by the new *Insovenzrecht* (Insolvency Law) which will enter into force on January 1, 1999.

But now we get back to the execution proceedings governed under the Code of Civil Proceedings: if a defendant does not voluntarily perform and fulfil his duties laid down in a judgment or court order, the creditor can file a demand for execution. The execution will then enforce the rights and claims laid down in the *Vollstreckungstitel* (title for execution). Judicially enforceable instruments are judgments (§ 704 ZPO) or other titles enumerated in § 794 ZPO, such as writs of execution, court settlements, court costs orders or enforceable notarial deeds drawn up by a notary.

The *Vollstreckungsorgan* (official organ for enforcement by execution) — for instance the court competent for enforcement measures or a bailiff — will examine whether the statutory requirements for execution are met; only then will measures to levy execution be carried out. At first, the creditor must file a demand for execution. Then, there has to be a title for execution bearing a *Vollstreckungsklausel* (court certificate of enforceability). Next, the service of the title for execution upon the debtor must be carried out. As far as the execution of the enforceable instrument depends on further prerequisites — such as a creditor's counter-performance, entry of a fixed calendar day or rendered security by the creditor — these requirements must also be fulfilled before steps to levy execution can be conducted. These requirements are examined *ex officio* by the *Vollstreckungsorgan*. Obstacles to execution — such as suspension of execution or debtor's bankruptcy — are only reviewed, if raised by one party. After affirming these requirements, the *Vollstreckungsorgan* fixes the enforcement measures which it will choose in accordance with the respective content of the executory title, *i.e.* different claims — such as monetary claims, claims for delivery or recovery of goods, claims for a specific performance or decrees according to which the defendant must give a certain declaration of intention — are enforced in different ways as outlined below.

B. ENFORCEMENT ON ACCOUNT OF MONEY DUE (*VOLLSTRECKUNG WEGEN GELDFORDERUNGEN*)

The executory title can be a monetary claim. In order to enforce such a claim, the relevant rules are laid down in §§ 803 to 882 a ZPO. As a rule, these claims will be enforced by attaching goods and their later realisation in order to meet the claim.

Bewegliche Sachen (movable property) can be liable to seizure. These proceedings are governed under §§ 808 to 827 ZPO and conducted by the *Gerichtsvollzieher* (bailiff) as *Vollstreckungsorgan*. Execution starts while the bailiff effects a seizure on the debtor's personal property. He may carry out execution by the writ of delivery of the debtor's valuable property or by seizing his valuable property. But in any case, the bailiff does not investigate property relations. Later, the seized objects are sold in public auction.

Forderungen (debts) or other rights are also liable to execution; proceedings are laid down in §§ 828 to 863 ZPO. The *Vollstreckungsgericht* (court competent for enforcement matters) — which is the *Amtsgericht* at the debtor's domicile or general residence — is the *Vollstreckungsorgan* (official organ for enforcement by execution). Execution is enforced by issuing a *Pfändungs- und Überweisungsbeschluß* (attachment order and transfer of garnished claim) and the respective procedure is as follows: after the creditor has lodged the petition for execution in which he identifies the debt to be collected, the court will review — besides the general requirements mentioned above — whether the debt to be collected is in existence and, in addition, is assignable. As far as the court can confirm these requirements, it will issue an attachment order, in which the respective debt is named and specified, the garnishee[23] is forbidden to pay the debtor and the debtor is informed that he is not allowed to dispose of this debt in any way. When the attachment order is served on the garnishee it is recognised in law. The next step is that the court will transfer the garnished claim to the creditor; in practice, the transfer is often performed together with the attachment order.

The execution imposed on the debtor's *unbewegliche Vermögen* (immovable property) is set forth in §§ 864 to 871 ZPO. The law provides different ways to execute immovable property — such as land and property treated as real property. The creditor's claim can be enforced while a *Zwangshypothek* (mortgage registered to enforce judgment debt) is registered in the

[23] A person who has been warned not to pay a debt to anyone other than the third party who has obtained judgment against the debtor's own creditor.

land register. This is undertaken by the *Grundbuchamt* (Land Registry) as the competent *Vollstreckungsorgan* on a corresponding petition of the creditor. In this case, his claim is not immediately satisfied but is a security out of which the creditor may take action.

Judicial execution imposed on the debtor's immovable property can also be carried out in the *Zwangsversteigerung* (sale by court order) which is the sale of property seized in execution in auctions ordered by court. Another possibility is the *Zwangsverwaltung* (sequestration or judicial enforced receivership) which is the administration of real property by an administrator appointed by the court in order to receive the rents and profits thereof. Details on how to conduct these proceedings — are laid down in the *Gesetz über die Zwangsversteigerung und Zwangsverwaltung* (Law on Compulsory Sale of Real Property and Sequestration). Any measure to conduct these proceedings is ordered by the court competent for execution of civil judgments.

C. EXECUTION ON ACCOUNT OF CLAIMS OTHER THAN MONETARY CLAIMS (*ZWANGSVOLLSTRECKUNG WEGEN ANDERER ANSPRÜCHE ALS GELDFORDERUNGEN*)

The creditor might also like to enforce his executory title which states a claim for delivery or recovery of goods. The relevant provisions to levy execution of such a kind are laid down in §§ 883 to 886 ZPO. The law distinguishes between different circumstances of the case and between whether the respective object is in custody of the debtor or a third party: if the respective good — which may be personal or real property — is in debtor's custody, the bailiff, as competent *Vollstreckungsorgan* will seize the good, deliver it to the creditor and restore the creditor's possession by that means. If the good is in the custody of a third party who denies the delivery, the bailiff is not allowed to seize the good. The claim for delivery will be enforced while the court, competent on enforcement matters (as the *Vollstreckungsorgan*), issues an attachment order and transfer of garnished claim. That is to say the creditor's claim for delivery against the third party will be attached and afterwards the garnished claim will be transferred to the creditor.

The debtor to an executory title can also be obliged to perform a certain act, to acquiesce in the plaintiff's acts or to refrain from certain acts. A debtor refusing to do so can be enforced to meet his obligation by the *Prozeßgericht erster Instanz* (trial court of first instance) which is the *Vollstreckungsorgan*. Proceedings governed by §§ 887 to 893 ZPO differentiate between the type of act to be enforced. A *vertretbare Handlung* (fungible act) which does not have to be performed by the debtor can be enforced while the trial court orders that the creditor or somebody else may carry out the fungible act at the expense of the debtor. An *unvertretbare Handlung* (non-fungible act) can also be liable for execution which is an act requiring personal performance by the debtor. This non-fungible act is enforced while the trial court imposes measures — such as a fine or a term of imprisonment — on the debtor in order to enforce performance. Next the debtor is obliged to acquiesce in the plaintiff's acts or refrain from certain acts, the trial court will impose a measure — such as a fine or a term of imprisonment — on the debtor in order to enforce compliance.

Finally, the debtor may be obliged by a decree to give a certain declaration of intent. Such an obligation cannot be enforced. But it is presumed by law that the debtor has made the respective declaration of intent as soon as the judgment becomes final, *i.e.* unappealable (§ 894 ZPO).

D. REMEDIES

As long as execution proceedings continue — namely: have been set going and have not yet been concluded — parties being affected by unlawful measures to levy execution have certain judicial remedies at hand. A party concerned may be a debtor, a creditor or a third party.

Any of these parties involved may file a *Vollstreckungserinnerung* (complaint against a measure of execution — § 766 ZPO) and may raise the objection that the respective *Vollstreckungsorgan* has carried out a step to levy execution which does not comply with the procedural requirements of execution. The court competent for enforcement matters will decide upon such a complaint.

Moreover, an appeal against a decision ordered by the court can be challenged only with filing the *sofortige Beschwerde* (immediate appeal, § 793 ZPO). With regard to this, an objection can be raised that the order, for instance, does not comply with the formal requirements of execution.

With filing a *Vollstreckungsgegenklage* (action raising an objection to judgment claim) the debtor — who is the only entitled party — pleads on the merits (§ 767 ZPO). He may raise the objection that the substantive claim to be enforced in execution proceedings does not exist. He has to substantiate his objections which may only be based on circumstances which have arisen after the final court hearing; for instance the creditor has waived the debt or the debtor has paid his debt thereafter. The action can only rest on new circumstances because otherwise the *lis pendens* of the judgment would prejudice the action.

The *Drittwiderspruchsklage* (third-party action against execution) is an action of a third party who demands the elimination of enforcement measures on property which does not belong to the debtor (§ 771 ZPO). It is a possibility that the third party can prove, for example, that the bailiff has not attached the property of the debtor but the personal property of the third party.

Finally, with the *Klage auf vorzugsweise Befriedigung* (action for preferential satisfaction) a further creditor of the debtor can demand satisfaction from an object liable for execution before the creditor can levy execution (§ 805 ZPO).

14. INTERLOCUTORY JUDICIAL RELIEF

The course of civil procedure — often over several stages — takes a long time before a final judgment is issued. During this time the creditor's rights may be endangered and, due to this, an interim regulation is necessary to secure claims or relationships. The Code of Civil Procedure provides summary proceedings seeking for interlocutory regulations or protection of rights or legal relationships, such as *Arrest* (civil arrest by court order) and *einstweilige Verfügung* (temporary injunction). Interlocutory judicial relief can be referred to as an injunction known in English civil litigation as the *Mareva* injunction (see *Mareva Compania Naviera SA v. International Bulkcarriers SA* [1975] 2 Lloyd's Rep. 509).

A. CIVIL ARREST BY COURT ORDER (*ARREST*)

Civil arrest by a court order is laid down in §§ 916 *et seq.* ZPO. It is a court order in a special procedure to obtain security for a future execution to satisfy a monetary claim or a claim which may become a money claim. There are two forms of civil arrest: the *dinglicher Arrest* (attachment or seizure) which is the seizure to preserve debtor's property in dispute, and the (seldom enforced) *persönlicher Arrest* (arrest of debtor) which is the detention of the debtor. Both forms have the same prerequisites.

First of all, an appellant seeking a civil arrest must have an *Arrestanspruch* (claim for arrest) which is a pecuniary claim or a claim which may become a pecuniary claim, whose future execution must be secured. The appellant has to set out such a claim for arrest. In addition, the appellant must demonstrate that there is an *Arrestgrund* (urgent reason for granting an order of civil arrest). This is the case when present reasons endanger future execution unless an order of civil arrest is to be issued; for instance, the appellant has to show in detail that the respondent is dissipating or removing property secretly or dishonestly and thereby preventing him from execution against the respondent's property. The appellant is able to start proceedings while filing an *Arrestgesuch* (application for a writ of attachment) in which he has to specify and to show the probable cause of both the claim and the reason for granting an order of civil arrest. In these summary proceedings, the appellant only has to furnish prima facie evidence for the existence of the claim and the reason. The means of proof are restricted to immediately available evidence; an *eidesstattliche Versicherung* (affidavit) is admissible too. Furnishing prima facie evidence with a lower standard of proof is the characteristic feature of temporary injunctions and distinguishes them from ordinary proceedings in which any party has to prove the prerequisites being beneficial to him. After filing the application, the *Arrestgericht* (competent court for arrest proceedings) hears the case and issues a judicial decision by order or judgment. This decision can be appealed by the opponent's objection and the competent court will then render a final judgment upon objection.

B. TEMPORARY INJUNCTION (*EINSTWEILIGE VERFÜGUNG*)

A temporary injunction is a provisional order obtained from a court on application of a party (§§ 935 *et seq.* ZPO). It may be issued in order to prevent a likely change of existing conditions which may render impossible or at least substantially more difficult, the realisation of one of the party's rights. This is the *Sicherungsverfügung* (preventive injunction) which secures a non-monetary claim, such as a claim for return of personal property. The *Regelungsverfügung* (regulative injunction) as another form of injunction is a preliminary adjudication of a dispute which is necessary for the prevention of substantial damage or for other reasons. This tries to settle disputes arising from a legal relationship, such as regulation in tenancy disputes. Contrary to the injunctions just mentioned, the *Leistungsverfügung* (injunction to perform the claim) as a third kind of injunction is not regulated in the Code of Civil Procedure but is specified by the courts. This injunction not only secures a claim but temporarily satisfies it, especially in maintenance cases in which the appellant needs an amount of money to meet the necessities of life. The procedure of the temporary injunction is conducted in a similar way to the civil arrest proceedings outlined above.

Schedule 2: Sequence of Courts starting from the *Amtsgericht*

First Instance		
Amtsgericht all pecuniary cases with a sum involved of not more than DM10.000 and all allotted cases, such as tenancy disputes (§ 23 No. 1, 2 GVG) One judge (§ 22 GVG)	***Amtsgericht*** Parent and Child Cases (§ 23a GVG) One judge (§ 22 GVG)	***Amtsgericht*** Family Law Cases (§ 23b GVG) One judge (§ 22 GVG)

Appeal

Second Instance	
***Landgericht* (§ 72 GVG)** *Zivilkammer* (Civil division) three judges (§ 75 ZPO)	***Oberlandesgericht* (§ 119 GVG)** *Familiensenat* (Family division) three judges (§ 122 I GVG

Schedule 3: Sequence of Courts starting from the *Landgericht*

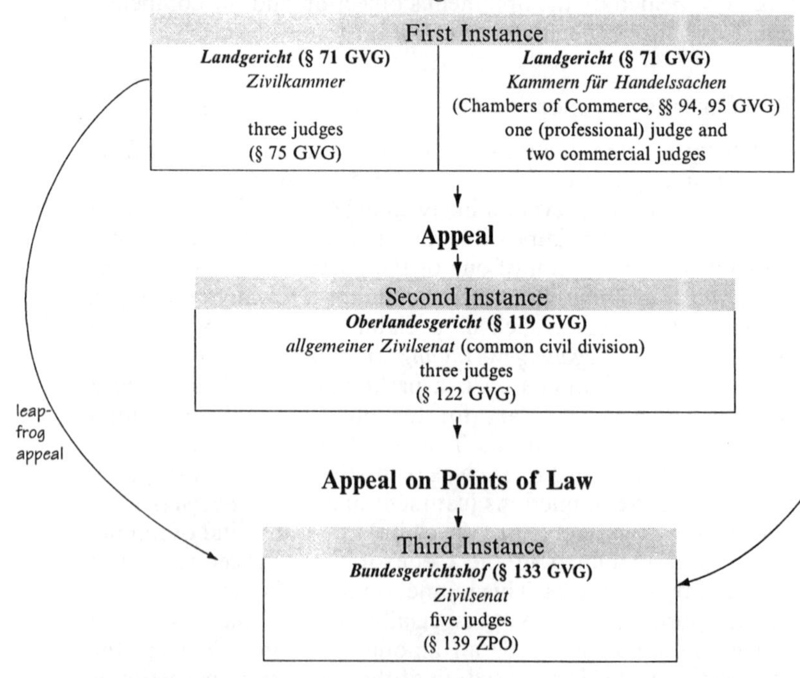

NOTE: a leap-frog appeal (566a ZPO) happens when the judgment is appealed and the opponent has consented to it. It occurs in cases in which the facts are clear and undisputed but legal questions of fundamental importance have to be decided. Then a second instance trial is unnecessary and the case will go straight to be heard in the *Bundesgerichtshof.*

SELECTED BIBLIOGRAHY

I. Commentaries

Baumbach, Lauterbach, Albers, Hartmann, *Zivilprozeßordnung* (56th ed. 1997).
Böttcher, *Gesetz über die Zwangsversteigerung und Zwangsverwaltung* (2nd ed. 1996).
Lüke, Walchshöfer, *Münchener Kommentar zur Zivilprozeßordnung*: Vol. 1: §§ 1–354, (1992); Vol. 2: §§ 355–802 (1992); Vol. 3: §§ 803–1048, EGZPO, GVG, EGGVG, IZPR (1992).
Thomas, Putzo, *Zivilprozeßordnung* (21st ed. 1998).
Kropholler, *Europäisches Zivilprozeßrecht* (6th ed. 1998).
Zöller, *Zivilprozeßordnung* (20th ed. 1997).

II. Textbooks

Arens, Lüke, *Zivilprozeßrecht* (6th ed. 1994).
Becht, *Einführung in die Praxis des Zivilprozesses* (1995).
Brox, *Allgemeiner Teil des Bürgerliches Gesetzbuch* (20th ed. 1996)
Jauerning, *Zwangsvollstreckungs- und Insolvenzrecht* (20th ed. 1996).
Medicus, *Bürgerliches Recht* (17th ed. 1996).
Rosenberg, Schwab, Gottwald, *Zivilprozeßrecht* (15th ed. 1993).
Tempel, *Materielles Recht im Zivilprozeß* (2nd ed. 1992).

Chapter Seven
Criminal Court Structure and Procedure

1. Criminal Procedure and its Legal Sources

The task of the *Strafverfahren* (criminal proceedings) is to prosecute criminal offences. Provisions carrying criminal penalties can mainly be found in the *Strafgesetzbuch* (Penal or Criminal Code) which governs whether an act or omission is regarded as a *Straftat* (criminal offence).

The answer to questions like how to prosecute a criminal offence; which legal means can be exercised to investigate the truth of the case; which rules apply to reach a true and just judgment; and how the accused can be punished if found guilty are laid down in the *Strafprozeßordnung* (Code of Criminal Procedure). It is the task of this Code to prescribe a lawful prosecution of a criminal case and to serve the realisation of substantive criminal law. It is quite important to notice that in Germany the claim for punishment against an offender is a matter entirely for the State.

Given these introductory thoughts, the criminal process is subject to extensive statutory regulations from a committed offence to the investigation of the facts of the case until the passing and implementation of the sentence:

(a) The main procedural provisions concerning criminal proceedings are laid down in the *Strafprozeßordnung* — the Code of Criminal Procedure. There, legal rules can be found regulating all aspects of the criminal process like appeal procedure and the rights and duties of the participating parties (*e.g.* accused, defence attorney and public prosecutor).

(b) The *Jugendgerichtsgesetz* (Juvenile Court Act) can be regarded as a further legal source. This provides rules for the composition of the juvenile criminal courts division and certain procedural rules involving persons under the age of 21 years in a criminal process; these persons are called

Jugendliche (young persons) if aged between 14 to 18 years and *Heranwachsende* (young adults) if they are 18 to 21 years of age.

(c) Moreover, the *Gerichtsverfassungsgesetz* (Judicature Act) governs the organisation and composition of criminal courts, their jurisdiction, the appointment of lay judges, voting of adjudicative process and the organisational structure of the *Staatsanwaltschaften* (public prosecutor's office).

(d) Further procedural regulations are scattered in various acts. For instance, a few procedural provisions are still laid down in the Penal Code — such as the application for prosecution (§§ 77 to 77 d StGB) and limitation periods (§§ 78 to 79 b StGB). Service is dealt with in provisions of the Code of Civil Procedure (§§ 166 *et seq.* ZPO) to which the Code of Criminal Procedure refers (§ 37 StPO).

(e) The *Grundgesetz* contains a catalogue of fundamental human rights and is another important source of law. The requirements of a humane and fair criminal trial are especially shown and expressed in the basic rights (Articles 1 to 19 GG)[1] and the special, judicial basic rights (Articles 101, 103 and 104 GG).[2]

(f) Further fundamental procedural guarantees are laid down in the *Europäische Menschenrechtskonvention* (European Convention on Human Rights) which, as directly applicable domestic law, must comply with those basic rights laid down in the German *Grundgesetz*. As far as the guarantees under the European Convention are more extensive than those under the *Grundgesetz*, the latter must be interpreted in the light of the value system laid down in the European Convention — this method of legal interpretation is called *menschenrechtskonforme Auslegung* (interpretation in conformity with human rights).

(g) In addition to the statutory legislation, there are general instructions which are called the *Richtlinien für das Strafverfahren und das Bußgeldverfahren* (guidance of criminal proceedings and of summary proceedings concerning administrative penalties). From a legal point of view these instructions are administrative directives. In practice they are of great importance because they give a detailed prescription about the way public prosecutors must prosecute criminal offences and conduct criminal proceedings.

---

[1] For more details, see *ibid.*, Chap. Three, 7.

[2] For more details, see *ibid.*, Chap. Five, 1.

2. CRIMINAL JURISDICTION (*STRAFGERICHTSBARKEIT*)

From a theoretical point of view, criminal jurisdiction belongs to ordinary jurisdiction (§ 13 GVG)[3] and is organised on four levels. The hierarchy of criminal courts starts with the *Amtsgericht* (County Court) and is followed by the *Landgericht* (Regional Court) and the *Oberlandesgericht* (Regional Appeal Court); the highest criminal court in Germany is the *Bundesgerichtshof* (Federal High Court of Justice) in Karlsruhe.

A court has to review *ex officio* whether it is competent to hear a submitted case. At first, a court must be locally competent, and the local jurisdiction governs the distribution of tasks among the German criminal courts which have jurisdiction as regards the subject matter. Its rules can be found in §§ 7 *et seq.* StPO: the most important local jurisdictions are the place of the commission of an offence, the domicile of the accused before trial or the place of arrest.

In addition, the court must have jurisdiction as regards the subject matter. The subject matter jurisdiction is regulated in the Judicature Act. This Act sets forth which criminal court has jurisdiction to hear a criminal case at first, second or final instance (see Schedules 4, 5 and 6). Jurisdiction of first instance normally depends on the nature and gravity of the committed offence in the individual case; appeals are generally heard by the next highest court.

(a) The *Amtsgericht* is competent for cases of minor importance and gravity (see §§ 22 to 58 GVG). These are cases of a low to medium level of seriousness in which the penalty does not exceed four years imprisonment (§ 24 GVG). The *Amtsgericht* is composed differently, depending on the nature and gravity of the individual case.

- The *Einzelrichter* (single judge) has jurisdiction for cases involving less serious offences, for cases subject to private prosecution or where the maximum anticipated prison sentence does not exceed two years (§ 25 GVG).

- The *Schöffengericht* (court with lay judges) consisting of one professional judge and two lay judges has jurisdiction to hear all the other cases in which it is likely that the penalty will not exceed four years' imprisonment (§ 24 GVG).

---

[3] For more details, see *ibid.*, Chap. Five, 2, A.

- The *erweitertes Schöffengericht* (extended court with lay judges) hears more significant cases which require the additional expertise of a further professional judge because of the extent or seriousness of the offence. It is composed of more professional judges than the *Schöffengericht*.

(b) The *Landgericht* may act as the court of first or of second instance (see §§ 59 to 78 GVG). If it acts as court of first instance, the court's composition depends on the nature and gravity of the individual case.

- At first, proceedings may take place before the *große Strafkammer* (grand criminal division) which consists of two or three professional judges and two lay judges (§ 76 I and II GVG). It hears serious criminal cases unless it is not required to by the *Schwurgericht* (criminal chamber of the regional court) or by the criminal division of the *Oberlandesgericht*.

- The *Schwurgericht* hears cases as a jury court with three professional judges and two lay judges if one of the most serious criminal offences enumerated in the canon of §§ 74 I and II, 74 a and 74 c GVG (*e.g.* death of a victim after being raped, wilful homicide, murder or manslaughter) has been charged.

Additionally, the *Landgericht* hears appeals on points of fact and law against judgments of the *Amtsgericht* and appeals are decided by the *kleine Strafkammer* (minor panel chamber). This chamber consists of one or two professional judges and two or three lay assessors (§§ 74 III, 74 c I, 76 and II GVG).

(c) The *Oberlandesgericht* also has a multiple function because it may act as court of first, second and third instance (see §§ 115 to 122 GVG). At first instance, its senates (also called criminal divisions) consist of five professional judges responsible for hearing cases involving crimes which are directed against the security of the State; these offences are enumerated in § 120 GVG (including high treason, destruction of and damage to military installations, membership of illegal political organisations). Apart from this, the *Oberlandesgericht* also acts as court of second instance and hears appeals on fact and law from the *Landgericht*. Finally, it decides on appeals of law at third instance from the *Amtsgericht*.

(d) The *Bundesgerichtshof* acts only as a court of appeal of last resort (see §§ 123 to 140 GVG). It hears appeals on points of law from decisions of the *Landgericht* or *Oberlandesgericht* (§ 135 GVG). Decision is rendered in chambers which are composed of five professional judges.

As mentioned the court's composition is laid down in the Judicature Act and depends on the gravity and seriousness of the offence charged. A criminal court may consist exclusively of professional judges, or is composed with professional judges and *Schöffen* (lay judges). Especially at courts of first instance (*e.g. Amtsgericht* or *Landgericht*) lay judges[4] are members of the court (see Schedules 4 and 5) and have to decide — together with professional judges — about the question of guilt at the end of the hearing. Any German citizen may take office as lay judge for a period of four years, and lay judges are elected from a list by a committee formed at the *Amtsgericht* (§ 36 GVG). Once a single person has been chosen, it is quite difficult to refuse this task — which is seen as a service of the individual for the advantage of society.

Finally, we would like to draw your attention to the fact that the subject matter jurisdiction has to be distinguished from the *Strafgewalt* (punitive power) which a court may possess (see Schedule 4). This difference becomes quite obvious whenever the *Amtsgericht* is concerned because its punitive power is limited up to a penalty not exceeding four years imprisonment. This means that the *Amtsgerichte* may only pass a sentence of no more than a four years imprisonment. Whenever the *Amtsgericht* comes to the conclusion that a fair conviction in the respective case will go beyond its punitive power, its subject matter jurisdiction is terminated. Then, the *Amtsgericht* is obliged to transfer the case to the competent court (such as the *Landgericht* or *Oberlandesgericht* — § 270 StPO).

3. PRINCIPLES OF CRIMINAL PROCEDURE

A. PRINCIPLE OF A CONSTITUTIONAL STATE

In addition to the general principles for judicial proceedings,[5] the *Grundgesetz* provides — especially in criminal proceedings — further guarantees to ensure that justice is administered

---

[4] For more details, see *ibid.*, Chap. Four, 2, A, (2).

[5] For more details, see *ibid.*, Chap. Five, 1.

properly and in accordance with the rule of law. One of these guarantees is that there is no capital punishment. Article 102 GG simply states that "The death penalty is abolished". A threat of the imposition and enforcement of capital punishment in criminal law is prohibited therewith. In Germany, the maximum penalty which can be imposed is life imprisonment.

A further guarantee is the constitutional prohibition on the retroactivity of criminal law. It is said in Article 103 II GG that "An act may be punished only if it constituted a criminal offence under the law before it was committed". Due to this norm, it is forbidden to impose a penalty on someone that had not come into operation at the time of commission of the offence. In addition, this principle states more generally that no punishment can be exercised unless it is explicitly ordered by law — a fundamental rule of law which is commonly known as *nulla poena sine lege* (no sentence without law).

Furthermore, it is said in Article 103 III GG that: "Nobody may be punished for the same act more than once under general criminal legislation". This constitutional guarantee forbids multiple punishment which means that someone who has already been punished for an offence or been finally acquitted not guilty of an offence is safeguarded from being prosecuted and punished for this act a second time.

It is worth mentioning in this context the important guarantee in the event of deprivation of liberty which is laid down in Article 104 I GG. Thereafter, someone's liberty can be restricted only if the measure ordering a deprivation of liberty is based on a law which has been legislated by Parliament and is conducted in the way prescribed by that law.

The principle of the constitutional state also has a strong influence on procedural law. Due to it, procedure has to be conducted in accordance with fixed principles, has to take place before a legally determined (Article 101 I 1 GG) and independent (Article 97 I GG) judge[6] and has to guarantee the basic rights. Given this, the following principles must be exercised in each criminal trial:

- The accused is not allowed to be degraded to a mere object of inquiry — in other words, he has to remain a procedural subject with procedural rights (Articles 1 and 2 I GG).
- In addition, before a decision is taken affecting his rights, the accused must be heard. Before a court, anyone shall be

---

[6] For more details, see *ibid.*, Chap. Five, 1, C.

entitled to a hearing in accordance with the law (principle of a hearing in accordance with the law — Article 103 I GG).

- The investigation of an offence cannot be exercised with any measure and at any price because it is prohibited to use compulsory measures to influence the will of the individual (§ 136 a StPO). Any investigating measure is subjected to the principle of reasonableness.
- A conviction presupposes a doubtless proof of guilt because of the presumption of innocence (*in dubio pro reo*) which means that the accused has to be given the benefit of any doubts. A doubt as to the accused's guilt prevents a finding of guilt because a finding of guilt can be given only under the condition that the court is totally convinced of the guilt (see § 262 StPO).

B. PRINCIPLE OF *EX OFFICIO* PROCEEDINGS

The *Offizialmaxime* (principle of *ex officio* proceedings) which is laid down in § 152 I StPO means that as a rule only the public prosecutor's office is entitled to bring public charges. Therefore, punishment as the responsibility of the State, is enforced *ex officio* by national institutions irrespective of whether the victim requests punishment. Criminal procedure generally is a matter for the State, and the institution of private prosecution — where individual citizens request a punishment — is the only exception. This is limited to certain offences such as the *Antragsdelikte*[7] (which are offences requiring an application for prosecution by victims, relatives or superiors pursuant to §§ 77 *et seq.* StGB), the *Ermächtigungsdelikte* (which are offences demanding a particular authorisation for prosecution pursuant to § 77e StGB)[8] and *Privatklagedelikte* (private prosecution offences which are enumerated in the catalogue in § 374 StPO).[9]

C. PRINCIPLE OF ACCUSATION

The *Akkusationsmaxime* (principle of accusation) which is also called *Anklagegrundsatz* (principle of *ex officio* prosecution) finds its expression in §§ 151, 155 and 264 StPO. This

---

[7] *e.g.* wilfully causing bodily harm and negligent bodily harm (§§ 232, 223, 230 StGB), theft within the family (§§ 247, 242 StGB).

[8] *e.g.* vilification of the President of the Federal Republic (§ 90 IV StGB) and prosecution against foreign states (§ 104 a StGB).

[9] For more details, see *ibid.*, Chap. Seven, 12, A.

principle is best described with the words of a German legal saying: "*Wo kein Kläger, da kein Richter*" ("where there is no plaintiff, there is no judge"). It means that without a previous action no judicial inquiry takes place. Charges must be brought before a court initiated by an investigation. And preferring a charge against an accused is the task of the public prosecutor's office which is an institution independent of the courts.

This principle also effects judicial decisions because courts may only pass a sentence in relation to actions which have been subject to the preferring of a charge. If during trial further offences by the accused come to light which have not been charged so far, the public prosecutor may file a *Nachtragsanklage* (supplementary indictment, § 266 I StPO) in order to amend and supplement the charges; in these cases an appropriate legal caution may also be given by the court and an unrestricted judgment on these offences is rendered (§ 265 StPO).[10]

D. PRINCIPLE OF LEGALITY

The *Legalitätsprinzip* (principle of legality) is laid down in §§ 152 II, 170 I StPO and provides that prosecution of an offence is mandatory for the public prosecutor. It demands that the public prosecutor starts investigations once a sufficient suspicion arises and that he prefer charges in cases of sufficient suspicion of an offence. To be certain that this duty is properly performed, there is an offence called *Strafvereitelung im Amt* (obstruction of criminal prosecution by an officer of the law — § 258 StGB) which can be used against an official who breaches his duty. However, in certain cases a public prosecutor may refrain from prosecuting offences for pragmatic reasons under the premises specified in §§ 153 *et seq.* StPO (*Opportunitätsprinzip* — principle of discretionary prosecution).

E. PRINCIPLE OF INVESTIGATION

In Germany, criminal proceedings are not based on the system of party prosecution. It is not the task of the parties (*e.g.* prosecutor, accused and defence council) to provide the facts and judicial evidences to court. On the contrary: the *Untersuchungsgrundsatz* (principle of investigation) governs criminal proceedings; finding out the truth is carried out *ex officio* in preliminary investigations by public prosecutors and during the

---

[10] For more details, see *ibid.*, Chap. Seven, 9, C.

main trial by courts. The reason for this is that in criminal proceedings it is in the public interest to establish what really happened; the material truth should be discovered. The court is not bound by a party's applications and submissions but rather must find out the facts and therefore inquires itself into the facts of the case; the prosecuting agencies are obliged to perform comprehensive investigations in order to bring the facts and truth to light.

F. PRINCIPLE OF EXPEDITION AND OF IMMEDIACY

The *Beschleunigungsgrundsatz* (principle of expedition) is intended to speed up the procedure in order to keep it as short as possible, mainly for the benefit of the accused. The Code of Criminal Procedure provides procedural rules to keep the duration of proceedings to a minimum; for instance there are two types of proceedings to speed up a trial: the *beschleunigte Verfahren* (expedited proceedings — §§ 417 *et seq.* StPO)[11] and the *Strafbefehlsverfahren* (summary proceedings without trial — §§ 407 *et seq.* StPO).[12]

A further procedural principle which applies in criminal proceedings is called the *Grundsatz der Unmittelbarkeit* (principle of immediacy). It demands that proceedings are conducted in person at the trial (§ 261 StPO) to ensure that all the participants involved in the case form an undiluted opinion of it (§ 226 StPO).

4. COURSE OF PROCEEDINGS

Criminal procedure may be subdivided into two main sections. The proceedings in which a criminal offence has been discovered, investigated, charged and then heard by court is called *Erkenntnisverfahren* (contentious proceedings). It terminates with the passing of a final sentence, and its rules are laid down in §§ 1 to 448 StPO. Once a final sentence has been pronounced, the sentence is enforced in the second part of proceedings (the *Vollstreckungsverfahren* — executive proceedings); details of which are regulated under §§ 449 to 463 d StPO.

Contentious proceedings as the procedural part in which the accused is convicted is the most important part of criminal procedure. It can be divided into three sections: the preliminary proceedings, the interlocutory proceedings and the trial itself.

---

[11] For more details, see *ibid.*, Chap. Seven, 12, D.
[12] For more details, see *ibid.*, Chap. Seven, 12, C.

(a) As a chronological starting point, any procedure starts with an offence. As soon as the prosecution authorities learn about that offence — for example by the injured party applying for prosecution or by filing a criminal information (§ 158 StPO) — the *Vorverfahren* (preliminary proceedings) have started; this procedural part is laid down in §§ 160 to 177 StPO. It is the preliminary investigation by the public prosecutor in order to prepare a case before the indictment. As a rule, the public prosecutor carries out his investigation with the extensive assistance of the police, and it should follow from the investigation whether it is likely that the person charged with a crime has committed the offence.

The public prosecutor has to investigate the facts of the case in a way which enables him to render a decision whether to file charges or not (§ 160 StPO). Only if he thinks — on the basis of the investigations — that the *Beschuldigte* (person charged) is likely to be found guilty in trial, will he prefer charges by submitting an indictment to court. Preferring charges requires that a *hinreichender Tatverdacht* (sufficient suspicion of an offence, § 170 StPO) against the person charged may be confirmed. In cases in which an insufficient ground for bringing charges is at hand, the public prosecutor will abandon the process. The person injured by the respective criminal act may appeal against the decision of dropping the case in the *Klageerzwingungsverfahren* (§§ 172 *et seq.* StPO) in which the decision of dismissing the case is reviewed at first by the next higher level of the public prosecutor's office and then by the Court of Appeal (the *Oberlandesgericht*).

(b) But once a charge has been filed with the court, the *Zwischenverfahren* (interlocutory proceedings) is conducted pursuant to §§ 199 *et seq.* StPO. With the formal indictment, control of proceedings is transferred from the public prosecutor to the court, and — as laid down in § 157 StPO — the *Beschuldigte* is now referred to as the *Angeschuldigte* (accused before trial).

The court reviews in the interlocutory proceedings whether to open a trial or dismiss the charge. It determines if proceedings should continue on the basis of the charge or if it should be dismissed in order to avoid an unnecessary trial. The court sends the case to trial if the matters charged constitute a crime. There must be sufficient grounds for suspicion against the *Angeschuldigte*, and court grants leave of the charges while rendering an *Eröffnungsbeschluß* (order committing for trial).

(c) This order committing for trial leads to the *Hauptverfahren* (trial procedure) in which the *Angeschuldigte* is now referred to as the *Angeklagter* (accused; see § 157 StPO). The case is now heard in court. The court starts preparing the case for the trial (§§ 213 *et seq.* StPO), sets a date for hearing and summons the accused, defence counsel, witnesses, and experts to appear. Then, the hearing itself takes place which can be regarded as the "heart" of trial procedure. The trial terminates with the pronouncement of the verdict. As far as an appeal is filed against the sentence passed in first instance, the case is heard in the court of second instance. Contentious proceedings conclude with the passing of a final and conclusive sentence. Such a sentence is enforced in the executive procedure.

5. PARTIES TO THE PROCEEDINGS

A. PUBLIC PROSECUTOR'S OFFICE (*STAATSANWALTSCHAFT*)

The public prosecutor's office[13] is judicial authority independent from the courts. It is primarily responsible for the investigative process, represents the State in intermediate proceedings and at the trial and, last but not least, is responsible for the enforcement of the sentence.

This public prosecutor's office is called "*Herrin des Vorverfahrens*" (master of preliminary proceedings) that is to say it is responsible for conducting investigations and should run the investigations as far as it has been decided whether or not to press charges (§§ 152 II and 170 II StPO). During this investigative procedure public prosecutors are bound to remain objective and to pursue evidence for and against the suspect (§ 160 II StPO). The public prosecutor receives assistance in carrying out the investigative process from the police. If the suspicion is found to be substantiated, charges are preferred and the actual bill of indictment is drafted by the public prosecutor's office.

The public prosecutor's office represents and acts on behalf of the State in the interlocutory proceedings and in the trial while it appears as the *Ankläger* (public prosecutor). A public

---

[13] For more details, see *ibid.*, Chap. Four, 2, C.

prosecutor contributes to the process of finding out the truth while it carries out procedural acts.

Finally, the department of public prosecution also acts as *Vollstreckungsbehörde* (law enforcement authority) because it implements and enforces the sentences.

B. POLICE

The public prosecutor is assisted by the police in carrying out the investigative process. With regard to their tasks, certain police officers — generally middle ranking officers in the police hierarchy — are called *Hilfsbeamte der Staatsanwaltschaft* (auxiliary officers of the public prosecutor's office). The police may be commissioned by the public prosecutor's office to carry out special measures; the police are obliged to comply with those instructions by law (§§ 152, 161 GVG).

In addition, the police may initiate proceedings provided that there is a suspicion that a crime has been committed; then the police have the right and duty to take the first step (§ 163 StPO). After the "first step" has been performed, the case has to be handed over for further prosecution to the public prosecutor's office, and furthermore, without delay.

The proceedings we just described relate to theory, in practice, the police — because of their experience — independently conduct proceedings until the case has been investigated to such an extent that charges can be pressed. The public prosecutor joins (in the majority of cases) the proceedings only at this point.

C. JUDGE (*RICHTER*)

Although the public prosecutor's office is the "master of preliminary proceedings", the judge may already be involved in the investigative procedure while he issues certain procedural measures requiring a judicial order, such as a court-ordered receivership (§§ 98 *et seq.* StPO), search (§§ 105 *et seq.* StPO) or warrant of arrest (§§ 114 *et seq.* StPO).[14] With regard to this, the judge then acts as a *Ermittlungsrichter* (examining judge); the judicial measures which he may carry out are specified in § 162 StPO. During the following interlocutory proceedings, the court reviews whether to open a trial based on the bill of indictment submitted by the public prosecutor's office (§ 203 StPO). If so, the presiding judge conducts the entire proceedings (for instance he has to take the evidence) and — as mentioned

[14] For more details, see *ibid.*, Chap. Seven, 6.

above — lay judges at the *Amtsgerichte* and *Landgerichte* may assist him in the adjudicative process.

Due to the German Code of Criminal Procedure, a judge can be excluded or rejected from performing his judicial office in a particular case to be heard by him provided certain criteria enumerated in the law are present (§§ 22 *et seq.* StPO). For instance, in cases of a conflict of interest a judge can be excluded provided that he himself was injured by the criminal act, has a close family relationship to either the injured party or the accused, or has previously been involved with the matter (*e.g.* as witness). In addition, the law provides the possibility that a judge be rejected because there are reasonable grounds to suspect him of partiality. Finally, it is regarded as a fundamental ground for appeal pursuant to § 338 No. 2 StPO if an excluded or rejected judge (or lay judge to which the same principles apply) participates in a sentence irrespective of whether the reason for exclusion is known or unknown.

D. VICTIM (*OPFER*)

The legal position of the victim as the injured party of a criminal act was laid down for the first time in April 1987. Only since then has the victim been equipped with a few rights governed in §§ 406 d to 406 h StPO during the course of proceedings. Therein, the victim has the right to be kept informed about the proceedings and to have access to the files. But both rights require the filing of a respective application. Generally, these rights can only be exercised properly with the help of a lawyer.

The victim may undertake a more active role in the criminal proceedings. He or she may take part in the trial as a witness, may join the public prosecutor in the prosecution as a *Nebenkläger* (joint plaintiff — §§ 395 *et seq.* StPO) or may act as a private prosecutor and initiate proceedings by bringing a *Privatklage* (private indictment). The latter requires that there has been no previous assistance from a public prosecutor and is possible as far as one of the criminal offences is fulfilled by the criminal which are enumerated in § 372 StPO (*e.g.* insult or bodily injury).[15]

E. PERSON CHARGED WITH A CRIME (*BESCHULDIGTER*)

The person charged with a crime is the person against whom investigation is directed. He or she is the object of investigation

---

[15] For more details, see *ibid.*, Chap. Seven, 12, A.

conducted by the police and public prosecutor. During the proceedings a person charged may suffer — under certain circumstances — massive infringements of his basic rights (such as being arrested). During proceedings, the person charged has to be referred to by investigating authorities in a certain way prescribed under § 157 StPO: the term *Beschuldigter* refers to a person charged with a criminal offence prior to the indictment and has to be used in preliminary proceedings. The term *Angeschuldigter* (accused before trial) has to be used for the accused before trial against whom a bill of indictment has been preferred; this term gives a name to the person in interlocutory proceedings. Finally, the *Angeklagter* (accused) is the word used for the accused once the opening of the trial has been decreed by the court.

During the criminal proceedings the legal status of the person charged with a crime is especially characterised by the principle of innocence — in other words: the person charged has to be regarded as being innocent until proved guilty (see also Article 6 II ECHR). In any stage of proceedings, the person charged has — as outlined before°— the right to be heard as laid down in Article 103 I GG and due to this, a judicial decision can only be based on those facts and evidence which have been shown to him previously. In addition, the person charged has no duty to contribute and assist in his own conviction. He has the right to remain silent — a fact that the police, prosecutor or court — has to point out before starting an examination (§ 136 I 2 StPO and § 243 IV StPO). As far as the accused refers to his right to remain silent, no conclusions and inferences may be drawn from this. Furthermore, criminal procedural law grants the person charged certain rights, for instance to engage a defence counsel at any stage of the criminal process (§ 137 StPO), to apply for the admission of evidence (§§ 219 and 244 to 246 StPO), to be present at the trial (§ 230 I StPO) and to ask questions (§ 240 II StPO). Finally, the accused also has duties. For instance, if a judge or public prosecutor has issued a summons requiring the person charged to appear before court or public prosecutor's office, he is obliged to appear in person. If he fails to do so, this duty to appear can be enforced by a *Vorführungsbefehl* (warrant to take a person before the judge).

F. DEFENCE COUNSEL (*STRAFVERTEIDIGER*)

The defence counsel has an important role as one of the major participants in the course of the proceedings. In performing this task counsel does not act as representative of the accused but as an independent body of the administration of justice (§ 1 BRAGO).

Due to this function, counsel is bound and obliged to sustain the process of finding out the truth of the case, but in practice the pure nature of the defence leads to the fact that counsel's assistance in finding out the truth is one-sided, because above all he has to deliver legal support for the accused who is his client. Defence counsel has to ensure that whether the accused is guilty or not has to be proven in a correct way legally and procedurally. It is counsel's task to advise the accused on questions of procedural and substantive criminal law, to carry out his rights, make declarations on behalf of the accused and, especially, to strive for the dismissal of the prosecution against his client — the accused.

Given this — and irrespective of a possible positive knowledge of the client's guilt — counsel is free to plead the *Freispruch mangels an Beweisen* (acquittal on account of insufficiency of proof). Counsel is not obliged to disclose circumstances which may be detrimental for the accused; and as far as counsel discloses circumstances on which he has to maintain silence according to the expressed will of the accused, he breaches his contractual duty to observe secrecy towards the accused as his client. In addition, such behaviour carries a penalty in order to protect the position of the accused (see § 203 I No. 3 StGB). Furthermore, it has to be pointed out that counsel is not allowed to prevent or impede in an active way — by means of inadmissible procedural measures — the process of finding out the truth. At least not if he wants to avoid becoming subject to a serious penalty himself which is the *Strafvereitelung* (obstruction of criminal prosecution, § 258 StPO).

At any stage of proceedings, the person charged with a crime has the right to demand the support and legal representation of his own counsel for defence (§ 137 I StPO) — a very important fact which has to be made clear to him at the beginning of the first examination (§§ 136 I, 163 a III and IIV StPO). The person charged has the right to choose his own counsel for defence who is called *Wahlverteidiger*. Otherwise, a *Pflichtverteidiger* (official defence counsel) is appointed by the court provided that trial takes place before the *Landgericht* or *Oberlandesgericht*, or the accused is charged with a crime punishable with imprisonment of not less than one year, or the legal or evidential circumstances are complicated, or the accused is unable to defend himself (§§ 140 and 141 StPO).

In practice, one of the most important rights of the defence is the *Akteneinsichtsrecht* (right to inspect the files) which is laid down in § 147 StPO. The right to inspect the files has to be granted in an unlimited way once investigations conducted by the public prosecutor are closed. In addition to this, defence counsel has the right of free circulation with his client even when he is taken into custody in a pending trial (§ 148 StPO). Counsel also has the right to be present during the entire course of criminal proceedings. Due to this, counsel has the right to be present if either a judge or a public prosecutor conducts the examination of his client (§§ 168 c and 163 a III StPO). However, such a right of presence does not exist if a witness is examined by a public prosecutor (see § 161 a StPO) or if a person charged or a witness is questioned by the police. But it is admissible to permit counsel to be present as well during such an interview. The person charged may indirectly influence the presence of his counsel when he is questioned by the police, because under § 136 StPO he or she is not obliged to give evidence without a defence counsel.

G. WITNESS (*ZEUGE*)

The function of a witness in criminal proceedings is to prove circumstances which may be relevant for conviction. It is the task of a witness to provide testimony about certain facts — which can be matters a witness has heard or even certain observations.

The legal position of the witness is governed in §§ 48 *et seq.* StPO, and as a rule a witness has three duties: he or she is obliged to appear in court or before a public prosecutor, to swear an oath and to testify truthfully regarding the object of examination. A practically quite "tricky" position, because false statements are punishable under §§ 153 *et seq.* StGB. But in certain cases the duty to testify and to swear an oath is cancelled.

(a) A witness may refuse to give evidence if he has a *Zeugnisverweigerungsrecht* which is the privilege of a witness to decline to answer questions. It grants a comprehensive right to refuse to say anything during the entire course of proceedings. Such a right to refuse to give evidence is held by the fiancee, spouse or close relative of the accused (§ 52 StPO). Such a witness is relieved from the burden of testifying. The legislative intention of this privilege is quite clear: in these cases there is obviously a conflict of interests, and the law should not force anyone to give evidence against relatives or persons he or she is in love with. It is required under law that such a witness has to be informed of his right to refuse to testify prior to the examination (§ 52 III StPO). The testimony of such a witness who was not (or not correctly) informed about his right to refuse to testify is subject to the ban on utilisation — this also applies to the privileges outlined below.

In addition to this right to refuse to give evidence because of personal grounds, there is a further privilege because of professional grounds. Due to § 53 StPO, persons holding professional secrets — such as lawyers, doctors and auditors — have the privilege to decline to answer questions. This privilege is extended to those persons assisting these professionals (§ 53 a StPO) and to judges and civil servants as to matters subject to their duties of official secrecy (§ 54 StPO).

(b) Furthermore, there is the *Aussageverweigerungsrecht* governed under § 55 StPO which grants a right to refuse to give information about any question which might expose the witness himself or his near relatives to the danger of prosecution for an offence. But this privilege only grants the right to refuse to answer a certain question which might leave him or his close relative liable to prosecution for an administrative or criminal offence. The *Zeugnisverweigerungsrechte*, however, guarantees the respective person a rather comprehensive right to say nothing during the course of the entire accusation.

H. EXPERT (*SACHVERSTÄNDIGE*)

An expert may also participate in criminal proceedings. Experts are consulted by the judge because of their expertise in certain areas which is required to conduct the trial and which the court does not possess. The expert has the duty to prove certain facts or circumstances; he is allowed to use scientific rules in order to conduct his research studies or investigations or to underline his results. The legal position of experts — which is determined in §§ 72 *et seq.* StPO — is nearly the same as the one of a witness and, due to this, an expert enjoys the right to refuse to furnish an expert opinion, too. Finally (and very much like judges), experts may be refused on the grounds of prejudice.

6. MEANS OF COERCION (*ZWANGSMITTEL*)

At any stage of procedure — like the preliminary and interlocutory proceedings, trial and executive proceedings —

means of coercion can be used but only under certain prerequisites specified in law because these restrict the basic rights of the respective person. Means of coercions are generally used in order to secure criminal evidence and to prevent the person charged from being absent when his presence is required.

A. WARRANT OF ARREST (*HAFTBEFEHL*)

Legal rules concerning the warrant of arrest can be found in §§ 112 *et seq.* StPO. A warrant of arrest, which is issued by a judge, is a written order to remand the person charged in *Untersuchungshaft* (remand in custody before or during a pending trial). Prior to pressing a charge, a warrant of arrest is issued by the court on application by the public prosecutor's office; after bringing an indictment, it is issued by the court which hears the case (§ 125 StPO). The execution of a warrant of arrest is carried out by taking the person into custody and apprehending a criminal is the task of the public prosecutor and police. After arresting a criminal, this person has to be brought before a judge without delay. The judge has to question the arrested and to decide whether to issue a warrant of arrest, to release the party or to issue a warrant subject to interim suspension. Besides this, the Code of Criminal Procedure provides further types of arrest warrant which can be issued under the following circumstances:

(a) There is the *Vollstreckungshaftbefehl* (warrant of arrest of execution) which is issued by a law enforcement authority (the public prosecutor's office) when a non-appealable convicted person does not appear at prison to serve a sentence or is a fugitive (§ 457 StPO).

(b) The *Sicherungshaftbefehl* is another warrant of arrest which provides security in cases in which the court has to decide on a revocation of a suspension of execution of sentence. The warrant allows the precautionary detention of a convicted person until a decision is rendered to ensure that he does not abscond (§ 453 c StPO).

(c) Normally, a warrant of arrest is issued in cases in which a verdict of guilt can be expected. But as far as the offence has been committed in a state of criminal incapacity (*e.g.* by a mentally disabled offender), no finding of guilt is rendered but a measure providing security such as confinement to a certain psychiatric institution (§ 63 StGB). In cases like this a *Sicherungsverfahren* (confinement proceedings) against mentally disabled offenders is carried out (§§ 413 *et seq.* StPO), and the *Unterbringungsbeschluß* (place of safety order) — as a certain warrant of arrest — serves as a safeguard for criminal proceedings (§ 126 a StPO).

Because of the serious restriction on the personal freedom of the person to be arrested, the law presupposes in §§ 112 and 112 a StPO that a warrant of arrest can only be issued under certain conditions. The presumption is first that the person charged is subject to a *dringender Tatverdacht* (urgent degree of suspicion). An urgent degree of suspicion is given when a high level of likelihood — according to the stage of investigation — exists that the person charged has taken part in a certain criminal offence. In other words: a great probability must be affirmed with regard to the investigations that the person charged has committed the offence as an offender or party to the offence. Moreover, a concrete *Haftgrund* (reason for arrest) must be given to ensure that custody is an appropriate measure in each case. The law provides final reasons for arrest in §§ 112 and 112 a StPO which are, for instance, escape, risk of escape, danger of collusion, strong suspicion of a capital offence and danger of recurrence or continuation of certain sex crimes or grave offences. Besides these reasons for arrest, the remand in custody may not offend the principle of proportionality (§ 112 I 2 StPO) because taking someone into custody is a serious restriction on someone's personal freedom. Consequently, a warrant of arrest cannot be issued lawfully as long as the deprivation of liberty as a basic right is not in proportion to the importance of the case.

The Code of Criminal Procedure provides legal protection for the benefit of the arrested because of the serious restriction on his personal freedom. At first, the arrested himself may file a *Haftbeschwerde* (complaint against a court order for arrest, §§ 304 *et seq.* StPO) or a *Haftprüfung* (review of a remand in custody, §§ 117 *et seq.* StPO) at any time in order to review the lawfulness of his arrest. In addition, after a period in custody lasting for at least three months the supposition is reviewed *ex officio* (§ 117 V StPO). Moreover, there is another safeguard for the accused person; a further review after a custody period of about six months. This review *ex officio* is also performed by the *Oberlandesgericht*. A continuation of the warrant of arrest for a period exceeding six months must be ordered either by the *Oberlandesgericht* or even the *Bundesgerichtshof* (see § 121 StPO).

B. PROVISIONAL DETENTION (*VORLÄUFIGE FESTNAHME*) AND WARRANT TO BRING A PERSON BEFORE COURT (*VORFÜHRUNGSBEFEHL*)

It can take too long to wait for the issue of a judicial warrant of arrest before apprehending the suspect. Therefore, the Code of Criminal Procedure provides further possibilities to take a person into custody.

One is the provisional detention under § 127 StPO which is the possibility of taking someone into custody without a judicial warrant if there is no time to wait for the issue of a warrant. § 127 I StPO sets out that anybody may exercise this right in cases where someone is caught red-handed, or where the respective person is being pursued and is likely to flee from justice or when his identity cannot be ascertained at once. Under these conditions, the use of physical force is justified as long as it is proportional and necessary for the seizure of the person. Only then may the person arresting justify the cause of an injury which has arisen in order to defend himself (see § 32 StGB). A public prosecutor or the police have a right of provisional arrest in cases of imminent danger (§ 127 II StPO). But in any case the person being arrested has to be brought — without delay — to a judge who may (if necessary) issue a warrant of arrest (see § 128 StPO and Article 104 GG).

Provisional arrest must be distinguished from the *Vorführungsbefehl* (warrant to bring a person before the court) which is the enforcement of the summoning of the person charged or of a witness who failed to appear.

(a) The person charged has the duty to appear in person but not to give evidence. This duty to appear in person arises if a judge or a public prosecutor has issued a summons requiring the person charged to appear before court or public procecutor's office. A *Vorführungsbefehl* may be issued by a judge (§ 134 StPO) or a public prosecutor (§ 163 a III StPO) against a suspect failing to do so in order to carry out examination. In addition, if the accused fails to appear at trial without an adequate excuse, the court may issue a warrant of arrest or a *Vorführungsbefehl* for the next hearing (§ 230 II StPO).

(b) If a witness who has the duty to appear in person and to give evidence in court or before a public prosecutor (§ 161 a StPO) fails to appear, these duties can also be enforced with the issue of a *Vorführungsbefehl* by a judge (§ 51 I 3 StPO) or by the public prosecutor (§ 161 a II 1 and § 51 I 3 StPO).

C. SECURITY (*SICHERSTELLUNG*)

Two different kinds of security have to be distinguished: the securing of judicial evidence intended to prevent its loss and, due to this, safeguards that the prosecution itself can be carried out (§§ 94 *et seq.* StPO); whereas the securing of *Verfalls- und Einziehungsgegenstände* (objects of forfeiture and confiscation) is intended to safeguard that the legal consequences ordered in the sentence can be enforced (§§ 111 b *et seq.* StPO).

Under §§ 94 *et seq.* StPO the object to be seized has to be an object which may become important as judicial evidence. It is said in § 94 StPO that driving licences may also be seized as criminal evidence and put in safe custody, for example because the accused is suspected of a committed *Urkundenfälschung* (forgery of an instrument or document, § 267 StPO). But in practice, a driving licence is normally not proof of evidence (*e.g.* driving while under the influence of alcohol) but is rather confiscated (§ 94 III StPO) together with the provisional withdrawal of the driving licence (§ 111 a StPO).

However, certain things are exempted from attachment and seizure, such as official papers (§ 96 StPO), and — in conformity with the right to refuse to give evidence[16] — certain written notices between the accused and the person entitled to refuse to give evidence (§ 97 I No. 1 StPO), just as notes and written communications are subject to privilege (§ 97 I No. 2 and 3 StPO). In addition, a prohibition of attachment may also directly follow from the basic rights. Therefore, diaries or personal letters, whose realisation would damage human dignity or the right of personality (Articles 1 and 2 GG), are exempted from seizure or attachment.

The attachment of certain objects is ordered either by the judge, or in cases of imminent danger, by the public prosecutor or their auxiliary officials (the police). Such an order presupposes an *Anfangsverdacht* (simple initial suspicion — see § 152 II StPO) and is exercised while the respective object is taken into official custody. The issue of a particular *Beschlagnahmeanordnung* (order of attachment) is not required if the respective object is in nobody's possession but is necessary if the person (either the accused or a third party) in possession of it is not willing to hand over the object on a voluntary basis.

The legal consequences of securing by custody are as follows: a bailment under public law is entered and the legal seizure attachment entangles the object. Furthermore, this relationship

---

[16] For more details, *see ibid.*, Chap. Seven, 5, G.

is protected under criminal law while an infringement carries the penalty of § 136 StGB which is the *Verstrickungsbruch* (interference with attachment), and under civil law a restraint of disposal exists (§§ 134, 135 BGB).

D. SEARCH (*DURCHSUCHUNG*)

Durchsuchungen (searches) are carried out to reveal the presence either of a suspect or certain objects. Details are laid down in §§ 102 *et seq.* StPO. As a rule, searches can only be ordered by a judge — as an exception to this principle (and as we have seen before) — in cases of imminent danger a search may also be ordered by the public prosecutor's office or their auxiliary officers (§ 105 StPO).

In order to issue a lawful search certain requirements must be satisfied which depend onto whom a search is ordered (suspect or a third party). Searches directed at a suspect require the presumption that the person intended to be apprehended or objects in demand may be found in the rooms where he or she is living (§ 102 StPO). This presumption must not follow from certain facts, but has to be the result of investigations and experience. Pursuant to § 102 StPO, a person becomes suspect of a certain crime in the case of a simple initial suspicion. Searches of persons who are not suspects have to match even stricter requirements which are specified in § 103 StPO. Due to this norm, concrete facts must be present which lead to the assumption that the person looking for the trace or the objects, may be found in the rooms to be searched (§ 103 StPO). Also during searches *Zufallsfunde* (finding of lost property by accident) which are objects indicating that another criminal offence has been commited, may be revealed; these objects may also be put into custody on provisional terms (§ 108 StPO).

E. FURTHER MEASURES

Taking a person into custody is pursuant to the confirmation of his identification and the lawfulness of such a measure is judged in accordance with §§ 163 b and 163 c StPO. The identification of a suspect or a person beyond suspicion may become necessary in order to prosecute an offence and can be initiated by the public prosecutor or the police. § 163 b I StPO relates to identification of suspects and performance of all measures being necessary for identification. The suspect can be searched, and all measures of police identification service (such as fingerprints and photographs) are also admissable. Identification of persons beyond suspicion, who may promote investigation, is only possible due to § 163 b II StPO. Any measure against such a person has to be appropriate and reasonable, and due to this, the searches and measures of the police identification service cannot be performed against his will.

§§ 81 to 81 c StPO allows certain specialised observing and investigative measures and, again, a difference has to be made if they are directed towards a suspect or a party beyond suspicion.

(a) In order to prepare a profile of the psychological conditions of the person charged, this person may be confined (not longer than six months) for observation in a public psychiatric hospital; such a measure is ordered by the court after a hearing of an expert and the defence counsel has taken place (§ 81 StPO).

Physical searches of the person charged (*e.g.* blood tests and DNA fingerprints) may be carried out in order to furnish certain facts which are important for the prosecution; these measures are generally ordered by the judge and, again, in cases of imminent danger, by the public prosecution or the auxiliary officers (§ 81 a StPO). § 81 b StPO allows photographs, fingerprints or similar measures (*e.g.* facial hair or altering head hair for purposes of an identity parade) to be taken of the person charged provided it is required for prosecution or identification, even against the expressed will of the person concerned.

(b) A person beyond suspicion — who may be a potential witness — may be searched without his consent only if it has to be stated for the finding out of the truth whether traces or effects of a crime may be found on the body of this person (§ 81 c StPO). A witness can refuse to be searched if he has a right to refuse to give evidence (see §§ 52 *et seq.* StPO).

Further means of investigation measures in order to detect and locate a suspect are, for example, the *Kontrollstellen* (checkpoints, § 111 StPO), *Steckbrief* (warrant for apprehension, §§ 131, 457 StPO), the *Netzfahndung* (network police investigation to detect and locate a suspect, § 163 d StPO), the *Rasterfahndung* (search for wanted persons by scanning devices, §§ 98 a, b StPO), the *polizeiliche Beobachtung* (police observation, § 163 e StPO), the *Datenabgleich* (counter-checking of data, § 98 c StPO), the *Überwachung und Aufnahme des Fernmeldeverkehrs* (observation and recording of telecommunication, §§ 100 a, b StPO) and secret investigations (§§ 100 c, d StPO).

F. LEGAL PROTECTION

Legal protection against means of coercion is complicated and depends on the question of whether imminent, continuing or completed measures are under appeal and by whom the relevant means have been ordered initially.

We begin with the legal protection against imminent or continuing measures:

(a) Legal protection against these measures ordered by a judge can be reached by lodging a *Beschwerde* (request for relief from a court order) pursuant to § 304 StPO.[17]

(b) An order made by a public prosecutor or the police in using their competence in cases of imminent danger (see §§ 98 II, 161 a II StPO) can be appealed with the *Antrag auf richterliche Entscheidung* (motion for judgment) which is governed under § 98 II 2 StPO. But what happens to the further means of coercion? The law explicitly provides legal protection only against certain means of coercion (such as the seizure attachment pursuant to § 98 II 2 StPO) and not against measures such as searches or blood tests: it has been specified by the courts, that in the interest of the guarantee of judicial protection (Article 19 IV GG)[18] § 98 II 2 StPO applies on an analogous basis to any other means of coercions, too. Given this, these measures are also subject to a judicial reservation of decision as long as the process is continuing.[19]

Another interesting legal question is whether the Criminal Code of Procedure provides a right of appeal against already concluded measures, especially with regard to Article 19 IV GG:

(a) It has been said by the courts[20] that as soon as means of coercion are concluded, there is no right of appeal against such a measure ordered by a judge. This has not been regarded as an infringement of Article 19 IV GG because this article does not protect an individual against acts carried out by judges.

(b) However, completed measures ordered by a public prosecutor or the police may be appealed by filing a motion for judgment

---

[17] For more details, see *ibid.*, Chap. Seven, 10, C.
[18] For more details, see *ibid.*, Chap. Five, 1, A.
[19] BGH NJW 1978, 1013.
[20] BGHSt 28, 57; BVerfGE 49, 329.

due to § 98 II 2 StPO (again, applied by analogy).[21] The reasoning is as follows: the person affected must have the opportunity to obtain a judicial decision stating the unlawfulness of the already concluded measure — this derives from the guarantee of legal protection as guaranteed under Article 19 IV GG. Anyway, to get a chance of a judicial decision the applicant must prove a special interest, for example a planned claim against the State, the danger of repetition, or even his personal interest in rehabilitation.[22]

7. PRELIMINARY PROCEEDINGS (*VORVERFAHREN*)

The preliminary proceedings are carried out and controlled by the public prosecutor and are intended to prepare his decision whether or not to press charges (§ 160 I StPO). The investigative proceedings may be set in motion if the injured person applies for prosecution; or if a *Strafanzeige* (information) is filed with the police, county court or public prosecutor's office which can be given by anyone (*e.g.* citizen, officer or public authority); or if the public prosecutor or the police themselves learn that a criminal offence has been committed (§§ 158 I and 160 StPO).

To fulfil the investigative task, the public prosecutor has to investigate the facts of the case, and to collect and examine all evidence in favour and against the person charged (§ 160 I and II StPO). Particular obligations have to be met especially in the course of questioning witnesses, experts and the person charged with a crime, which are laid down in the Code of Criminal Procedure. As far as these duties have not been satisfied in a legally correct way, testimony can generally not be used in court as evidence. This means: prior to the interview a witness has to be informed about existing rights to refuse to give evidence or information (§§ 52 III and 55 II StPO). Before being examined for the first time by a judge or a public prosecutor, the person charged has to be told about the offences he has been charged with as well as the respective criminal provisions; the suspect has also to be informed about his legal rights granted under the Code of Criminal Procedure — for example his freedom to testify or to ask for a defence counsel (§ 163 a StPO). Moreover, during the interview, it is prohibited to influence the suspect's will in an inadmissible way or manner. Therefore, methods leading to maltreatment or exhaustion are strictly forbidden as are

[21] BGHSt 28, 57; OLG Karlsruhe NJW 1988, 84; BGH NJW 1990, 2758.
[22] See BGH NJW 1990, 2758, 2759.

physical force, drugs, torment, deception or hypnosis (§ 136 a StPO).

During the investigative procedure, the assistance of a judge — who then is called *Ermittlungsrichter* (examining or pre-trial judge) — may become necessary, if the public prosecutor comes to the conclusion to issue certain compulsory measures (such as warrant for arrest, a search warrant or a seizure attachment). These measures can only be issued by court.

At the end of the investigative process, the public prosecutor may either abandon the process or press charges. If the public prosecutor is persuaded that — on the basis of the investigation — the person charged is likely to be found guilty in a later trial, which means that a *hinreichender Tatverdacht* (sufficient suspicion) can be confirmed, he presses charges and submits a bill of indictment to the court having jurisdiction in the respective case. Such a bill of indictment has to satisfy the requirements being specified in § 200 StPO.

The public prosecutor may also come to the decision to terminate the investigative process. Then, he issues a *Einstellungsverfügung* (stop notice, § 170 I StPO). The following grounds are the reasons for not preferring charges but terminating proceedings:

(a) That a sufficient suspicion of an offence is not present. In this case, the injured person may enforce formal accusation by instituting the *Klageerzwingungsverfahren* (§§ 172–177 StPO) — proceedings to force the public prosecutor's office to charge a certain offence. In this proceeding the stop-notice is reviewed on points of law and fact. These proceedings are intended to protect the injured party and to supervise the decisions of the public prosecutor's office.

(b) When it is likely that only a *Privatklagedelikt* (private prosecution offence) — which are minor offences against individuals enumerated in § 374 StPO — has been committed and the public prosecutor denies the public interest in the sense of § 376 StPO.[23]

(c) As a consequence of the principle of discretionary prosecution, the public prosecutor refrains from prosecuting minor criminal offences governed under §§ 153 to 154 e StPO.

[23] For more details, see *ibid.*, Chap. Seven, 12, A.

8. INTERLOCUTORY PROCEEDINGS (*ZWISCHENVERFAHREN*)

In interlocutory proceedings the court — which is composed only of professional judges and is sitting *in camera* — has to decide whether and on what counts of the indictment the trial against the accused will be opened (see §§ 199 *et seq.* StPO). The reason for conducting interlocutory proceedings is that judicial control takes place prior to pressing a charge in order to safeguard the position of the accused before trial. In addition to this, the *Angeschuldigte* again has the opportunity to plead his objections and to submit a motion for submission of evidence, and that in the knowledge of the actual bill of indictment. The court may order a further hearing of evidence before rendering a decision. But if there seem to be adequate reasons of suspicion against the accused, the court will send the matter to trial and render a *Eröffnungsbeschluß* (order committing the accused for trial).

The court quite obviously refuses to send the matter to trial if, for instance, procedural requirements are missing or the act charged with does not constitute a criminal offence under law. Finally, there will be no trial if the facts of the case or legal reasons indicate that a judgment of guilt against the accused is unlikely (*e.g.* the criminal evidence seems to be insufficient). The court will then issue an order in which it refuses to send the matter to trial; the public prosecutor may appeal against this decision by filing a *Beschwerde* (request for relief from a court order).

9. MAIN PROCEEDINGS (*HAUPTVERFAHREN*)

A. COURSE OF THE TRIAL

After the court has prepared the trial — *i.e.* issuing summonses requiring witnesses and experts to appear before court — the actual hearing begins with the calling of the case. The actual course of how the trial has to be proceeded is laid down in § 243 StPO.

After the matter has been called the presiding judge states the presence of the accused, defence counsel and the summoned witnesses and experts. Then the witnesses are advised on their rights and duties. After the witnesses have left the courtroom the accused is questioned with regard to his personal status in order to state his or her personal identification and to ascertain his or her capacity to proceed in court. Afterwards the public prosecutor reads out the charges laid down in the bill of indictment and the accused is advised on his right either to respond to the charges or to remain silent. If he is willing to answer the questions, the examination as to the matters charged is carried out. Then the hearing of the evidence takes place by the presiding judge who, for instance, examines witnesses and experts. The presiding judge may grant the right to ask questions to his associate judges, the public prosecutor, the accused and the defence counsel as well. But questions not belonging to the subject matter or unsuitable questions can be refused to be asked by the presiding judge. After the taking of evidence has been terminated, the closing speeches of the public prosecutor, the defence counsel and the accused are delivered in which they outline their personal views of the case. The accused has the last word. This is a right which gives the accused the chance to address the judge and the public prosecutor for one last time.

The trial terminates with the delivery of the verdict. The reasons for the verdict and the legal description of the act of which the accused has been found guilty (or has been acquitted) are read out in court at the end of the trial by the presiding judge. The verdict is passed "*Im Namen des Volkes*" ("In the Name of the People") and is later set down in writing. The judgment might be a finding of guilt, an acquittal, or the abandonment of the proceedings.

B. TAKING OF EVIDENCE (*BEWEISAUFNAHME*)

After the accused has been examined, the taking of evidence is carried out. This is practically the most important part of trial which lies in the hands of the court. The court is obliged to extend *ex officio* the taking of evidence to all facts of the case and all criminal evidence which is material for the decision in order to find out the truth of the case (§ 244 II StPO). The investigating of evidence — which might concern internal and external facts — is exercised in order to examine the reasons of the charges against the accused.

The Code of Criminal Procedure provides two different types of criminal evidence; one is the *Strengbeweis* (stringent evidence) and the other is called the *Freibeweis* (informal evidence).

(a) For all circumstances concerning the question of guilt and punishment, stringent evidence has to be furnished. Its rules are governed under §§ 244 *et seq.* StPO. Because of the material importance of these circumstances such proof can only be produced with formal evidence, like a defence or confession entered by the accused, witnesses (§§ 48 to 71 StPO), experts (§§ 72 to 85 StPO), inspections (§§ 86 to 93 StPO) and documents (§§ 249 to 256 StPO).

(b) Circumstances concerning procedural questions — for example the minimum age for taking an oath or lodging a demand for prosecution in due time — can be investigated by the informal evidence. In contrast to the stringent evidence, the court is not bound by any rule relating to how to furnish informal evidence — this is left to the court's discretion.

The extent of the court's duty to investigate the matter does not depend on the fact that the participants have applied for the introduction of evidence. The court itself must take judicial evidence *ex officio* as far as circumstances — known to the court — require to furnish evidence for further investigation. Otherwise, the court is in breach of its duty to investigate the matter.

But despite the court's own *ex officio* duty to investigate, defence counsel, public prosecutors, joint plaintiffs and private prosecutors also have a right to motion for the introduction of evidence. A *Beweisantrag* (motion for the admission of evidence) is a request for evidence to be taken. It can be offered in a trial until judgment is delivered and has to be made in a certain form of evidence acknowledged by the Code of Criminal Procedure. The respective points at issue and the offered criminal evidence have to be named along with the facts with a view that the evidence must concern an allegation of a question of guilt or sentencing. If one of the participants has applied to introduce evidence, the court generally has to perform such an application. Motions for the admission of evidence can only be denied by court order — provided that a statutory reason for a denial is present. These grounds are enumerated in § 244 III to V StPO and are, for instance: the matter to be proved is obvious, common knowledge or has already positively been demonstrated; or the matter to be proved bears no relation to the event under consideration or is entirely unsuitable as evidence; or the taking of evidence is inadmissible or is inaccessible or is an attempt to delay. If the court denies a motion for admission of evidence because of reasons other than the statutory grounds for denial prescribed by law, this is a fundamental error which forms the legal basis to lodge an appeal on points of law (so-called *absoluter Revisionsgrund*, § 338 No. 8 StPO).[24]

[24] For more details, see *ibid.*, Chap. Seven, 10, B.

As far as a mistake has happened during the course of taking of evidence, the question arises whether this leads to a *Beweisverwertungsverbot* (exclusion of evidence improperly obtained) in trial. Only the prohibited methods of examination are prescribed by law. § 136 a I StPO enumerates these prohibited methods like maltreatment, exhaustion, physical force, medication, torment, deception or hypnosis. Results which have been gained by these methods cannot be utilised in trial and taken into account in the judgment irrespective of whether the person concerned has consented to the use.

For further cases of unlawfully obtained evidence the Code of Criminal Procedure does not provide any legal rule. It then has to be stated in evaluating the circumstances in the individual case whether an exclusion of improperly obtained evidence exists. The criteria for this are controversial, but generally the protective purpose of the infringed legal norm and the affected interest (*e.g.* untouchable basic rights) are taken into account and have to be balanced against one another in order to ascertain whether an exclusion of evidence improperly obtained is given. This is the task of the court too. A few practical examples shall demonstrate what is meant by such an exclusion: omission to caution either the witness (§ 52 II StPO) or the accused (§ 136 I StPO); inadmissible telephone tapping (§ 100 a StPO); a non-enforceable refusal given by a relative to testify at trial with regard to a statement made previously (§ 257 StPO); and — finally — diary entries which are protected by the law as well.

A further question is whether the exclusion of evidence improperly obtained includes further indirectly obtained evidence as well. As a rule, the courts have decided that such evidence (*e.g.* fingerprint) gained on the basis of excludable evidence may be used in court. This leads to the fact that the so-called "*Früchte des verbotenen Baums*" (or "fruit of the poisonous tree doctrine") which has been developed in the United States is not applicable at all.[25] The reasons for the rejection of this theory by the German criminal courts is that it does not fit in the process of the German criminal proceedings and that otherwise even a minor mistake by the police could bring the investigative proceedings to a stand still.

A further reason is that according to the courts the "educating thought" behind this theory does not fit into the German legal system because the law already provides security for observance of correct proceedings while criminal offences like *Rechtsbeugung* (perversion of justice — § 336 StGB) or an

---

[25] See BGHSt 27, 358; BGHSt 32, 71.

Aussageerpressung (extortion of testimony by duress — § 343 StGB). Therefore, such an exclusion of evidence is not required within German criminal proceedings. The approach in the United States is different. First, by means of this theory (the "fruit of the poisonous tree doctrine") the constitutional rights of a suspect should be guaranteed. Then it follows from the rule of law that the police should be prevented from infringing and violating the constitutional rights of a suspect.

After the taking of evidence the court judges in accordance with the personal convictions to which it has come to during the course of proceedings (§ 261 StPO). The only barrier is that the court is bound by the laws of logic. This principle is called *Grundsatz der freien Beweiswürdigung* (principle of free evaluation of the evidence). This does in practice mean that — apart from a few statutory exceptions — the admission and weighting of evidence, including for instance hearsay, lies within the discretion of the court. The court is free in assessing the evidence and is not bound by any rules when deciding the question of whether a matter has been proved or not. But, as far as proof cannot be furnished without any doubt, the court renders a decision giving the accused the benefit of the doubt. This principle is called "*im Zweifel für den Angeklagten*" — the Latin expression is *in dubio pro reo* which can be translated as proof beyond any reasonable doubt and simply means that in criminal proceedings any uncertainty about the guilt of a person prevents a judgment against the accused.

C. SUPPLEMENTARY INDICTMENT, JUDGMENT AND COSTS

The subject matter of the adjudicative process is the criminal offence as it has been charged by the public prosecutor. The court can only give a ruling on those criminal offences which are the subject matter of the bill of indictment. But what happens if further offences committed by the accused come to light in the course of the trial? Then, the public prosecutor has to file a *Nachtragsanklage* (supplementary indictment) pursuant to § 266 StPO in which a charge is made with regard to the criminal offences being newly discovered. And, if a legal aspect were subject to change during the course of proceedings with the legal consequence that another criminal provision applied as charged, the court will give an appropriate legal caution (see § 265 StPO).

As mentioned above, the court may only give a ruling on those offences which have been charged. But it has to be stressed that the court is not bound by the legal appreciation in the bill of indictment. The point is that the judgment is the ruling given by the court on the basis of the result of trial. The most important practical effect is that it concludes proceedings at the relevant instance. The judgment may be a *Prozeßurteil* (judgment on procedural grounds) or a *Sachurteil* (judgment on the merits of the case). Only in the latter case, is a decision delivered related to the material content of the charge and it may be a conviction, a verdict of not guilty, or a measure for the prevention of crime and the reformation of the offenders (see § 69 StGB).

A judgment becomes final — in other words: non-appealable — when a notice of appeal is not given in due time, the right of appeal has been waived, or when the appeal has been withdrawn or is inadmissible. The legal consequence is that a final judgment can no longer be challenged at all. In addition, "finality" is the supposition of penal execution and the registration in the Federal Central Register (and in the Central Register of Traffic Violations if penal travel cases have been committed). But a distinction must be drawn between the formal and the material "finality". Whereas a *formal finality* means that a judgment cannot be appealed anymore, *material finality* has the effect that a further penalty and conviction for the same criminal act is impossible and excluded (this fundamental legal principle is called "*ne bis in idem*" — a Latin expression which is laid down in Article 103 III GG).

The law relating to costs and compensation is laid down in §§ 464 *et seq.* StPO. Due to these norms costs of the proceedings are fees, expenses of the public treasury and the necessary expenses of the participants. The costs of the proceedings have to be met by the accused to the extent that it was originally occasioned by an act of which he was found guilty or in relation to which a measure of correction and public security was ordered against him. A different result is given if there is no conviction at the end of the trial; then the costs of the proceedings and the necessary expenses of the accused have to be met by the public purse (§ 467 StPO). The costs of an appeal which remains unsuccessful or is withdrawn have to be met by the appellant himself.

10. APPEAL PROCEDURE

A judicial decision can be challenged by filing a right of appeal.[26] With regard to this aspect the Code of Criminal

[26] For more details concerning the term right of appeal, see *ibid.*, Chap. Six, 11.

Procedure provides the *Berufung* (appeal), *Revision* (appeal on points of law) and the *Beschwerde* (request for relief from a court order).

A. APPEAL (*BERUFUNG*)

Appeals are governed under §§ 312 to 332 StPO and are admissible against judgments of the *Strafrichter* (criminal court judge) or the *Schöffengericht* (criminal court with lay judges; see Schedule 5). Judgments of the *Landgericht* cannot be challenged with an appeal.

The following parties are generally entitled to lodge an appeal: the accused, the public prosecutor — and also for the benefit of the accused — the defence counsel with the consent of the accused. Furthermore, this right is given to the private prosecutor and the joint plaintiff (see §§ 296, 297, 390 and 401 StPO). The entitlement to lodge an appeal presupposes that the appellant himself or the third party on whose behalf the appeal is lodged is aggrieved by the judgment under appeal. Such a *Beschwer* (grievance) is given if the appellant is able to assert that he or the third party has been effected by the judgment under appeal; the public prosecutor's office, for instance, is always effected by a wrong judgment whereas the accused is only aggrieved by his conviction.

Such an appeal has to be filed with the court of first instance, and that within one week after the judgment has been pronounced; if the pronouncement of the judgment has taken place in the absence of the accused, the period begins to run with judgment's service. The application may be in writing or may be entered on record at the court's office and, at this time, need not be supplied with reasons. A well founded appeal, namely an appeal supported by reasons, has to be lodged within a further week after the expiry of the period for lodging an appeal.

The appeal is heard by the court of appeal which is the *Landgericht*. The case is reviewed on point of facts and law. The Court of Appeal as a second trial court not only examines whether the judgment resting on the facts of the case determined in the first instance is correct but also whether new facts and judicial evidence may be introduced and have to be taken into consideration. An appeal is successful if it is admissible and well founded; the latter is the case if the challenged judgment is wrong. If the appeal is successful, the Court of Appeal quashes the first instance judgment and delivers an entirely new judgment on the merits of the case. The prohibition of *reformatio in peius* also has to be observed. It means that the judgment may not be amended to the detriment of the accused as far as he himself or a persons entitled to do so on his behalf has lodged the appeal. This prohibition also applies to the appeal on points of law mentioned below.

B. APPEAL ON POINTS OF LAW (*REVISION*)

The appeal on points of law is governed under §§ 333 to 358 StPO and is permissible from first-instance judgments of the *Landgericht* or *Oberlandesgericht* and appeal judgments of the *Landgericht*. In addition, this appeal on points of law is permissible as a *Sprungrevision* (leap-frog appeal — § 335 StPO) from judgments of the *Amtsgericht* instead of taking an appeal. In other words: the second instance is skipped in this situation.

The appeal on points of law has to be lodged within one week after the pronouncement of the judgment with the court whose judgment is under appeal and, again, it may be in writing or be entered on record at the court's office. If the pronouncement has taken place without the accused, the time limit begins to run with judgment's service. It has to be legally justified within one month since the expiry of the time limit for lodging the appeal or since the service of the judgment.

The appeal on points of law is heard by the *Bundesgerichtshof* or the *Oberlandesgericht* (see Schedules 5 and 6) and its intention is to find out whether the law has been applied correctly. The finding on facts cannot be challenged because the review is restricted to determining whether the judgment is based on properly applied procedural and substantive law. The appeal on points of law can only be based on the fact that the judgment "*beruht*" (rests) on the breach of law (§ 337 StPO). This can be an error related to procedural or substantive law.

Errors related to procedural law have to be indicated, and the infringed procedural provisions must be named by the appellant. The court then examines the judgment under appeal only with regard to the asserted procedural error. But, as far as an error is related to substantive law, it is sufficient that the applicant only has to assert that substantive law has been infringed; definite errors do not have to be indicated. In this case, the court reviews the entire judgment with regard to correctly applied substantive law.

An error can be an *absoluter Revisionsgrund* (fundamental error) provided it is enumerated in the canon of § 338 StPO, *e.g.* the wrong composition of trial court or a participation in judgment of an excluded or rejected judge or lay judge. The legal consequence is that the causation between the procedural mistake and the judgment will be presumed and is irrefutable. Obviously, the appeal on points of law is then well-founded. In addition, there are the *relative Revisionsgründe* (reversible errors). In these cases the appeal on points of law is only successful, when the reversible error has happened during the trial and — this is the important legal barrier — the judgment rests upon this error (§ 337 StPO). In practice, this does not require a proved causality. Rather it is sufficient if it can't be excluded that without the mistake a different judgment would have been rendered.

If the court of last resort comes to the conclusion that the appeal is substantiated, the judgment is quashed. As a rule, the matter is sent back to the court of lower instance in order to render a new decision after considering the findings of the court of last resort.

C. REQUEST FOR RELIEF FROM A COURT ORDER (*BESCHWERDE*)

The request for relief from a court order is the correct remedy against decisions other than judgments (§§ 304 to 311 a StPO). Any judicial ruling or court order from the dispositions of the courts in first instance or the appellate procedure or the presiding judge, the judge in the investigative proceedings or the commissioned or requested judge can be appealed from by a request for relief from a court order as long as the law does not expressly preclude it. Generally, the request is excluded against decisions before the delivery of judgment except for means of coercion (§ 305 StPO). The complaint is not subject to any time limit and has to be lodged with the court which has issued the decision under appeal. This court itself may grant relief; otherwise the court at next instance has the jurisdictional power. The challenged decision is reviewed on points of facts and law.

In certain cases a *sofortige Beschwerde* (immediate appeal) has to be lodged as far it is prescribed by law (*e.g.* § 81 IV StPO). The immediate appeal is subject to a time limit and, due to this, the appeal has to be lodged within one week after the pronouncement of the decision.

11. LEGAL REMEDIES

A. RESTORATION TO ONE'S ORIGINAL POSITION (*WIEDEREINSETZUNG IN DEN VORHERIGEN STAND*)

The restoration to one's original position is the suitable legal remedy whenever the participating party has failed to observe the time limit (§§ 44 *et seq.* StPO). In practice, the most relevant cases are the failure to observe the period for appeal.

B. REOPENING OF THE CASE (*WIEDERAUFNAHMEVERFAHREN*)

The reopening of a case is an extraordinary remedy specified in §§ 359 to 373 a StPO. The resumption of proceedings is directed at reopening a trial which had been previously finalised and, therefore, in general terms no longer the subject of an appeal. This provides the possibility of eliminating judicial errors. The preconditions for reopening an already concluded trial for the benefit of the convicted are specified in § 359 StPO, and those that are to his detriment are enumerated in § 362 StPO. The most important grounds for reopening the case are the introduction of new facts or evidence. The proceedings of a new trial can be subdivided into three parts: review of admissibility, review of the reasonable justification and finally the new trial itself. If an application for resumption of process is admissible and legally justified, it is accepted and, as a rule, a new trial will proceed.

12. SPECIAL PROCEEDINGS

A. PRIVATE PROSECUTION OR INDICTMENT (*PRIVATKLAGE*)

A person injured by a criminal offence may prosecute a case in a *Privatklage* (private prosecution). Such a private criminal action is governed under §§ 374 to 394 StPO and may be brought for certain offences enumerated in the canon of § 374 StPO. These offences — *e.g. Hausfriedensbruch* (unlawful entering of another person's house, § 123 StGB), *Beleidigung* (insult, §§ 185 *et seq.* StGB), *Sachbeschädigung* (criminal damage, § 303 StGB) — have in common the fact that they generally attack only the rights of the directly concerned persons (offender — victim) and, due to this, no public interest in prosecution is given or has to be protected.

The public prosecutor, therefore, can refrain from pressing charges as far as exclusively offences in the sense of § 374 StPO are concerned. Instead, the injured person themself has the opportunity to pursue a private criminal action. But for certain offences (*e.g.* unlawful entering of another person's house, insult, slight bodily injury) it is required under law that prior to bringing a private prosecution an attempt of reconciliation should have been tried — but failed (see § 380 StPO). At any stage of the proceedings under a private indictment, the public prosecutor's office may take over the prosecution with the legal consequence that the proceedings proceed to public prosecution (§ 377 II StPO) and the private prosecutor retires from proceedings; he may only take part in proceedings as a joint plaintiff.

B. ACCESSORY PROSECUTION (*NEBENKLAGE*)

The accessory prosecution by an injured party or his relatives is regulated in §§ 395 to 402 StPO. It is a further possibility that the victim's side (*e.g.* the injured person, or his relatives) may participate in a trial as a *Nebenkläger* (joint plaintiff or additional private prosecutor). He or she may join the public prosecutor in the prosecution of certain grave offences enumerated in § 395 StPO such as (attempted) manslaughter, (attempted) murder or rape. The joint plaintiff is a further party participating in proceedings, provided with procedural rights and may influence proceedings to a certain extent (see § 397 StPO).

C. SUMMARY PROCEEDINGS WITHOUT TRIAL (*STRAFBEFEHLSVERFAHREN*)

Summary proceedings without trial serves the purpose of obtaining a conviction as quickly as possible and without high costs and time-consuming trial proceedings (§§ 407 to 412 StPO). It comes into question for cases of lesser criminality in which the facts of the case have been ascertained in the investigative proceedings and in which the criminal has confessed to a crime.

The course of proceedings is as follows: at first, the public prosecutor presses a charge and applies for the issue of a *Strafbefehl* (order imposing punishment). Contrary to the bill of indictment — a certain legal consequence to be imposed on the person charged has to be requested. In summary proceedings without trial only the legal consequences enumerated in § 407 II StPO can be imposed — such as a fine, driving ban, refraining from penalty or an imprisonment up to one year if the sentence is suspended and the accused is represented by defence counsel.

The judge reviews — on record without trial — the application for the issue of an order imposing punishment as regards to jurisdiction and sufficient grounds for suspicion. The application is declined if the judge regards the person charged as not being sufficiently suspicious. But if there are no objections, the judge has to comply with the public prosecutor's application and has to issue an order imposing punishment as applied for.

This order imposing punishment may be appealed against by

the person charged within two weeks after it has been served on him, with the legal consequence that the (normal) trial procedure is conducted. If, however, there is no timely and admissible appeal, the fixed order imposing punishment acquires the character of a final judgment and becomes non-appealable.

D. EXPEDITED PROCEEDINGS (*BESCHLEUNIGTES VERFAHREN*)

Besides the proceedings mentioned above another type of proceeding is the expedited proceedings which are governed under §§ 417 *et seq.* StPO. The public prosecutor is obliged to apply for expedited proceedings as far as the facts of the case are simple and straightforward and due to this, the case qualifies for immediate trial. Then, the trial is conducted at once or within a short period without proceeding with the interlocutory procedure. The taking of evidence is simplified. But the legal consequences are restricted and only a fine or a sentence of imprisonment not exceeding one year may be imposed.

13. PENAL EXECUTION (*STRAFVOLLSTRECKUNG*) AND EXECUTION OF A CUSTODIAL SENTENCE (*STRAFVOLLZUG*)

We now come to the *real* end of criminal proceedings: the legal consequences of the final judgment may be the execution of a custodial sentence. Execution is governed under §§ 449 to 463 d StPO in which the enforcement of non-appealable judgments is initiated and supervised by the public prosecutor's office as law enforcement authority. At any *Landgericht* there are divisions for execution. These divisions are competent for those decisions which may become necessary with regard to the enforcement of prison sentences such as the revocation of the suspension of sentence on probation. The execution of a custodial sentence is the performance of the term of imprisonment. Proceedings are laid down in the *Strafvollzugsgesetz* (Prison Act).

In Germany there are certain panel registers: the Federal Public Prosecutor in Berlin registers any final conviction in the *Bundeszentralregister* (Federal Central Penal Register); the public prosecutor's office registers any relevant data concerning the preliminary proceedings; and finally any road traffic case is registered in the *Verkehrszentralregister* (Central Register of Traffic Violation).

Schedule 4: First-Instance Jurisdiction (o = judge; x = lay judges)

COURT	JURISDICTION AS REGARDS THE SUBJECT MATTER	PUNITIVE POWER
Amtsgericht (County Court)		
Einzelrichter (single judge) o	§ 25 GVG 1. private prosecution 2. criminal offences if the maximum anticipated prison sentence does not exceed two years	
Schöffengericht (court with lay judges) x o x	§§ 24, 28 GVG any *Verbrechen, Vergehen*[27] but **except for** the following offences: 1. jurisdiction of the *Landgericht* under § 74 II GVG (criminal chamber as the *Schwurgericht*) or § 74 a GVG (criminal chamber for state security matters) or jurisdiction of the *Oberlandesgericht* under § 120 GVG is present;	§ 24 II GVG 1. a pecuniary penalty or a prison sentence not exceeding four years imprisonment 2. any rule except for a confinement to an psychiatric institution or a preventive detention
Erweitertes Schöffengericht (extended court with lay judges) x o o x	2. a prison sentence of more than four years, a confinement to a psychiatric institution or a preventive detention is the minimum punishment; 3. public prosecutor presses charges with the *Landgericht* because of the particular importance.	
Landgericht (Regional Court)		
Große Strafkammer (grand criminal division) x o o (o) x	§§ 74 and 76 II GVG: any *Verbrechen* and *Vergehen*, if: 1. more than four years imprisonment, a confinement to a psychiatric institution or a preventive detention is the minimum punishment provided that no jurisdiction to a criminal division such as a *Schwurgericht* (§ 74 II GVG) or *Oberlandesgericht* (§ 120 GVG) is given; 2. the public prosecutor brings charges at the *Große Strafkammer* because of the particular importance of the case despite a minor expectation of penalty.	unrestricted
Schwurgericht (criminal chamber of the regional court) x o o o x	§§ 74 II and 76 I GVG exhausted catalogue of jurisdiction, especially wilful homicide and offences with fatal outcome	unrestricted
Oberlandesgericht Regional Appeal Court		
Strafsenat (Criminal division) o o o o o	§ 120 GVG State security-related matters and genocide	unrestricted

[27] *Vergehen* are minor offences which are punished by up to one year or by pecuniary penalty (§ 12 II StGB). *Verbrechen* are criminal offences punished with at least a one-year sentence of imprisonment (§ 12 I StGB).

Schedule 5: Sequence of courts starting from the *Amtsgerichte*

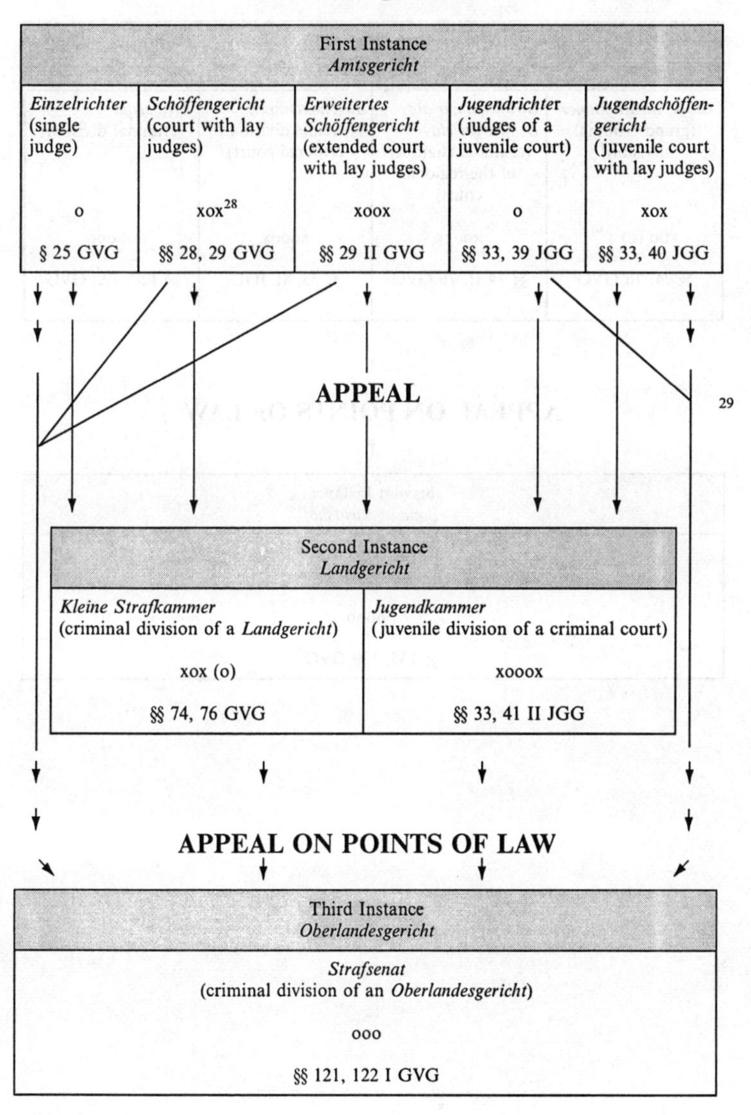

[28] o = judge; x = lay judge

[29] If criminal law relating to young offenders does apply and the judgment of first instance should be appealed there is a right to choose whether to file an appeal with the *Landgericht* or the appeal on points of law with the *Oberlandesgericht*.

Schedule 6: Sequence of courts starting from the *Land-* and *Oberlandesgericht*

First Instance			
Landgericht	*Landgericht*	*Landgericht*	*Oberlandes-gericht*
Große Strafkammer (grand criminal division)	*Strafkammer als Schwurgericht* (criminal chamber of the regional court)	*Jugendkammer* (juvenile division of criminal court)	*Strafsenat* (criminal division)
xoo (o) x[30]	xooox	xooox	ooooo
§§ 74, 76 GVG	§§ 74 II, 76 GVG	§§ 33, 41 JGG	§§ 120, 122 GVG

↓

APPEAL ON POINTS OF LAW

↓

Second Instance *Bundesgerichtshof*
Strafsenat (criminal division)
ooooo
§§ 135, 139 GVG

[30] o = judge; x = lay judge.

SELECTED BIBLIOGRAPHY

I. Commentaries

Callies, Müller-Dietz, *Strafvollzugsgesetz* (7th ed., 1998).
Kleinknecht, Meyer-Goßner, *Strafprozeßordnung* (43th ed., 1997).
Lackner, *Strafgesetzbuch* (22nd ed., 1997).
Schönke, Schröder, *Strafgesetzbuch* (25th ed., 1997).
Tröndle, *Strafgesetzbuch* (48th ed., 1997).
Pfeiffer, *Karlsruher Kommentar zur Strafprozeßordnung und zum Gerichtsverfassungsgesetz mit Einführungsgesetz* (4th ed., 1999).

II. Textbooks

Dahs, *Handbuch des Strafverteidigers* (1998).
Fetzer, *Strafprozeßrecht* (2nd ed., 1995).
Hassemer, *Einführung in die Grundlagen des Strafrechts* (2nd ed., 1990).
Luther, *Grundzüge des Strafverfahrensrechts* (1991).
Roxin, *Strafprozeßrecht* (15th ed., 1997).
Roxin, *Strafverfahrensrecht* (25th ed., 1998).
Schroeder, *Strafprozeßrecht* (2nd ed., 1997).
Weiland, *Einführung in die Praxis des Strafverfahrens* (2nd ed., 1996).
Wetterich, Hamann, *Strafvollstreckung* (5th ed., 1994).

Chapter Eight Administrative Court Structure and Procedure

1. Introduction

The public administration has its own specific field of law in order to carry out administrative tasks. This branch of law is called *Verwaltungsrecht* (administrative law) and regulates the activities of the State or any other administrative authority — even those which do not exercise legislative, judicial or governmental tasks.[1] Administrative law contains all the rules concerning the administrative apparatus, its tasks and administrative procedure. Administrative law is public law and, due to this, has to be demarcated from private law such as civil or commercial law. Public law regulates, in general terms, the relations between citizens and public administration whereas private law governs the relations among citizens. The field of administrative law consists of the general administrative law which is laid out in the *Verwaltungsverfahrensgesetz* (VwVfG — Code of Administrative Procedure) and specific administrative law which concerns the different branches of administration such as the *Polizei- und Ordnungsrecht* (police and regulatory law), the *Baurecht* (building laws), the *Beamtengesetz* (Civil Service Code) and the *Gemeindeordnungen* (Local Government Codes).

Public administration is mainly carried out by regulations and charters, plans, internal administrative decisions and, most importantly, by administrative acts. These administrative decisions are rendered in the *Verwaltungsverfahren* (administrative procedure), and thereby, the substantive administrative law — such as police and regulatory law, law on building, local governmental law and environmental law — is implemented by those decisions. The Code of Administrative Procedure differentiates between the various types of administrative procedure. Unless otherwise prescribed by law, the common administrative procedure applies as set out in §§ 9 to 62 VwVfG. But where a special procedure is prescribed statutorily — such as the formal admin-

---

[1] For more details, see *ibid.*, Chap. Three, 3, C.

istrative procedure (§§ 63 to 71 VwVfG), the plan approval procedure (§§ 72 to 78 VwVfG) or the procedure of administrative remedy (§§ 79 and 80 VwVfG) — it has to be followed.

The common administrative procedure is set in motion when a public authority is statutorily obliged to follow it, or when a citizen has applied for it, or when the authority, in its best judgment, considers it the appropriate way to fulfil statutory obligations. Its most distinctive features are the principles of informality and of investigation. In addition, the parties involved have a right to be heard and have access to files before an administrative decision is delivered. But on the other hand, they have certain duties. They are obliged to contribute in investigating the facts of the case and, for instance, must disclose the relevant information and other evidence known to them. Proceedings are concluded with the issue of an administrative decision which may be a *Verwaltungsakt* (administrative act, § 35 VwVfG) or an *öffentlich-rechtlicher Vertrag* (public law contract, §§ 54 *et seq.* VwVfG) agreed with the respective citizen.

The *Verwaltungsgerichtsordnung* (VwGO — Rules of the Administrative Courts) provide certain judicial remedies for citizens (which will be outlined in detail below) who may be affected by an administrative decision. A citizen seeking relief to obtain protection against an administrative act or its omissions having an onerous effect on him has to initiate the *Widerspruchsverfahren* (protest procedure) which takes place before the administrative authorities. It is a preliminary proceeding prior to suing a public authority in which an individual administrative act is reviewed after a protest by the aggrieved party. The protest procedure is mainly regulated in §§ 68 to 73 and 80 VwGO.

After the conclusion of an (unsuccessful) protest procedure, the citizen may seek relief and file a suit. This is the *Verwaltungsgerichtsverfahren* (legal proceedings in an administrative court) and is governed in the Rules of Administrative Courts. A citizen may go to administrative courts at once without conducting protest procedure when the decision under appeal is not an administrative act.

2. ADMINISTRATIVE JURISDICTION (*VERWALTUNGSGERICHTSBARKEIT*)

A. ADMINISTRATIVE COURTS

Structure, powers and procedural rules of administrative jurisdiction are governed under the Rules of Administrative Courts (VwGO). The administrative jurisdiction is guaranteed by Article 95 GG and exercised by the *Verwaltungsgerichte* (administrative courts) who are independent from the administration. Any administrative court is composed of a president, several presiding judges and further professional and honorary judges (§ 5 I, § 9 I and § 10 I VwGO).

The administrative jurisdiction is organised on three different levels (see Schedules 6 to 8). As a matter of principle, decisions are taken at first instance by a *Verwaltungsgericht* (Administrative Court), at second instance by an *Oberverwaltungsgericht* (Higher Administrative Court) and at third and final instance by the *Bundesverwaltungsgericht* (Supreme Federal Administrative Court).

— First, there are the *Verwaltungsgerichte* which are courts of the *Länder*. Their panel of judges are called *Kammern* (chambers). Chambers generally hear cases in the composition of three professional judges and two honorary judges but transfer the matter to one of its panel members (who then acts as a single judge), if the legal matter is not of principle importance and does not contain factual or legal difficulties (§ 6 I No. 1 and 2 VwGO).

— *Oberverwaltungsgerichte*[2] are also courts of the *Länder*. In any *Bundesland*, there is at least one *Oberverwaltungsgericht*. These courts render judicial decisions in panels of judges which are called *Senate* (senates). A *Senate*, as a rule, delivers decisions with three (professional) judges in attendance, and as far as the law of a *Land* deviates from this principle, they may sit with five judges, two of them may be honorary judges (§ 9 III VwGO).

— The *Bundesverwaltungsgericht* as the highest administrative court in Germany is a court of the Federation which still sits in Berlin but will move to Leipzig (which — as a city for the highest German courts — has a long tradition in legal history). Its panel of judges are senates which consist of five professional judges; only three judges may participate in the judicial process, if a judicial decision is issued in chambers like the *Beschluß* (court order), which is a judicial decision delivered *in Camera* (10 III VwGO).[3]

---

[2] In some *Bundesländer*, courts of second instance bear the name *Verwaltungsgerichtshof* (VGH, Higher Administrative Court).

[3] Sometimes the higher administrative courts have to set up a *Großer Senat* (Great Senate), for instance the *Bundesverwaltungsgericht* has to do so as far as one of its senates intends to diviate from the adjudication of another senate or of the *Großen Senat* (§ 11 II VwGO).

B. JURISDICTION

The jurisdiction is regulated in the Rules of Administrative Courts. These rules are simple but rigid. The Act contains no exclusive jurisdictions, and — contrary to civil proceedings — stipulations as to the venue cannot be agreed between the participating parties in administrative court proceedings.

The question of whether or not to have jurisdiction sometimes might not be answered by trial court. The court may be unable to exercise jurisdiction on legal or factual grounds, or because more than one court has been confirmed as having to have jurisdiction. Then, the next highest administrative court or the *Bundesverwaltungsgericht* can be called by the parties or the trial court to take a decision on the court's jurisdiction (§ 53 VwGO). Sometimes, a court may lack local jurisdiction or jurisdiction as regards to the subject matter. In such a case, the court concerned has to transfer the case — on application by the plaintiff — to the competent court (§ 83 VwGO and §§ 17 to 17 b GVG).[4] Administrative courts have to examine *ex officio* whether they are competent to give a ruling on a case.

At first, the court has to have jurisdiction as regards the subject matter. The subject matter jurisdiction determines which of the administrative courts within the sequence of courts is competent to hear the case (see Schedules 6 to 8). Contrary to civil procedure, this kind of jurisdiction does not relate to the sum involved but is rather acting in accordance with the respective matter in dispute. This, for instance, can be an act, omission, claim or allegation.

(a) The *Verwaltungsgericht* as a court of first instance hears any legal dispute to which the recourse to administrative court is at hand (§ 45 VwGO) unless otherwise prescribed by the law.

(b) Judgments of the *Verwaltungsgericht* under appeal (on points of facts and law) are heard by the *Oberverwaltungsgericht* (§ 46 VwGO). In addition, the *Oberverwaltungsgericht* may also act as a court of first instance provided that specific matters are in dispute such as judicial proceedings on the constitutionality of laws (§ 47 VwGO) or a legal matter enumerated in § 48 VwGO (for example proceedings under the Atomic Energy Act or a project-determination procedure).

(c) The *Bundesverwaltungsgericht* may act as court of last instance (§ 49 VwGO) and, due to this, decides on appeals

---

[4] For more details, see *ibid.*, Chap. Five, 2.

on points of law against judgments of the *Oberverwaltungsgericht* (§ 132 VwGO). It also hears leap-frog appeals against judgments of the *Verwaltungsgericht* (§§ 134, 135 VwGO). In a few cases, the *Bundesverwaltunggericht* performs a dual role as court of first and last instance. These legal matters are enumerated in § 50 VwGO and can concern — for instance — public law disputes of a non-constitutional manner between federation and *Länder* or between the *Länder inter se*, or complaints against the prohibition against an association which has been issued by the Federal Ministry of Interior pursuant to the Law Regulating Association.

The local jurisdiction determines which court is locally competent to hear the case. The local jurisdiction is regulated in § 52 VwGO. Due to this norm, in disputes concerning immovable property or rights or legal relationships which are attached to a certain district, this district determines the venue (§ 52 No. 1 VwGO). Furthermore, if there are actions to rescind[5] against public authorities (such as federal or other authorities or corporations under public law), the court then has local jurisdiction in which this authority has its seat (§ 52 No. 2 VwGO). In all remaining actions to rescind, except for those mentioned in No. 1 and 4, the court is competent in whose district the administrative act has been issued (§ 52 No. 3 VwGO). Furthermore, in actions concerning the status of a public official or a corresponding employment, the local court is determined in accordance with the domicile of the officer concerned (§ 52 No. 4 VwGO). Finally, any other court in whose district the defendant has his seat will have jurisdiction (§ 52 No. 5 VwGO).

3. THE PROTEST PROCEDURE (*WIDERSPRUCHSVERFAHREN*)

The protest procedure is mainly regulated in §§ 68–73 VwGO, §§ 79 and 80 VwVfG. It is an administrative proceeding to review an individual administrative decision upon a protest by the aggrieved party. It is a preliminary proceeding prior to suing a public authority which takes place before the administrative authorities. A concluded protest proceeding is a procedural prerequisite for filing certain administrative suits, such as the action to rescind.

These administrative proceedings pursue three aims: at first,

---

[5] For more details, see *ibid*, Chap. Eight, 4, B, (1).

the citizen concerned obtains a non-judicial remedy; next, the issuing authority gains a further opportunity to review once again and internally the legality and expediency of the respective administrative act; and finally, it discharges administrative courts of claims that otherwise would be heard in the courts.

A. THE COURSE OF PROCEEDINGS

The protest procedure takes place between the *Widerspruchsführer* (person filing a protest) and the administration. It is initiated by filing a protest with the *Ausgangsbehörde* (issuing public authority). A properly lodged protest observing the deadline has two effects: it delays the onset of finality, which means, the administrative act's enforcement is postponed (suspensive effect) and proceedings are brought — as a rule — to the next highest public authority (devolutive effect).

After filing a protest, the *Abhilfeverfahren* (redress proceedings) is the first thing to take place, in which the issuing authority gets the opportunity to review once more the legality and expediency of its administrative decision which has to be an administrative act. The further course of proceeding is determined by the outcome of this examination. If the issuing authority considers the protest as legally justified, the protest is allowed and a decision as to the costs is given as well. But, if the protest is not allowed, the issuing authority submits the legal matter for decision to the *Widerspruchsbehörde* (protest authority). Now, the proper protest procedure takes place before the protest authority which, as a rule, is the *nächsthöhere Behörde* (public authority of the next highest ranking). The protest authority delivers a decision in the form of a *Widerspruchsbescheid* (ruling on a protest). The protest authority may quash the administrative act under appeal if the protest is admissible and well founded; otherwise the protest will be dismissed.

B. ADMISSIBILITY

In order to be successful, the protest must be admissible and, due to this, has to meet certain prerequisites. First of all, the dispute must relate to a public law issue which has not specifically been assigned to another court (§ 40 VwGO in analogous interpretation).[6] At this stage, private law disputes have to be demarcated from public law disputes because the public admin-

[6] This provision applies only by analogy because it concerns administrative court proceedings. For more details, see *ibid.*, Chap. Eight, 4, A.

istration is only responsible to decide on disputes referring to public law questions.

Next, the protest has to be *statthaft* (permissible) — that is to say, prior to filing certain actions (such as the action to rescind and the action for the issue of an administrative act) a protest must be filed in order to review the decision under appeal which can only be an administrative act (§ 35 VwVfG[7]). A protest against non-administrative acts, for instance physical acts, legal norms or internal decisions is not permissible.[8] As a result, the plaintiff can directly file a suit to challenge a non-administrative act. In addition, § 68 I 2 VwGO enumerates cases in which the law discharges a citizen from the obligation to lodge a protest prior to filing action. These cases are as follows:

1. In particular legal matters for which it has statutorily been prescribed, such as formal administrative proceedings (§ 70 VwVfG);
2. A supreme federal authority or supreme *Land* authority has issued the challenged administrative act; or
3. A third party is affected by a ruling on a protest for the first time.

In these cases, the legislator has regarded a re-examining of the lawfulness and expediency of the administrative acts as not being necessary.

The person filing a protest also has to meet specific procedural requirements. First, he must have the *Widerspruchsbefugnis* (right of protest). This capacity presupposes that he may claim to argue to have been infringed in his individual rights by the administrative act or omission which has an onerous effect on him (§ 42 II VwGO in analogous interpretation[9]). In addition, he must be capable of taking part in the procedure. This *Beteiligtenfähigkeit* (capacity to be a participant) is governed under § 11 VwVfG and, due to this norm, any natural person, legal entity, association possessing a right[10] just as any public authority enjoys this legal advantage. Besides this, the participant must also possess the *Handlungsfähigkeit* (capacity to act) which is the ability to act in such a way as to

---

[7] For more details, see *ibid.*, Chap. Eight, 4, B, (1).

[8] There is an exception: irrespective of whether an administrative act is present, cases concerning the status of a public officer require the course of procedure of administrative remedy under § 126 III BRRG.

[9] This provision applies only by analogy because it concerns administrative court procedure. For more details, see *ibid.*, Chap. Eight, 4, B., (1).

[10] This right must be one which is controversial in the proceedings.

produce legal consequences (§§ 12, 14 VwVfG). Any party is allowed to conduct proceedings by himself or by an authorised person. Participants, therefore, may effectively be represented by an authorised person. Mandatory representation by lawyers exists only before the *Bundesverwaltungsgericht* as the highest administrative court (§ 67 I VwGO).

A protest must be lodged in the correct form, which means it has to be filed in writing or to be recorded with the issuing public authority, and also it must be filed within one month after the announcement of the administrative act (§ 70 VwGO). As far as a party fails to meet the deadline in § 70 VwGO, the administrative act becomes final and non-appealable.[11] With regard to time limits, the advice of legal remedies relating to the administrative act can be quite important as well because the time limit for filing a protest is extended from one month to one year when the advice has not taken place or has been performed incorrectly (§§ 70 II, 58 II VwGO).

Last but not least, the appellant must have a *Rechtsschutzbedürfnis* (legitimate interest to take legal action) this is not the case if the claiming party may reach the satisfaction of his claim in a different, easy and more simple way.

C. REASONABLE JUSTIFICATION

In addition to the protest's admissibility, the protest must also be *begründet* (well-founded) which is the case when the administrative act under appeal is unlawful and not expedient. The lawfulness and expedience of an administrative act is, due to § 68 VwGO, the test standard of a protest's reasonable justification. An administrative act or the omission to issue the administrative act is unlawful as far as this judicial decision breaches substantive administrative law and through that infringes the appellant's individual rights. The expedience of the administrative act under appeal has been examined as well, and discretionary decisions are reviewed not only with regard to an abuse of discretion but also with a view to inexpedience, inefficiency and further alternative decisions which perhaps would put a lesser burden on the citizen.

Within the protest procedure, the administrative authority reviews the position of the case and its legal situation at the moment in which the ruling on a protest is delivered. This is the

---

[11] The party which failed to meet the deadline can apply for restitution to the previous condition (§§ 70 II, 60 VwGO) provided that he may show that he has not given the cause for the failure to meet the deadline.

relevant moment in time. As far as the factual or legal basis of the challenged administrative act has changed after its issue, the amended circumstances are taken into account in the decision-making process by the public authority. The administrative act obtains — for the first time — its finalised feature with the ruling on the protest.

The protest authority delivers decision in a *Widerspruchsbescheid* (ruling on a protest). It is an administrative act in the sense of § 35 VwVfG and, due to this, has to be in writing, must contain advice to the addressee of his legal remedies and has to be served upon him (§ 73 III VwGO). The ruling on a protest must be justified; the facts of the case and the legal reasoning on which the decision is resting must be laid down in a simple and understandable way. The authority, moreover, has to enter in detail into particulars of the arguments presented by the person having filed the protest. A ruling on a protest which does not contain substantiation or lack of supporting arguments, contains a procedural mistake and, as a result, is unlawful and can sucessfully be challenged by an action (§ 79 II VwGO).

The protest authority may quash the protest if it is either inadmissible or admissible but not well-founded; and as far as the protest is well-founded, the respective administrative act will be quashed or the act applied for will be issued depending on the legal consequences petitioned with the protest. The protest authority also renders a cost order (§ 73 II 2 VwGO and § 80 VwVfG). The administration must reimburse the appellant's necessary expenses of effective prosecution, if the protest has been successful; otherwise, the appellant must reimburse the necessary expenses of effective defence of the administration. The costs, however, will have to be split or reasonably divided as far as the protest has only partly been successful (see § 155 I VwGO).

4. THE ACTION (*KLAGE*)

Any citizen can seek judicial relief in the administrative courts and can obtain protection against unlawful administrative decisions which have an onerous effect on the citizen. Administrative actions are successful, if they meet certain prerequisites, namely, are admissible and well-founded.

A. RECOURSE OF ADMINISTRATIVE COURTS

The first precondition for a successful administrative action is the ability to have recourse to the administrative courts. This is comprehensively governed under § 40 VwGO. As a matter of principle, the administrative courts are responsible for any litigation which belongs to the sphere of public law, which is of a non-constitutional manner and is not specifically assigned to another court by federal law. Judicial relief in remaining legal disputes is not part of the administrative jurisdiction and can be reached, for example in criminal, civil, fiscal or social courts.[12]

Certain cases are specifically allotted by federal law to the administrative courts — such as actions based on the status of public officials (§ 126 BRRG), claims based on public law contracts (§ 40 II 1 VwGO), or compensatory claims for pecuniary prejudice because of the withdrawal of an unlawful administrative act (§ 40 II 2 VwGO and § 48 VI VwVfG).

In addition, public law disputes may be expressly delegated by federal law to another jurisdiction.[13] For example, § 32 FGO constitutes the fiscal court jurisdiction of the tax courts for cases concerning tax law; § 51 SGG furnishes the social jurisdiction in matters concerning social law; and § 40 II VwGO establishes the ordinary jurisdiction regarding claims to compensation against a public authority for the sacrifice of the common good, pecuniary claims in public law, deposits or claims for damages based on failures to comply with duties under public law which do not rest on a contract under public law. Ordinary jurisdiction is also constituted regarding claims for damages based on expropriation (Article 14 III 4 GG) or breach of official duties (Article 34 GG and § 839 BGB).

As far as a legal matter is not specifically assigned to a court, the question of whether administrative courts are competent to hear the case — is answered by applying § 40 I 1 VwGO. This comprehensive clause makes clear that the administrative courts are responsible for any litigation from the sphere of public law. Due to this, any case has to be classified as concerning either public or private law. A demarcation has to be drawn because civil courts are only competent to hear cases subject to a private law claim, and administrative courts are responsible for subjects to a dispute under public law only.

Administrative courts have to review *ex officio* whether a suit is subject to public law and thereby take into consideration only the true legal nature of the asserted claim; in this respect, the parties' legal opinions are not relevant at all. This decision looks simple at the first sight. But in some cases, the line between private and public law is difficult to be drawn, especially because of the fact that this question is not codified in any

---

[12] For more details, see *ibid.*, Chap. Five, 2.

[13] For more details, see *ibid.*, Chap. Five, 2.

detail in the law. Due to this, various theories[14] have been developed which attempt to define and determine the features of a public law dispute and its delimitation to private law. Historically and dogmatically, these theories are less productive, because, especially in borderline cases they can contribute little to decide a case but serve only as a "*Faustregel*" (rule of thumb), especially in cases which have not been decided yet. In practice, a distinct, developed case law and the acknowledged fields of either private or public law are helping to determine the interpretation of § 40 VwGO:

— The *Eingriffsverwaltung* (interventive administration) is acknowledged as a typical branch of public law. It represents the traditional branch of administrative tasks. Its purpose and intention is to protect law and order against dangers which may threaten the public interest or the individual citizen. To it belongs, for example, police and security law,[15] municipal revenue law, law regulating the rights and duties of civil servants, law concerning the State's organisation and administration and law on environmental protection against noxious intrusions.

— Those branches of law in which the administration takes part in trade and commerce and acts like an ordinary citizen are acknowledged as typical fields of private law. These branches include, for instance, the administration of state property, or the exercise of legal transactions on behalf of the State in order to fulfil the administrative task (such as to enter tenancy agreements for administrative offices or the purchase of office requirements).

Finally, as far as a public law dispute can be described, it must be demarcated from cases involving constitutional law. This is required under § 40 I VwGO which specifically excludes litigation in constitutional matters. The reason is that constitu-

---

[14] One theory is the *Subordinationstheorie*. Due to this, a distinct feature of public law is that under it administration is regarded as being above citizens and citizens are regarded as subordinate to the administration; characteristic of private law is that both administration and citizens are placed on the same footing.

Another theory is the *Subjektstheorie*. Thereafter, it should be decisive who is entitled or obliged out of the legal rule in question: a dispute belongs to public law, if only the State or a comparable corporation under public law is entitled or obliged thereof; a legal relation or act is subject to private law, as far as private persons are entitled or obliged thereof.

[15] Such as the right of assembly, law concerning foreign nations, buildings regulations law, traffic law, trade and industry law, etc.

tional questions do not belong to administrative courts but only to constitutional courts. Litigation involving constitutional law may be regarded as disputes between constitutional organs of the Federal Government or between the Federal Government and the *Länder*.

B. TYPE OF ACTIONS (*KLAGEARTEN*)

Before filing an administrative action, the plaintiff should review exactly which of the following types of actions will help to realize his claim at best. Under the Rules of Administrative Courts (VwGO) different types of actions can be lodged. A plaintiff pursuing different types of relief may also combine his different claims in one action. Such a joinder of causes of actions is admissible under the requirements set forth in § 44 VwGO. Any administrative action has its own specific, procedural requirements to be met in order to be admissible and its legal justification varies and acts merely in accordance with the substantive administrative law.

(1) Action to rescind (*Anfechtungsklage*)

The action to rescind may be regarded as the "classical" action of administrative trial governed under § 42 I 1. Alt. VwGO. The action to rescind is directed to quash the administrative act under appeal which has an onerous effect on the plaintiff. While filing such a suit the citizen can defend himself against a *belastender Verwaltungsakt* (administrative act imposing obligations) and demand a return to the status quo. Due to this, the administrative decision appealed from can only be an administrative act.

Therefore, the action to rescind presupposes the presence of an effective administrative act. § 35 VwVfG defines an administrative act as an order, decision or other measure made under public law in order to regulate an individual case on the field of public law which achieves an immediate legal effect on external subjects. It follows from this definition that the administrative act has five characteristic and compulsory elements: first, the administrative act must be a measure (order or decision); this is any act containing a specific declaration. Next, only public authorities — as defined in § 1 IV VwVfG — may issue administrative acts. Any office exercising the task of public administration is acknowledged as a public authority. Moreover, administrative acts must be attributable to the sphere of public law. Therefore, they stand in contrast to instruments under private law. In addition, a very decisive element of administrative acts is its regulative feature because the act must be issued in order to determine, regulate, change or modify a legal consequence. Given this, an administrative act can establish new rights or impose obligations. Furthermore, the administrative act must regulate a concrete, individual case; this element distinguishes the administrative act from legal norms which have an abstract and general legal nature. Finally, the administrative act must be issued to establish an immediate external legal effect; it, therefore, has to be distinguished from internal orders or internal administrative regulations not related to achieve any kind of legal effect on external subjects.

Filing an action to rescind also supposes the plaintiff's *Klagebefugnis* (right of action). Due to § 42 II VwGO, the plaintiff must claim to argue that his individual rights are infringed by the administrative act under appeal. Thus, the addressee of an administrative act is, as a rule, always empowered to file a suit because he may always claim that the administrative act to be appealed restricts at least his basic right of liberty of action governed in Article 2 I GG. A question may be put with regard to the purpose behind the right of action — and the answer is clear: it excludes popular actions and demarcates in a clear way an infringed person from a person merely factually concerned or bothered. As a rule within the German legal system, the latter have no right of action.

Anyway, as outlined above, the legal situation is quite clear if the addressee of the administrative act files a suit; but what happens if a third party seeks judicial relief? The third party only has the right of action if he can assert to have an individual right which is infringed through the issue of the administrative act under appeal. To establish such an individual right which also protects the third party's interest is not easy but can be put forward as follows: it may be derived — for instance — from basic rights (which are specified by the courts) or from certain legal rules[16] which especially intend to safeguard the third party's protection. These legal rules are called *Schutznormen*. A legal rule is to be seen as a *Schutznorm* as far as its legal protection is allocated just to the third party. This occurs under the following conditions: there is a clear and fixed group of potential plaintiffs to which the plaintiff belongs; the purpose of the legal rule is at least directed for the plaintiff's protection.

As outlined before, prior to filing an action to rescind, the

---

[16] As *Schutznormen* have been acknowleged by the courts, for instance §§ 30, 34 and 35 BauGB (Federal Town and Country Planning Code), §§ 4 I, 5 I No. 1 BImSchG (Federal Law on protection against harmful effects on the Environment).

protest procedure must have been conducted unsuccessfully, that is to say, the administration has not quashed the administrative act under appeal. Such a protest procedure is a further specific procedural requirement of this kind of action. Moreover, the action to rescind has to be filed within just one month after the ruling on the objection has been serviced on the plaintiff (§ 74 I VwGO); this deadline is extended to one year provided that the advice given of the plaintiff's legal remedies has not been carried out at all or has been incorrect (§ 58 II VwGO). A plaintiff failing to observe the time limit has only one opportunity to seek judicial relief: he can put in a claim for the *Wiedereinsetzung in den vorigen Stand* (restitution to the previous condition) in which he can only assert that the default does not rest on a mistake arising in his own sphere (§ 60 VwGO). Only if this pleading is successful, can he sue. Otherwise the action will be dismissed because of the non-observance of the time limit.

The reasonable justification of the action to rescind is roughly specified in § 113 I 1 VwGO. Due to this legal norm, action is legally justified as far as the administrative act under appeal is unlawful (which is a question of substantive administrative law) and, therefore, infringes the individual rights of the plaintiff. The administrative act and the ruling on a protest are quashed when the action is well founded. Otherwise the action is dismissed on the merits.

(2) Action for the issue of an administrative act (*Verpflichtungsklage*)

The action for the issue of an administrative act is governed under § 42 I 2. Alt. VwGO and demands the performance of a denied or omitted administrative act for the benefit of the plaintiff. Contrary to the action to rescind, the purpose of this action is not the reversal but the issue of a *begünstigender Verwaltungsakt* (administrative act establishing rights) such as a building permission. A plaintiff files such an action in order to extend his status quo, he claims to establish new rights.

The plaintiff filing this kind of action must have a right of action (§ 42 II VwGO). He must assert to have been infringed in his individual rights because the performance of the administrative act has been denied or failed to do so although he has a corresponding claim. Such a claim can be based on basic rights, legal rules of protection or a special public law relationship such as a public law contract or a binding administrative promise. In addition, prior to filing this suit, the plaintiff must have unsuccessfully conducted the protest procedure which — as shown by the action to rescind — is the procedural prerequisite for commencement of this action. Moreover, the plaintiff also has to observe a time limit of one month after the decision has been serviced on him (§ 74 II VwGO).

As far as the admissibility of an action can be confirmed, the question of its reasonable justification arises. This is laid down in § 113 V VwGO. Due to this norm, the action is well-founded provided that the administrative act's denial or omission has been unlawful and through that infringes the individual rights of the plaintiff. As far as the action is well-founded, the court puts the obligation on the respective public authority to perform the petitioned official act provided that the case has the necessary requirements for a court decision. Otherwise, the court only states the obligation of the public authority to give notification under consideration of the court's legal opinion laid down in the judgment.

(3) Action for performance (*Leistungsklage*)

The action for performance is not expressly regulated in the Rules of Administrative Courts but is specified by the courts.[17] In filing the action for performance, a plaintiff's claim must be to compel the performance of a reasonable and definite obligation which might be an act, toleration or an omission. Therefore, the issue of an administrative act cannot be enforced with this kind of action. The object at issue in this action is only the *Realakt* (physical act) — which can also be named as *schlichtes Verwaltungshandeln* (simple administrative action) — such as an indication, notice, report, warning or payment.

There are two different actions for performance: the positive action for performance demands performance of a certain physical act, and the negative action for performance — also called *Unterlassungsklage* (prohibitory action) — claims to prevent a certain act; it is the defence of a disturbance which has already taken place or is about to take place. Like any other administrative action, the action for performance must meet a certain procedural prerequisite in order to be admissible, namely the plaintiff must have a right of action (§ 42 II VwGO analogous).[18] Further requirements do not exist. The protest procedure (provided that it is not prescribed by law — such as in § 126 III BRRG — Civil Service Law) does not have to be

---

[17] BVerwGE 31, 301; 60, 144.

[18] This provision applies only by analogy because it concerns expressively only the action to rescind or the action for the issue of an administrative act.

conducted nor has a certain deadline to be observed. In addition to the procedural prerequisites, the action for performance must be legally justified which presupposes that the plaintiff has an entitlement to performance of the act, toleration or omission. Like any other action it is a question of substantive administrative law whether the plaintiff has such a claim.

(4) Declaratory action (*Feststellungsklage*)

A further administrative action is the *Feststellungsklage* (declaratory action). The Code of Administrative Procedure provides different declaratory actions. One of these is governed under § 43 I 1. Alt. VwGO with which the plaintiff may claim the declaration of the existence or non-existence of a legal relationship. The action is called positive or negative declaratory action as the case may be. In these actions, the term "legal relationship" as the subject matter of action is decisive and may be defined as reasonable concrete legal relations under public law between two persons or a person and an object. Such a relationship can concern certain obligations, entitlements or contracts. The plaintiff filing such a suit must assert the existence or non-existence of the legal relationship as mentioned above and set forth to have an interest in the way that the declaration will soon be performed. The latter is called *Feststellungsinteresse* (interest to seek a declaratory judgment) which is present if the judicial decision can improve the legal position of the claiming party. In addition, the plaintiff filing such a suit must have a right of action (§ 42 II VwGO). Further procedural prerequisites do not have to be met. The protest procedure (unless it is prescribed by law, *e.g.* in § 126 III BRRG) does not have to be conducted and there is no deadline for filing the suit. The declaratory action is legally justified when a plaintiff's claim to declare something exists as a question to be answered in accordance with substantive administrative law.

A further declaratory action is the *Nichtigkeitsfeststellungsklage* (action for cancellation of a declaration) which is laid down in § 43 I 2 Alt. VwGO. It claims to declare the annulment of an administrative act. The plaintiff must assert that the void administrative act has an onerous effect on him and infringes his individual's rights. He also has to specify that he has an interest in seeking a declaratory judgment.

The *Fortsetzungsfeststellungklage* (declaratory action for continuation) is another declaratory action which demands the declaration that an administrative act has been finally disposed of and whose completion may have happened prior to filing the suit (§ 113 I 4 VwGO analogous) or during trial (§ 113 I 4

VwGO). The completion of an administrative act — which must have been in existence prior to completion — may have factual grounds (such as lapse of time) or legal grounds (such as the withdrawal or revocation of the administrative act). The plaintiff filing such a suit claims the declaration that the respective administrative act to be disposed of was unlawful and therefore has infringed his individual rights. Such a claiming party must have the right of action, must have conducted unsuccessfully the protest procedure and has to file action within the time prescribed by law, namely within one month after the service of the administrative act under appeal (§ 74 VwGO). In addition to this, the plaintiff has to show the presence of a *besonderes Feststellungsinteresse* (special interest to seek a declaratory action) which can be confirmed if the claiming party establishes the danger of repetition,[19] the interest of rehabilitation,[20] the impairment of substantial basic constitutional rights[21] or the preparation of a lawsuit for official liability or compensation.[22] In addition to those procedural prerequisites mentioned above, the suit must be well-founded which is the case when the administrative act to be disposed of was unlawful and through that has infringed the plaintiff's rights. Whether the administrative act was unlawful, can be answered only by applying the substantive administrative law.

(5) Judicial review (*Normenkontrolle*)

§ 47 VwGO governs judicial review, which is the examination on the constitutionality of laws. Courts review subordinated laws and determine their constitutionality. But this objective review is only a test of the constitutionality of subordinated law and must be demarcated from the test of the constitutionality of supreme laws which takes place before the constitutional courts. The latter is laid down in the German *Grundgesetz* (Article. 93 I No. 2, No. 4a GG and Article. 100 GG).[23]

Back to judicial review governed under § 47 VwGO: these proceedings are set in motion by filing an application, and the applicant may demand to review the constitutionality of charters or regulations being issued on the basis of the Town and

---

19 See BVerwGE 42, 318, 326; 80, 355, 365; VGH München, BayVBl. 1983, 434.
20 See BVerwGE 26, 168; BVerwGE NJW 1991, 581.
21 The adjudication has accepted such an impairment partly together with other reasons, for instance the bugging campaign (BVerwGE 87, 23) or the infringement of the right of assembly (OVG Bremen, NVwZ 1987, 235).
22 BVerwGE 9, 196, 198; another view VGH Mannheim, NVwZ-RR 1991, 518.
23 For more details, see *ibid.*, Chap. Three, 8, B, (2).

Country Planning Code or any legal rule of a lower ranking than the *Land* law — as far as it is prescribed by law. The applicant has to show his *Antragsbefugnis* (legal ability to institute proceedings). Due to § 47 II VwGO, the legal ability to institute proceedings requires that the applicant (a human being, legal entity or public authority) has suffered or soon expects to suffer a disadvantage under the legal source under appeal. The proceedings have to be initiated against the public authority, corporation or foundation which has issued the legal rule under appeal. The application for judicial review is legally justified if the respective legal rule is unlawful. This again is a question of substantive administrative law.

C. THE PARTICIPANT (*BETEILIGTER*)

The Rules of Administrative Courts set a certain standard of the capacity to be a party in the process. § 63 VwGO enumerates the parties who may take part in proceedings. First, there are the plaintiff and the defendant. Their role generally is as follows: the claiming citizen seeks judicial relief from the defendant who might be the State — acting through its organs such as the Federal Government, the *Länder* or the local authorities — or a corporation under public law. In addition, a third party can also be a participant in proceedings. The third party is the *Beigeladener* (summoned third party). The court issues a summons to interested parties who are not party to the proceedings, but whose legal interests may be affected. These third parties, then, attend proceedings. The summons to interested parties must show and specify the present position of the case and grounds for the summons. Finally, public authority attorneys[24] may also take part in proceedings. They are called *Vertreter des öffentlichen Interesses* (agent of the public interest) in trials before the *Verwaltungs-* and *Oberverwaltungsgericht*, and *Oberbundesanwalt* (Chief Public Attorney) in trials before the *Bundesverwaltungsgericht*.

In an administrative court procedure more than one party on the plaintiff's side or on the defendant's side can take part. This, then, is known as joint parties and is admissible under § 64 VwGO which refers to the corresponding rules in civil proceedings (see §§ 59 to 63 ZPO).[25] All participants must have certain capacities, otherwise the action is not admissible. With regard to this, a capacity is the *Parteifähigkeit* (capacity of being a party

---

[24] For more details, see *ibid.*, Chap. Four, 2, D.
[25] For more details, see *ibid.*, Chap. Six, 6, B.

in a lawsuit) whose qualifications are laid down in § 61 VwGO. It is the capacity to participate in proceedings as a subject of individual, procedural rights and duties. Those capable of being a participant in the process are natural persons, legal entities,[26] associations as far as a right is due to them and public authorities as far as prescribed by *Land* law. The parties participating in proceedings must have the *Prozeßfähigkeit* (capacity to sue and be sued). This capability is set forth in § 62 VwGO and is the capacity to conduct proceedings in one's own name or to appoint a representative to conduct proceedings. This ability to carry out effective acts in court has nothing in common with the *Postulationsfähigkeit* (right of audience). The latter is the capacity to act in person before (for instance) the *Verwaltungs-* or *Oberverwaltungsgericht*. Only lawyers have a right of audience before the *Bundesverwaltungsgericht* because in this court there is mandatory representation by lawyers (§ 67 I VwGO) due to the importance of the decisions.

D. GENERAL PROCEDURAL REQUIREMENTS

Besides the specific conditions outlined above, any administrative action must fulfil a few general procedural requirements. First, action has to be filed in written form with the court or must be recorded at the court's office with the *Verwaltungsgericht*; the latter is only possible at the *Verwaltungsgericht* (§ 81 VwGO). Moreover, the action has to take into consideration the compulsory content set forth in § 82 VwGO. Thereafter, the statement of claim has to designate the plaintiff and defendant and must specify the cause of action. It also has to contain a certain and definite demand for relief. Moreover, the plaintiff should indicate and define the grounds for claims and show the facts and judicial evidence that — in his opinion — provide the basis of his legal claim. Finally, the administrative decision under appeal and the ruling on the protest have to be enclosed as well.

A further requirement is that the action must be filed against the correct defendant. This is in some cases difficult to state. Due to § 78 VwGO the correct defendant is specified regarding the action to rescind and the action for the issue of an administrative act is as follows:

---

[26] There are corporations and insitutions which do not have the legal capacity under law. But they are regarded as legal entities and, due to this, are also capable of being a party in the process, provided that they have the ability to exercise their own rights on their behalf such as political parties, trade unions, general partnerships and limited partnerships.

1. As a matter of principle, actions are generally filed against the Federation, *Land* or corporation whose public authority has issued the administrative act under appeal or denied to issue the administrative act applied for.
2. But it must act against the public authority which has issued the administrative act under appeal or has denied to issue an administrative act to be applied for provided that this is prescribed by the *Land* law.[27] Although, this provision of § 78 VwGO applies expressively only to certain actions mentioned before, it is acknowledged that it has to make use of the remaining types of action as well by analogy.

The final procedural requirements are that the action is only admissible provided that no other suit with the same matter of dispute has already been made pending, that no further final judgment on the same dispute has been rendered, and that the plaintiff has not declared a waiver of the action. Finally, the legitimate interest to take legal action must be given as well.

5. PROCEDURE OF FIRST INSTANCE

A. PRINCIPLES OF PROCEDURE

As in any other court proceedings in Germany, there are some general principles — such as the principle of right of orality and of public trial[28] — which apply equally in administrative court proceedings. In addition, there are certain specific principles which give administrative court procedure its distinct feature.

One is the *Untersuchungsgrundsatz* (principle of investigation) which finds its expression in § 86 VwGO. Administrative court procedure is designed to establish what really has happened. Courts have to investigate the facts of the case *ex officio*. Courts inquiring into the state of affairs *ex officio*, therefore, are not bound by allegations of the parties, by statements and offers to take evidence. The parties take part in the process as far as they are called by court to clarify the circumstances of the case. Parties are obliged to participate and cooperate as far as this is concerned. In case of unanswered questions, parties must submit, adduce and furnish proof upon the facts of such a kind which are within their sphere of responsibility. In this

---

[27] Such as § 5 AG VwGO NW — Implementing a statute according to the Rules of the Administrative Courts in Northrine-Westphalia.

[28] For more details, see *ibid.*, Chap. Five, 1, D.

respect, a true onus of presentation and of proof is incumbent upon them.

A further quite important procedural principle is the *Verfügungsgrundsatz* (principle of party disposition). Parties may dispose of the demand for relief to be applied for and through that the matter in dispute. Courts become active only on application (see §§ 42 I, 80 V, 123 VwGO) and are bound by a party's demand for relief. But — contrary to civil proceedings — courts are not bound by the wording of the demand for relief. They have to draw — as far as it is necessary — the party's attention to the completion of the claim (§ 82 II VwGO), to the removal of defects in form, to the supplementation of the demands for relief and to a petitioned demand for relief being appropriate to the point (§ 86 VwGO). Nevertheless, the court cannot award any more or differently than that which has been applied for (§ 88 VwGO). Moreover, the parties are also able to dispose and determine the matter in dispute upon which trial has been conducted. The parties determine the start and termination of the trial, they may change the object in dispute by amending the action, and may conclude the lawsuit either by withdrawal of action or by court settlement.[29]

A further procedural principle is the *Beschleunigungsgrundsatz* (principle of expedition) which is designed to speed up proceedings and aims to keep the trial as short as possible. For instance, the hearing has to be prepared in such a way that it can be conducted at one stroke and as soon as possible. Another principle is the *Grundsatz der Unmittelbarkeit* (principle of immediacy) which demands of the court to obtain the most direct and immediate impression of the case. Consequently only judges who have attended the entire hearing can take part in the adjudicative process and may deliver the final ruling at the end of trial; administrative courts generally give ruling on the basis of the hearing (§ 101 VwGO).

B. BEHAVIOUR OF PARTIES DURING PROCEEDINGS

During the proceedings, substantial changes may occur, and the trial has to be adapted to circumstances. The corresponding procedural instrument is the *Klageänderung* (amendment of action) which is governed under § 91 ZPO. The amendment of action which may become necessary because of a change of the matter in dispute or of the litigants must be declared in court, and is admissible provided either that the remaining parties give

---

[29] For more details, see *ibid.*, Chap. Eight, 5, B.

their consent to the amendment of action or the court regards the amendment as expedient and appropriate to the point.

Sometimes the parties may dispose of the lawsuit in such a way that the court does not have to give a ruling on the merits. As far as a party acts in such a way, courts are bound by these acts even though they consider them as wrong or inappropriate. The Rules of Administrative Courts provide the following possibilities:

(a) Prior to the hearing, the plaintiff is free to withdraw action which he has to put forward in court (§ 92 VwGO). But, after the parties have moved their applications in court, the withdrawal of action requires in addition the consent of the defendant and, as far as a *Vertreter des öffentlichen Interesses* takes part, his consent as well. The plaintiff may withdraw action until the *res judicata* of the judgment. If the withdrawal of action has been effective, the court discontinues trial by court order and imposes the legal costs of the lawsuit on the plaintiff, including those arising for the defendant.

(b) During the running trial, the matter in dispute may finally be disposed of because of legal reasons (such as an administrative act under appeal is withdrawn by administration) or factual grounds (such as the defendant pays the amount sued for by the plaintiff). The Rules of Administrative Courts provides two different ways of concluding the substantive dispute. First, both participants may together declare the conclusion of the trial, and may leave the issue of costs to be decided by court order. In this case, the court will not review whether proceedings were really finally disposed of because it is bound by the declaration of both parties. The second possibility is that only one of the parties declares the dispute to be terminated over the opponent's objection. Then, this declaration is treated as a motion for a judgment declaring the action to be terminated. In this case, the court examines whether the trial is in fact finally disposed of. But — quite differently from civil trials — the question of whether the action was initially admissible and well founded, does not have to be answered by the administrative court. The court declares the action as being terminated by court order provided that it comes to the conclusion that trial is in fact finally disposed of and, therefore, terminated,

(c) The litigant parties may also enter into a *Prozeßvergleich* (court settlement) and thereby amicably settle the legal dispute (§ 106 VwGO). This is a mutual settlement in which the litigants may settle their entire relations, including claims beyond the suit.

In administrative court procedure, the defendant is not restricted to a mere defensive role. To the contrary — he can take an active defence and has the opportunity to file a *Widerklage* (counterclaim). Taking this move means attacking the action by bringing a claim against the plaintiff. The counterclaim is an independent action filed against the plaintiff. Its requirements are set out in § 89 VwGO: due to this legal rule, the counterclaim requires for its admissibility that the original action be pending, that a different matter is in dispute than the original action and, finally, a factual connection between original action and the matter of the counterclaim. A further active defence is the *Aufrechnung* (set-off) specified in §§ 387 *et seq.* BGB analogous. The set-off must be declared in court in order to enforce a right of claim against the plaintiff and thereby removes — in case of its legal justification — the plaintiff's substantial claim. Contrary to civil procedure, a defendant in an administrative trial will make use of the counterclaim or set-off quite rarely in order to defend his rights actively.

C. COURSE OF PROCEEDINGS

Administrative court procedure is set in motion by filing an action with the court and through that the legal dispute becomes *lis pendens* (§ 90 VwGO). With an action becoming *lis pendens* no further lawsuit with the same matter in dispute can be filed. Prior to the hearing, either the presiding judge or the reporting judge issues any general instruction in order to prepare the lawsuit for the hearing. During this preparatory period, the court may — for instance — draw a litigant's attention to incorrect applications and insufficient presentation of the facts and may summon all participants to appear. As a rule, with the arrival of an action at court, the court will arrange for all necessary steps to be taken in order to prepare, advance and conduct the trial.

The Rules of Administrative Courts delegate single tasks to the different judges sitting in the panel of judges. For instance, the presiding judge conducts proceedings and prepares the decision. But in practice, however, the continuation of proceedings is rather more incumbent upon the *Berichterstatter* (reporting judge) as one of the judges sitting in the panel of judges: he reviews the factual and legal position of the case, prepares the courts instructions and orders, corresponds with participants and evaluates their statements at first. Finally, as far as a case is transferred to the *Einzelrichter* (single judge), he will act as a trial court and deliver findings.

As a matter of principle, the court delivers its finding on the basis of the hearing, provided that nothing else is prescribed by law. With regard to the latter, the court can give a ruling without a hearing in court by a *Gerichtsbescheid* (summary court decision) if the case does not contain particular difficulties on points of facts or law, and the facts of the case are clarified (§ 84 VwGO). But this is an exception. Generally a hearing has to be conducted and its course is specified in §§ 103 and 104 VwGO. The hearing begins with the calling of the case. The presiding judge opens trial and gives a talk on the substantial content of the files. The motioning and justification of the demands for relief by the parties is then followed by discussing the case in court. Thereafter, the hearing of the evidence — as far it is necessary — takes place. Admissible means of proof are inspections, witnesses, experts, documents or interrogation of parties (§ 96 VwGO). The way to conduct the taking of evidence is in accordance with the principles of the civil procedure as outlined before.[30] After the taking of evidence, the court retires, enters into deliberation and prepares its finding. The administrative court procedure terminates with the pronouncement of the judgment provided that decision will not be appealed.

D. JUDICIAL DECISION

As a rule, actions are ruled on by judgment unless nothing else is prescribed by law (§ 107 VwGO). There are two other forms of judicial decision to be distinguished from judgments which both have in common that they do not — unlike judgments — require the course of a hearing in court. One is the *Gerichtsbescheid* (summary court decision): actions are ruled on by this form of decision as far as the case does not show a particular difficulty on points of facts or law and the facts of the case are clarified (§ 84 VwGO). A further form of judicial decision is the *Beschluß* (court order). The court may render this kind of decision in order either to conduct proceedings (*e.g.* order for evidence and order for transfer of action) or to decide the lawsuit (*e.g.* rejection of appeal and interlocutory court order).

As far as the litigation will be decided by judgment, there are judgments of a different kind which have to be distinguished

[30] For more details, see *ibid.*, Chap. Six, 9.

from each other. There is the *Prozeßurteil* (judgment on procedural grounds) which is a judgment on questions of procedure only and the *Sachurteil* (judgments on the merits) which renders decision on the plaintiff's claim. Both judgments conclude trial. In addition, the court may also render a *Zwischenurteil* (interlocutory judgment adjudicating only one of the matters in dispute — § 109 VwGO), a *Teilurteil* (partial judgment — § 110 VwGO) and a *Vorbehaltsurteil* (judgment on the basis of the cause of action reserving the amount to a later decision — § 111 VwGO). These latter forms of judgment do not terminate trial but give a ruling on a part of the entire trial.

§ 117 VwGO specifies the form and content of judgments. Any judgment must be rendered "*Im Namen des Volkes*" ("In the Name of the People"), has to be in written from, must contain a heading, an operative part including a decision as to costs and as to the preliminary enforceability of the decree, and the finding of facts just as the legal reasons for decision. The judgment must be signed by the participating judges. In order to become effective, the judgment must be pronounced, which may happen either in court or with its service on the participants (§ 116 VwGO). After the pronouncement of the judgment the court is bound by the decision. As a result, corrections and supplementations of the judgment are only admissible under exceptional circumstances — for instance, in order to correct typographical errors, errors of calculation or mistakes of the facts (§§ 119 and 120 VwGO).

As far as no appeal has been lodged, the judgment becomes final and absolute. Compared to civil or criminal judgments, administrative judgments will then obtain the formal and substantial status of *res judicata* (see § 173 VwGO and §§ 705 *et seq.* ZPO and § 121 VwGO).[31] As a rule, a final and absolute judgment cannot be challenged. But under exceptional circumstances the *Wiederaufnahme des Verfahrens* (reopening of the appeal) is possible. The reopening of the appeal is governed under § 153 VwGO and is an extraordinary remedy which seeks to remove a final judgment by opening proceedings for annullment or for restitution.

In any case, courts also give a ruling on costs in the final judgment. A decision as to costs is rendered without a motion by one of the parties. In cost orders, the court delivers a finding whether the plaintiff or the defendant has to bear the costs of the lawsuit. As a rule, the defeated participant bears full costs of proceedings, including court fees as well as the opponent's

---

[31] For more details, see *ibid.*, Chap. Six, 10, and Chapter Seven, 9, C.

necessary expenses including lawyer's fees (§ 154 I VwGO). In cases in which both parties partly have won and lost the case, the legal costs will be split or shared in a way that each side bears half the court costs and its own lawyer's fees and expenses (§ 155 I VwGO). After rendering a judgment, the participants apply for a *Kostenfestsetzungsbeschluß* (order regulating the determination of costs) which determines in detail the reimbursement of costs and expenses (§ 164 VwGO). This order is an executory title (§ 168 I No. 4 VwGO). As mentioned before, the courts also give a ruling on the enforceability of judgments. Due to § 167 VwGO, the enforceability of administrative judgments has to comply with the provisions laid down in the eighth book of the ZPO. Therefore, we refer to the corresponding statement outlined above.[32]

6. APPELLATE REMEDIES

The Rules of Administrative Courts provide three different rights of appeals — the *Berufung* (appeal), the *Revision* (appeal on points of law) and the *Beschwerde* (request for relief from court order). Like any appellate remedy, they have a suspensive and devolutive effect[33] and are successful as far as they are admissible and well-founded.

A. APPEAL (*BERUFUNG*)

The appeal is governed under §§ 124 to 131 VwGO. It seeks a reversal of the judgment under appeal. Only final judgments of the *Verwaltungsgericht* are appealable including partial and interlocutory judgments. The appeal is heard and decided on by the Court of Appeal which is the *Oberverwaltungsgericht* (see Schedule 7). A party who has taken part in first-instance proceedings and is now aggrieved by the judgment is allowed to lodge an appeal. The appellant has to file the appeal in written form within one month after the service of the complete judgment. He has to address the appeal with the court whose decision will be challenged or with the court of appeal. The petition must indicate the judgment under appeal and has to contain a certain demand for relief. Moreover, it has to set forth the facts of the case which — in the plaintiff's opinion — provide the basis of the appeal and offer evidence.

---

[32] For more details, see *ibid.*, Chap. Six, 13.
[33] For more details, see *ibid.*, Chap. Six, 11.

In addition to these requirements concerning admissibility, the appeal must be well-founded. An appeal is legally justified as far as the judgment under appeal has been unlawful and through that aggrieves the appellant's rights. The Court of Appeal reviews and rehears the first-instance judgments on points of both fact and law and also takes into account new submitted facts and judicial evidence. If the appeal is well-founded, the judgment will be quashed; then, the court of appeal can deliver its own finding or can remand the case back to the lower court for decision which has to take into consideration the legal viewpoint of the court of appeal on rehearing (§ 130 II VwGO). As far as the appeal does not meet one of the procedural requirements, the court of appeal dismisses the appeal on procedural grounds.

B. APPEAL ON POINTS OF LAW (*REVISION*)

An appeal on points of law is governed under §§ 132 to 145 VwGO and is the review of a case on points of fact. Judgments of the *Oberverwaltungsgericht* and, by way of exception, judgments of the *Verwaltungsgericht* are appealable (see Schedules 7 and 8). The latter requires the consent of the parties and an order granting leave to appeal on points of law; it is called *Sprungrevision* (leap-frog appeal). Judgments to be rendered in the judicial proceedings on the constitutionality of laws are non-appealable (§ 47 VwGO). The *Bundesverwaltungsgericht* as court of last resort hears the case provided that the appellate court has granted leave to appeal on points of law which will be the case under the following circumstances:

1. The lawsuit is of principle importance.
2. The judgment under appeal deviates from a decision of the *Bundesverwaltungsgericht* or the *Gemeinsamer Senat der obersten Gerichtshöhe des Bundes* or the *Bundesverfassungsgericht* and rests on this deviation.
3. Procedural mistakes have been claimed on which the decision is resting.

Moreover, the appealing party must be entitled to appeal in a way that he can show to be aggrieved by the challenged judgment. The appeal has to be lodged within one month after service of the complete judgment with the court of last resort, and the statement of grounds for appeal can be filed within two months after the service of the judgment.

In addition to the procedural prerequisites to be met, the

appeal on points of law must be well-founded which is the case if the appeal rests on a violation of procedural or substantive law. Contrary to the appeal, the challenged judgment is only reviewed to see whether the law has been violated. The judgment is examined to see whether it contains a mistake (which may be a violation of either procedural or substantive law) and whether it rests on this mistake. The challenged judgment must rest on a breach of federal law or on a breach of a provision in a *Land's* Code of Administrative Procedure which corresponds with the one in the corresponding Federal Code of Administrative Procedure. As a result, appealable sources of law are, for instance, *einfache Bundesgesetze* (German Federal Acts), and non-appealable are administrative rules or the remaining provisions of *Land* law. In order to be successful, the appellant must set out and prove that the judgment under appeal causally rests on the infringement of law. In cases containing fundamental errors the judgment is regarded in any case as resting on the infringement of federal law (§ 138 VwGO).

After rehearing the case, the appeal is dismissed on procedural grounds if it is inadmissible. The appeal on points of law is dismissed if it is unfounded. But, if an appeal is found to be substantiated, the court of last resort may quash the challenged judgment and deliver a new finding or transfer the case for a new hearing and decision back to a lower court which then has to take into consideration the legal viewpoint of the court of last resort during the decision-making process (§ 144 VI VwGO).

C. REQUEST FOR RELIEF FROM A COURT ORDER (*BESCHWERDE*)

The request for relief from a court order is a further appellate remedy which reviews the lawfulness of court orders (§§ 146 to 152 VwGO). Any judicial decision is appealable — such as court orders — which cannot be classified as a judgment or summary court decision. Unless prescribed by law, requests for relief against decisions of the *Verwaltungsgericht* are heard by the *Oberverwaltungsgericht*. In any case, the appellant must be entitled to appeal and show his grievance against the challenged court order. He has to file the request for relief within two weeks after the decision has been pronounced, with the court whose decision is appealed against. The complaint is well founded if the court order is unlawful and through that infringes the rights of the appellant. The case will be reviewed on points of both facts and law. The *Verwaltungsgericht* may itself address requests for relief. When the request from relief cannot be redressed, the case is submitted to the *Oberverwaltungsgericht* for decision. If the request for relief is admissible and well-founded, the decision under appeal is quashed by court order. A request which is inadmissible or unfounded is dismissed.

7. INTERLOCUTORY JUDICIAL RELIEF

During the course of an administrative court procedure — which can sometimes last for years — the chance of the claiming party to enforce his rights may be endangered. In order to secure the party's legal position, the Rules of Administrative Courts provide two different interlocutory judicial remedies — such as provisional judicial relief against onerous administrative acts and interim orders — which are both summary proceedings.

A. PROVISIONAL RELIEF AGAINST ONEROUS ADMINISTRATIVE ACTS

The *vorläufige Rechtsschutz gegen belastende Verwaltungsakte* (provisional judicial relief against onerous administrative acts) is set forth in §§ 80 *et seq.* VwGO. Provisional relief seeks to restore the suspensive effect of administrative acts according to § 35 VwVfG. As a rule, a suspensive effect is furnished with the filing of a protest or an action to rescind and means that this act cannot be enforced as long as the suspensive effect is established. Under certain circumstances the suspensive effect is cancelled, for instance in cases concerning:

1. Demands of public charges or costs;
2. Unpostponable orders and measures of police officers;
3. Cases in which it is prescribed by federal law[34]; or
4. Orders of immediate enforcement issued by a public authority.

With regard to the latter case, a public authority issues an order of immediate enforcement when the public interest or an overwhelming interest of one of the participants requires the immediate enforcement of the respective administrative act. The judicial justification of the immediate enforcement must be set forth in this order.

A citizen can seek to restore the suspensive effect of an administrative act under § 80 V VwGO. Such a motion requires recourse to the administrative courts and is permissible only as far as the correct action in the main issue would be the action to

[34] For example § 42 AuslG, § 75 AsylVfG (law regulating the right to asylum).

rescind. Thus, the motion must turn against the enforcement of an administrative act. The party filing such a motion must have the *Antragsbefugnis* (ability to institute proceedings) and has to show that his rights would be infringed through the enforcement of the administrative act. The appellant does not have to observe a particular deadline but the administrative act should not become final; this happens after the time for filing a protest or suit is expired. As in any other administrative court proceedings, the participating parties — such as the appellant and respondent — must be able and capable of taking part in proceedings (see §§ 61 *seq.* VwGO).

The case is heard by the same court as the main action. The decision as to whether the motion is well-founded is taken by balancing the public law interest in enforcing the administrative act and the appellant's interest in suspending the administrative act. The appellant's interest will succeed when the administrative act has been unlawful and through that the rights of the appellant have been infringed. The court will then restore the suspensive effect of the administrative act. Otherwise the motion under § 80 V VwGO will be dismissed.

B. INTERIM ORDER

The e*instweilige Anordnung* (interim order) is governed under § 123 VwGO. All remaining cases which are not subject to the proceedings specified in §§ 80 *et seq.* VwGO are regulated by the interim order. It is a summary proceeding which satisfies the need for the protection of rights and relationships. It is started by filing a motion, is heard by the court of the main issue and requires recourse to the administrative court. These proceedings are not admissible in cases in which the restoration of the suspensive effect of an administrative act is demanded because this is subject only to proceedings pursuant to §§ 80 *et seq.* VwGO. But, in the remaining cases, the interim order is the correct way to obtain provisional relief. The appealing party must show that his right is infringed or endangered and by this means shows his legal capability of instituting proceedings. The appellant has to set forth that he has a claim against the administration which is called *Anordnungsanspruch* (claim for order). In addition urgent reasons for granting such an order must demonstrate an *Anordnungsgrund* (reason for order). For the existence of both the claim and the reason for order the appellant has to furnish *prima facie* evidence.

There are two different kinds of interim orders: one is called *Sicherungsanordnung* (preventative order) which claims the protection of the existing *status quo*. The applicant demanding such an order must set forth that through a change of the existing situation the realisation of a right is frustrated or rendered more difficult. The second interim order is called *Regelungsanordnung* (regulatory order) which is simply designed to settle a dispute arising from legal relationships on a provisional basis. This must be demonstrated by the appealing party as well.

In addition to the interim order governed under § 123 VwGO, German law provides an interim order under § 47 VIII VwGO. This motion is intended to secure the legal position in judicial proceedings on the constitutionality of laws.[35] Such an interim order is intended to avert a material danger or other important grounds.

[35] For more details, see *ibid.*, Chap. Eight, 4, B, (5).

Schedule 7: Sequence of courts of the *Verwaltungsgerichte*

Verwaltungsgericht at First Instance

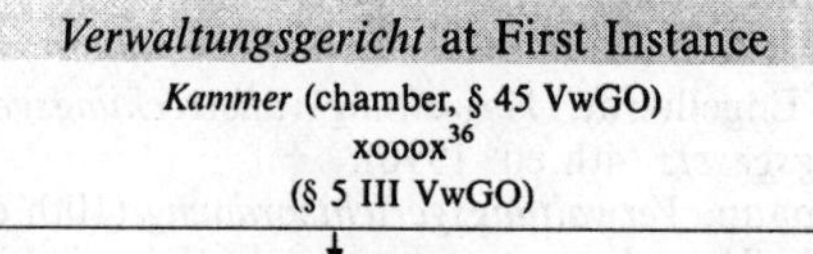

↓

Appeal

↓

Oberverwalungsgericht at Second Instance

Senat (senate, §§ 46 VwGO)

ooo (xx*)

(§ 9 III 1, 1.HS. VwGO; *§ 9 III 1, 2.HS VwGO)

Leap-Frog Appeal

↓

Appeal on Points of Law

↓

Bundesverwaltungsgericht at Third Instance

Senat (§ 49 VwGO)

ooooo

(§ 10 III GVG)

Schedule 8: Sequence of courts of the *Oberverwaltungsgerichte*

Oberverwaltungsgericht at First Instance

Senat (§ 48 VwGO)

ooo (xx*)

(§ 9 III 1, 1.HS. VwGO; *§ 9 III 1, 2.HS VwGO)

↓

Appeal on Points of Law

↓

Bundesverwaltungsgericht at Second Instance

Senat (§ 49 VwGO)

ooooo

(§ 10 III GVG)

Schedule 9: Sequence of courts of the *Bundesverwaltungsgerichte*

Bundesverwaltungsgericht at First and Sole Instance

Senat (§ 50 VwGO)

ooooo

(§ 10 III GVG

---

[36] o = judge; x = lay judge

SELECTED BIBLIOGRAPHY

I. Commentaries

App, Engelhardt, *Verwaltungsvollstreckungsgesetz, Verwaltungszustellungsgesetz* (4th ed. 1996).
Eyermann, *Verwaltungsgerichtsordnung* (10th ed. 1998).
Knack, *Verwaltungsverfahrensrecht* (5th ed. 1996).
Kopp, Schenke, *Verwaltungsgerichtsordnung* (11th ed. 1998).
Kopp, *Verwaltungsverfahrensgesetz* (6th ed. 1996).
Schoch, Schmidt-Aßmann, Pietzner, *Verwaltungsgerichtsordnung* (1998).
Stelkens, Bonk, Sachs, *Verwaltungsverfahrensgesetz* (5th ed. 1998).

II. Textbooks

App, Wettlaufer, *Verwaltungsvollstreckungsrecht* (3rd ed. 1997).
Götz, *Allgemeines Verwaltungsrecht, Fälle und Erläuterungen für Studienanfänger* (4th edi. 1997).
Hufen, *Verwaltungsprozeßrecht* (3rd ed. 1998).
Maurer, *Allgemeines Verwaltungsrecht* (11th ed. 1997).
Peine, *Allgemeines Verwaltungsrecht* (4th ed. 1998).
Schenke, *Verwaltungsprozeßrecht* (6th ed. 1998).
Schmitt Glaeser, *Verwaltungsprozeßrecht* (13th ed. 1994).
Ule, Laubinger, *Verwaltungsverfahrensrecht* (4th ed. 1995).
Wolff, Bachhof, Stober, *Verwaltungsrecht I* (10th ed. 1994).
Wolff, Bachhof, Stober, *Verwaltungsrecht II, Besonderes Organisations- und Dienstrecht* (5th ed. 1987).

Glossary

Abgeordnetengesetz	Regulations for the members of the *Bundestag*
Abhilfeverfahren	Redress Proceedings
Akt der öffentlichen Gewalt	Act in the power of the public
Akkusationsprinzip	Principle of accusation
Akteneinsichtsrecht	Right to examine files
Aktiengesetz	Law relating to public companies
Allgemeines Freiheitsrecht	Common right of liberty
Allgemeines Persönlichkeitsrecht	Right of personality/right to live one's own life
Amtsbetrieb	*Ex officio* proceedings
Amtsgericht	District court/Lower Court
Analogie	Analogy
Anerkenntnis	Acknowledgement
Anfangsverdacht	Simple initial suspicion
Anfechtungsklage	Application to rescind
Angeschuldigter	Accused before trial/suspect
Angeklagter	Accused
Anklagegrundsatz	Principle of *ex officio* prosecution
Ankläger	Public prosecutor
Antrag	Motion, Application, Petition
Antrag auf richterliche Entscheidung	Application for judicial decision

Anhängigkeit	Pending litigation or *lis pendens*
Anordnungsanspruch	Claim for an order
Anordnungsgrund	Reason for an order
Antragsbefugnis	Authority to institute proceedings
Antragsdelikte	Offences requiring an application for prosecution by victim
Antragsschrift	Written application/ Petition
Arbeitsgericht	Labour court
Arbeitsgerichtsbarkeit	Jurisdiction in labour matters
Arbeitsgerichtsgesetz	Labour Courts Act
Arbeitsrecht	Labour Law
Arrest	Civil arrest by court order
Arrestanspruch	Claim for arrest
Arrestgesuch	Application for an arrest
Arrestgrund	Urgent reason for granting an order of civil arrest
Artikel	Article
Asylrecht	Right of asylum
Aufklärungszeit	Era of Enlightenment
Aufrechnung	Set-off
Auflage	Edition
Aussageverweigerungsrecht	Right to refuse to give information/evidence
Ausgangsbehörde	Issuing public authority
Auslagen	Expenses
Ausschließlicher Gerichtsstand	Exclusive jurisdiction
Baurecht	Building law
Beauftragter Richter	Commissioned judge
Beamtengesetz	Civil Service Code

Beigeladener	Summoned third party
Beleidigung	Insult
Berichterstatter	Reporting judge
Beschuldigter	Accused
Besonderes Feststellungsinteresse	Special interest to seek declaratory action
Bewegliche Sachen	Movable assets
Begründet	Well-founded or legally justified
Begünstigender Verwaltungsakt	Administrative act establishing rights
Belastender Verwaltungsakt	Administrative act imposing obligations
Berufsfreiheit	Freedom of profession
Berufung	Appeal
Besatzungsmächte	Occupying powers
Beschlagnahmeanordnung	Order of confiscation
Beschleunigungsgrundsatz	Principle of expedition
Beschleunigtes Verfahren	Expeditious proceedings
Beschluß	Court order (or ruling or decision)
Beschwer	Grievance
Beschwerde	Complaint against a court order
Bestimmtheitsgrundsatz	Principle of certainty
Besonderer Gerichtsstand	Place of special jurisdiction
Beteiligtenfähigkeit	Capacity to be a participant
Beweisantritt	Offer of proof
Beweisaufnahme	Taking of evidence
Beweisbeschluß	Order to take evidence
Beweisantrag	Application for the admission of evidence
Beweisgebühr	Court fee for evidence

Beweisverwertungsverbot	Exclusion of evidence improperly obtained
Beweiswürdigung	Consideration of evidence
Bodenreform	Land reform
Brief-, Post-Fernmeldegeheimnis	Privacy of letters, post and telecommunications
Bürgerliches Gesetzbuch	German Civil Code
Bund-Länder-Streitigkeiten	Disputes between Federation and *Länder*
Bundesanzeiger	Federal Gazette
Bundesarbeitsgericht	Federal Labour Court
Bundesauftragsverwaltung	*Land's* administration on behalf of the Federation
Bundesbank	Central Bank of Germany
Bundesdisziplinarhof	Supreme Federal Disciplinary Tribunal
Bundesfinanzhof	Federal Fiscal Court
Bundesgesetzblatt	Federal Law Gazette
Bundesgericht	Federal Court
Bundesgerichtshof	Federal Supreme Court of Justice
Bundeshaushaltsordnung	Federal budgetary regulation
Bundeskanzleramt	Office of Federal Chancellor
Bundespräsident	Federal President
Bundesrat	Federal Council
Bundesregierung	Federal Government
Bundesrechtsanwaltsordnung	Federal rules and regulations for lawyers
Bundesrechtsanwaltsgebührenordnung	Attorney's Fees Act
Bundesrechnungshof	Federal Audit Office
Bundestag	Federal Parliament

Bundestagsabgeordneter	Deputy or Member of the Bundestag
Bundesstaat	Federal State
Bundessozialgericht	Federal Social Court of Justice
Bundespatentgericht	Federal Patent Tribunal
Bundesverfassungsgericht	Federal Constitutional Court
Bundesverfassungsgerichtsgesetz	Code of Procedure of the Federal Constitutional Court
Bundesversammlung	Federal Electoral Assembly
Bundesverwaltung	Federal administration
Bundesverwaltungsgericht	Supreme Federal Administrative Court
Bundeszentralregister	Federal central panel register
Bundeszwang	Federal enforcement
Civiates	Communities
Demokratie	Democracy
Dinglicher Arrest	Attachment or seizure of property
Dreiklassenwahlrecht	Electoral proceedings of three classes
Dispositionsmaxime	Principle of party disposition
Deutsche Demokratische Republik	German Democratic Republic
Dringender Tatverdacht	Strong degree of suspicion
Drittwiderspruchsklage	Third-party action against execution
Durchsuchung	Search
Ehe und Familie	Marriage and family
Eidesstattliche Versicherung	Affidavit
Eigentumsgarantie	Guarantee of property

Einfache Beschwerde	Ordinary appeal from a court order
Einfache Bundesgesetze	German Federal Acts
Eingriffsverwaltung	Interventive administration
Einheitliche Europäische Akte	Single European Act
Einigungsvertrag	Treaty of Re-Unification
Einrede	Defence
Einspruch	Objection
Einstellungsverfügung	Stop notice
Einstweilige Anordnung	Interim or provisional order
Einstweilige Verfügung	Temporary injunction
Einzelrichter	Single judge
Endurteile	Final legal judgments
Entscheidungen	Decisions
des Bundesfinanzhofs	of the Federal Fiscal Court
des Bundesgerichtshofs in Zivil- und Strafsachen	of the Federal Court of Justice in civil and criminal matters
des Bundessozialgerichts	of the Federal Social Court
des Bundesverfassungsgerichts	of the Federal Constitutional Court
Enumerationsprinzip	Principle of enumeration
Erbrecht	Law of Succession, Law of Inheritance
Erkenntnisverfahren	Contentious proceedings
Erledigung der Hauptsache	Termination of the substantive dispute
Ermächtigungsdelikte	Offences demanding a particular authorisation for prosecution
Ermittlungsrichter	Examining or pre-trial judge
Eröffnungsbeschluß	Order committing for trial
Ersuchter Richter	Requested judge

Europarecht	European Community Law
Europäisches Gerichsstands- und Vollstreckungsabkommen	European Convention on Jurisdiction and Enforcement of Judgments in Civil and Criminal Matters
Europäische Konvention zum Schutz der Menschenrechte und Grundfreiheiten	European Convention on Human Rights
Ewigkeitsgarantie	Guarantee of eternity
Familiengericht	Family court
Familiensenat	Family law panel
Fraktion	Parliamentary Group
Feststellungsklage	Declaratory action or action for a declaratory judgment
Feststellungsinteresse	Interest to seek a declaratory judgment
Feststellungsurteil	Declaratory judgment
Finanzgericht	Fiscal court
Finanzgerichtsbarkeit	Jurisdiction of the fiscal courts
Finanzgerichtsordnung	Rules of Procedure of the fiscal courts
Folgesachen	Ancillary proceedings in divorce cases
Formelle Rechtskraft	Formal *res judicata* or unappealability
Fortsetzungsfeststellungsklage	Declaratory action for continuation of proceedings
Frankenreich	Salic-Frank Empire
Fränkische Zeit	Salic-Frank Period
Freibeweis	Informal evidence
Freiheit der Kunst und Wissenschaft	Freedom of Arts and Science

Früher erster Termin zur mündlichen Verhandlung	Preliminary hearing for trial
Funktionelle Zuständigkeit	Jurisdiction limited to the type of case
Fürsprecher	Mediator
Gaugericht	District court
Gebühren	Fees
Gemeindeordnung	Local Government Code
Gemeinsamer Senat der obersten Gerichtshöfe des Bundes	General Senate of the Highest Federal Courts of Justice
Gemeinschaftsaufgaben	Joint tasks
Gerichtsbarkeit	Jurisdiction
Gerichtsbescheid	Summary court decision
Gerichtsverfassungsgesetz	Judicature Act
Gerichtsvollzieher	Bailiff
Gesamtvollstreckungsverfahren	Law on Universal Execution
Geschäftsordnung	Rules of procedure for business
Geschäftsverteilungsplan	Court work schedule
Gesellschaftsrecht	Company Law
Gesetz	Law, act or statute
Gesetzesauslegung	Statutory interpretation
Gesetzgeber	Legislator
Gesetzgebung	Legislation
Gesetzgebungsauftrag	Legal order
Gesetzgebungsverfahren (ausschließliche und konkurriende)	Legislative procedure (exclusive and concurrent)
Gesetzgebungszuständigkeit	Legislative Power
Gesetz zur Regelung des Rechts der Allgemeinen Geschäftsbedingungen	Code regulating the Law of General Terms and Conditions of Trade or Business

Gesetz über die Zwangsversteigerung und Zwangsverwaltung	Law on Compulsory Auction or Sequestration of Real Property
Gerichtsverfassungsgesetz	Judicature Act
Gestaltungsklage	Action for a change of a legal right or status
Gestaltungsurteil	Judgment changing a legal right or status
Gewaltenteilung	Separation of powers
Gewohnheitsrecht	Customary law
Glaubens- und Gewissensfreiheit	Freedom of Religion and Conscience
Glaubhaftmachung	Substantiating prima facie evidence
Gleichheitsrecht	Equal rights principle
Gleichheitsgrundsatz	Principle of equality
Glosse	Comment
Grafengericht	Earl's court
GmbH-Gesetz	Code on Limited Liability Companies
Großer Senat	Great senate
Grundgesetz	Constitution/Fundamental or Basic Law
Grundrechte	Basic or constitutional rights
Grundrechtsträger	Entitlement to basic rights
Grundherr	Lord of the manor
Grundherrliches Gaugericht	Manor Court
Grundhöriger	Subject
Grundsatz der freien Beweiswürdigung	Principle of free evaluation of the evidence
Grundsatz der gesetzmäßigen Verwaltung	Principle of lawful administration
Grundsatz der Öffentlichkeit	Principle of public trial
Grundsatz der Unmittelbarkeit	Principle of immediacy

Grundsatz des rechtlichen Gehörs	Principle of the right of audience
Grundbuchamt	Land Registry
Grundurteil	Judgment on the basis of the cause of action reserving the amount to a later decision
Güteverhandlung	Conciliation proceedings
Haftbefehl	Warrant of arrest
Haftbeschwerde	Complaint against a court order for arrest
Haftgrund	Reason for arrest
Haftprüfung	Review of a remand in custody
Handelsgesetzbuch	Commercial Code
Handlungsfähigkeit	Capacity to act
Hauptverfahren	Main trial proceedings
Hausfriedensbruch	Unlawfully entering another person's property
Haushaltsplan	Budget
Heiliges Römisches Reich Deutscher Nationen	Holy Roman Reich of the German Nations or *Sacrum Imperium Romanum*
Heranwachsender	Young adult
Herrschende Meinung	Prevailing view/opinion
Hilfsbeamte der Staatsanwaltschaft	Auxiliary officer of the public prosecutor's office
Hinreichender Tatverdacht	Sufficient suspicion of an offence
Historische Rechtsschule	Historical law school
Hoheitsakt	Act of the State
Im Namen des Volkes	In the Name of the People
Immunität	Immunity
Indemität	Indemnity

Inquisitionsprozeß	Inquisitorial proceedings
Insolvenzrecht	Insolvency law
Internationale Zuständigkeit	International jurisdiction
Jugendgerichtsgesetz	Juvenile Court Act
Jugendliche	Young people
Kabinettsvorlage	Cabinet bill
Kaisergesetze	Emperor's law
Kammer	Chamber
Klage	Legal action
Klagearten	Type of actions
Klage auf vorzugsweise Befriedigung	Action for preferential satisfaction
Klageänderung	Amendment of action
Klagebefugnis	Right of action
Klageerhebung	Commencement of an action
Klageerwiderung	Statement of Defence
Kläger	Plaintiff
Klagerücknahme	Withdrawal of an action
Klageschrift	Statement of claim
Klageverzicht	Waiver of an action
Kommunikationsgrundrecht	Basic right of communication
Kommunalverfassungsbeschwerde	Constitutional complaint of the local authority
König der Franken	Salic-Frank King
Königsgericht	King's court
Königswahlrecht	Law of succession to the throne
Konkursordnung	Bankruptcy Act
Kontrollstellen	Check-points
Konzentrationsmaxime	Principle of concentration

Kostenerstattungsanspruch	Entitlement to costs
Kostenfestsetzungsbeschluß	Order regulating the determination of costs
Kostenverzeichnis	Costs schedule
Landesarbeitsgericht	Regional Labour Court of Appeal
Landeshoheit, Landesherrschaft	National sovereignty
Landessozialgericht	Regional Social Appeal Tribunal
Land	Territory
Landesrecht	*Land* law
Landgericht	Regional Court
Legalitätsprinzip	Principle of legality
Leistungsklage	Legal action for performance
Leistungsurteil	Judgment which obliges a party to perform or refrain from a certain act
Leistungsverfügung	Injunction to perform the claim
Mahnantrag	Application for a default summons
Mahnbescheid	Default summons
Mahnverfahren	Summary proceedings for order to pay debts
Materielle Rechtskraft	Substantial *res judicata* or force of a final judgment
Meinungsfreiheit	Freedom of speech, opinion
Menschenrechte	Human rights
Menschenrechtskonvention	Human Rights Convention
Menschenrechtskonforme Auslegung	Interpretation in conformity with human rights
Menschenwürde	Human dignity
Ministerpräsident	Minister-President

Mischverwaltung	Mixed Administration
Missetaten	Offences
Monarchie	Monarchy
Nächsthöhere Behörde	Public authority of the next highest ranking
Nachtragsklage	Supplementary indictment
Nachverfahren	Subsequent proceedings
Nebenklage	Accessory prosecution
Nebenkläger	Joint plaintiff
Netzfahndung	Police investigation network to detect and locate a suspect
Nichtigkeitsfeststellungsklage	Action for declaration of cancellation
Nebenintervention	Intervention of a third party in support of a plaintiff or defendant
Normenkontrolle	Judicial Review
Oberlandesgericht	Regional Court of Appeal
Oberverwaltungsgericht	Regional Administrative Court of Appeal
Oberbundesanwalt	Chief Public Attorney
Öffentliche Sicherheit und Ordnung	Public peace and order and public security
Organstreitverfahren	Court proceedings between administrative bodies
Örtliche Zuständigkeit	Local jurisdiction or venue
Öffentlich-rechtlicher Vertrag	Public law contract
Opfer	Victim
Opportunitätsprinzip	Principle of discretionary prosecution
Ordentliche Gerichtsbarkeit	Ordinary jurisdiction
Palamentarischer Rat	Parliamentary council
Partei	Party

Parteifähigkeit	The capability to be a party (to a lawsuit)
Parteienbeitritt	Joining a party (in a lawsuit)
Parteiengesetz	Law regulating political parties
Parteienwechsel	Change of parties
Patentgesetz	Patent Act
Persönlicher Arrest	Arrest of debtor
Petitionsrecht	Right of petition
Pfalzgraf	Count Palatine
Pfändungs- und Überweisungsbeschluß	Attachment order and transfer of garnished claim
Pflichtverteidiger	Official defence counsel
Polizei- und Ordnungsrecht	Police and regulatory law
Postulationsfähigkeit	Lawyer's right of audience
Preußisches Allgemeines	Prussian Common Law
Principes	Earls
Privatklage	Private prosecution
Privatklagedelikte	Private prosecution offences
Polizeiliche Beobachtung	Police observation
Pressefreiheit	Freedom of the Press
Prozeßfähigkeit	Capacity to sue and be sued
Prozeßführungsbefugnis	Right of action or *locus standi*
Prozeßgericht erster Instanz	Trial court of first instance
Prozeßhindernisse	Impediments to an action
Prozeßurteil	Judgment on procedural grounds
Prozeßvergleich	Court settlement
Prozeßvoraussetzungen	Procedural prerequisites
Rahmengesetzgebung	Skeleton legislation
Rahmenvorschriften	General or outline provisions

Rasterfahndung	Search for wanted persons using scanning devices
Realakt	Physical act
Recht auf Leben	Right to life
Recht der europäischen Gemeinschaften	Law of the European Union
Rechtsanwalt	Lawyer
Rechtsanwaltsgebühr	Lawyer's fee
Rechtsbehelf	Legal address in written proceedings
Rechtshängigkeit	Pendency of a suit or *lis pendens*
Rechtskraft	*Res judicata*
Rechtsmittel	Right of appeal
Rechtsordnung	Statutory instruments or ordinances
Rechtspfleger	Judicial official
Rechtspflegergesetz	Act outlining the powers of the *Rechtspfleger*
Rechtsschutz	Question of legal protection
Rechtsschutzbedürfnis	Legitimate interest in having legal protection
Rechtsschutzgarantie	Guarantee of legal protection
Rechtsstaat	Constitutional State
Rechtsprechung	Jurisdiction
Rechtsprechungsmonopol	Judicial monopoly
Rechtsverordnung	Statutory instruments or ordinances
Reichskreise	Districts of the Reich
Reichsregiment	Army of the Reich
Reichsstrafgesetz	Criminal Code of the Reich
Regelungsanordnung	Regulatory order
Regelungsverfügung	Regulatory injunction

Regierung	Government
Regierungsentwurf	Government bill
Repräsentative Demokratie	Representative Democracy
Republik	Republic
Reservatrechte	Prerogative rights
Revision	Appeal on points of law
(absoluter) und (relativer) Revisionsgrund	(fundamental) and (reversible) error
Revisionsbegründungsschrift	Statement of grounds for appeal
Richter	Judge
Richterdienstgericht	Disciplinary Court of Judges
Richterdienstgesetz	German Law of the Judiciary
Rubrum	Recitals
Rückwirkende Gesetze	Retroactive legislation
Sachbeschädigung	Criminal damage
Sachliche Zuständigkeit	Jurisdiction over the subject matter
Sachverständiger	Expert
Sachurteil	Judgment on the merits of the case
Satzung	Charters or byelaws
Scheckprozeß	Cheque proceedings
Schiedsgericht	Arbitration tribunal
Schiedsgerichtsverfahren	Arbitration proceedings
Schiedsspruch	Arbitration award
Schiedsvertrag	Arbitration treaty
Schlichtes Verwaltungshandeln	Simple administrative action
Schöffen	Lay judges
Schöffengericht	Specialist criminal chamber of the *Amtsgericht* consisting of a professional judge and lay assessors or judges

Schöffenspruch	Findings of lay magistrates or judges
Schriftliches Vorverfahren	Written pre-trial process
Schutz vor Ausbürgerung und Auslieferung	Protection against expatriation and extradition
Schwurgericht	Criminal chamber of the *Landgericht*, hearing only the most serious cases
Selbständiges Beweisverfahren	Independent proceedings for the introduction of evidence
Senat	Senate
Sicherungsanordnung	Preventive order
Sicherungshaftbefehl	Warrant of arrest for precautionary detention
Sicherstellung	Securing
Sicherungsverfahren	Confinement proceedings
Sicherungsverfügung	Preventive injunction
Sofortige Beschwerde	Immediate appeal from a court order
Sozialgericht	Social Security Tribunal
Sozialgerichtsbarkeit	Jurisdiction of the social courts
Sozialgerichtsgesetz	Law concerning Social Courts and its Procedure
Sozialstaat	Social State
Sozialstaatliche Chancengleichheit	Social equality of opportunities
Sprungrevision	Leap-frog appeal
Staatsanwaltschaft	Public prosecutor's office
Staatsform	Form of Government
Staatsgewalt	State authority
Staatsverträge	State treaty
Stadtgericht	Municipal court
Städtischer Rat	Town council

Stadtrecht	Town law
Standesgericht	Professional tribunal
Statthaft	Permissible
Strafbefehl	Order imposing punishment
Strafbefehlsverfahren	Summary proceedings imposing punishment
Strafgesetzbuch	Criminal Code
Streitgegenstand	Matter in dispute
Streitgenossen	Joint parties (as plaintiffs or defendants)
Strafgesetz	Code of Criminal Proceedings
Strafgesetzbuch	Panel or Criminal Code
Strafgewalt	Punitive power
Strafkammer (klein)	Panel chamber (minor)
Strafprozeßordnung	Code of Criminal Procedure
Strafrichter	Criminal court judge
Straftat	Criminal Offence
Strafvereitelung (im Amt)	Obstruction of criminal prosecution (by an officer of the law)
Strafverfahren	Criminal proceedings
Strafverteidiger	Defence Counsel
Strafvollstreckung	Penal execution
Strafvollzug	Execution of a custodial sentence
Streithelfer	Party intervening on the side of a litigant
Streitverkündung	Third party notice
Strengbeweis	Stringent evidence
Stufenklage	Action by stages
Subjektives Recht	Subjective right
Tatbestand	Facts of a case
Tatopfer	Victim

Teilurteil	Partial judgment or part-judgment
Teleologische Reduktion	Teleological reduction
Thing	Concilium or council
Truppendienstgericht	Federal Military Court
Üeberwachung und Aufnahme des Fernmeldeverkehrs	Observation and recording of telecommunication
Unbewegliches Vermögen	Immovable assets
Unterlassungsklage	Prohibitory action
Unterbringungsbeschluß	Place of safety order
Unverletzlichkeit der Wohnung	Protection of private residential space
Untersuchungsausschuß	Investigation committee
Untersuchungsgrundsatz	Principle of investigation
Unvertretbare Handlung	Non-fungible act
Urkundenfälschung	Forgery of an instrument or document
Urkundenprozeß	Trial by record
Urkundsbeamter der Geschäftsstelle	Clerk to the court's office
Urteil	Judgment, sentence
Urteilsbegründung	Reason for the judgment, sentence
Urteilstenor	Operative part of the judgment, sentence
Verbraucherkreditgesetz	Consumer Credit Act
Verfassungsbeschwerde	Constitutional complaint
Verfahrensgebühr	Court fees of proceedings
Verfassungsrecht	Constitutional law
Verfassungsgerichtsbarkeit	Constitutional jurisdiction
Verfassungskonforme Auslegung	Interpretation conforming to the Constitution
Verfügung	Order

Verfügungsgrundsatz	Principle of party disposition
Vergleichsordnung	Law on Composition Proceedings
Verkehrszentralregister	Central register of traffic violation
Verpflichtungsklage	Action for the issue of an administrative act
Vertreter des öffentlichen Interesses	Representative of the public interest
Verhältnismäßigkeitsgrundsatz	Principle of proportionality
Verhältniswahlsystem	Proportional representation
Verhandlungsgrundsatz	Principle of party presentation
Versammlungsfreiheit	Freedom of assembly
Versäumnisverfahren	Default proceedings
Versäumnisurteil	Judgment by default
Versicherung an Eides Statt	Affirmation in lieu of an oath
Verstrickungsbruch	Interference with attachment
Vertrauensgrundsatz	Fidelity clause
Vertretbare Handlung	Fungible act
Verwaltung	Administration
Verwaltungsakt	Administrative act
Verwaltungsgericht	Administrative Court
Verwaltungsgerichtshof	Administrative Court of Appeal
Verwaltungsgerichtsbarkeit	Administrative jurisdiction
Verwaltungsgerichtsordnung	Rules of the Administrative Courts
Verwaltungsgerichtsverfahren	Legal proceedings in an Administrative Court
Verwaltungsrecht	Administrative law
Verwaltungsverfahren	Administrative procedure

Verwaltungsverfahrensgesetz	Code of Administrative Procedure
Verwaltungsvorschriften	Administrative provisions or regulations
Völkerrecht	Law of nations or Public International Law
Vollstreckungsbehörde	Law enforcement authority
Vollstreckungsbescheid	Writ of execution
Vollstreckungserinnerung	Complaint against a measure of execution
Vollstreckungsgegenklage	Action raising an objection to judgment claim
Vollstreckungsgericht	Court responsible for enforcement matters
Vollstreckungshaftbefehl	Warrant of arrest of execution
Vollstreckungsklausel	Court certificate of enforceability
Vollstreckungsorgan	Official organ for enforcement by execution
Vollstreckungstitel	Title for execution
Vorbehaltsurteil	Judgment on the basis of the cause of action reserving the amount to a later decision
Verfalls- und Einziehungsgegenstände	Objects of forfeiture and confiscation
Vorführungsbefehl	Warrant to bring a person before a judge
Vorläufige Festnahme	Provisional arrest
Vorläufiger Rechtsschutz gegen belastende Verwaltungsakte	Provisional judicial protection against incriminating administrative acts
Vorverfahren	Preliminary proceedings
Wahlverteidiger	Counsel chosen by the defendant
Währungsunion	Monetary Union

Wechselprozeß	Summary bill-enforcement procedure
Weitere Beschwerde	Further appeal on points of law
Wertungsjurispudenz	Jurisdiction of valuation
Widerklage	Counterclaim
Widerspruch	Protest, objection or complaint
Widerspruchsbefugnis	Right of protest
Widerspruchsbescheid	Ruling on a protest
Widerspruchsführer	Person filing a protest
Widerspruchsverfahren	Protest procedure
Wiederaufnahme des Verfahrens	Resumption of Proceedings
Wiedereinsetzung in den vorherigen Stand	Restoration to one's original position or restitution to the previous condition
Zeugnisverweigerungsrecht	The right to decline to answer questions
Zivilprozeßordnung	Code of Civil Procedure
Zivilverfahren	Civil proceedings
Zufallsfund	Finding lost property by accident
Zwangsmittel	Means of coercion
Zwangsversteigerung	Auction by court order
Zwangsversteigerungsgesetz	Compulsory Auction of Immovable Property Act
Zwangsverwaltung	Sequestration or judicial enforced receivership
Zwangsvollstreckung	Execution, enforcement
Zwangsvollstreckungsverfahren	Execution proceedings
Zweizeugenbeweis	Evidence by two witnesses
Zwischenverfahren	Interlocutory proceedings
Zwischenurteil	Interlocutory judgment adjudicating only one of the matters in dispute

Index